Copyright in the Music
Industry

Elgar Practical Guides

Rich in practical advice, *Elgar Practical Guides* are handy, concise guides to a range of legal practice areas.

Combining practical insight and step-by-step guidance with the relevant substantive law and procedural rules, the books in this series focus on understanding and navigating the issues that are likely to be encountered in practice. This is facilitated by a range of structural tools including checklists, glossaries, sample documentation and recommended actions.

Elgar Practical Guides are indispensable resources for the busy practitioner and for the non-specialist who requires a first introduction or a reliable turn-to reference book.

Titles in the series include:

A Practical Guide to Using International Human Rights and Criminal Law Procedures
Connie de la Vega and Alen Mirza

Art Law and the Business of Art
Martin Wilson

Proceedings Before the European Patent Office
A Practical Guide to Success in Opposition and Appeal, Second Edition
Marcus O. Müller and Cees A.M. Mulder

The UN Human Rights Council
A Practical Anatomy
Eric Tistounet

Start-up Law
Edited by Alexandra Andhov

Copyright in the Music Industry
A Practical Guide to Exploiting and Enforcing Rights
Hayleigh Bosher

Copyright in the Music Industry

A Practical Guide to Exploiting and Enforcing Rights

HAYLEIGH BOSHER

Senior Lecturer in Intellectual Property Law, Brunel University London, and Legal Consultant specialising in Intellectual Property, Media and Entertainment Law, UK

Elgar Practical Guides

EE Edward Elgar
PUBLISHING

Cheltenham, UK • Northampton, MA, USA

Published by
Edward Elgar Publishing Limited
The Lypiatts
15 Lansdown Road
Cheltenham
Glos GL50 2JA
UK

Edward Elgar Publishing, Inc.
William Pratt House
9 Dewey Court
Northampton
Massachusetts 01060
USA

A catalogue record for this book
is available from the British Library

Library of Congress Control Number: 2020952041

This book is available electronically in the **Elgar**online
Law subject collection
http://dx.doi.org/10.4337/9781839101274

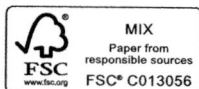

MIX
Paper from
responsible sources
FSC
www.fsc.org   FSC® C013056

ISBN 978 1 83910 126 7 (cased)
ISBN 978 1 83910 128 1 (paperback)
ISBN 978 1 83910 127 4 (eBook)

Printed and bound in Great Britain by TJ Books Limited, Padstow, Cornwall

This one's for you,
Jonathan.

Content overview

Table of contents

Foreword I

David Martin

In *Copyright in the Music Industry: A Practical Guide to Exploiting and Enforcing Rights*, Dr Hayleigh Bosher has succeeded in doing something many would have thought impossible. She has made copyright fun.

The book takes an in-depth look at areas of copyright and enforcement in a way that humanises and contextualises them with practical examples and clear explanations. The intended audience of artists, producers and other creators and industry personnel will discover a text that is written specifically with them in mind. Opening with the fundamentals, such as what copyright is and why it matters, and progressing to more complex matters, such as artificial intelligence and blockchain, in an almost whimsical manner, ultimately, here is the proof that you don't need to have decades of legal experience in order to grasp the key concepts of copyright within the music industry.

Copyright and its exploitation sit at the very centre of most creators' businesses. Understanding the basics is key to realising the value and potential of one's work. *Copyright in the Music Industry* should become a staple for creators who are serious about their work and about protecting it.

As the CEO of the Featured Artists Coalition, the UK's trade body representing the rights and interests of artists, I see first-hand how frequently conflicts that arise within artists' careers might have been headed off with a better understanding of some of the basics covered in this book. There's helpful advice on the simple steps that can be taken to document working arrangements and wise words on seeking expert advice before entering into deals. A solid grounding in these issues can undoubtedly stave off some of the heartache that many creators in our industry suffer, many cases of which have been famously publicised and are documented in detail in this text.

The book walks the reader through the history of copyright, its initial purposes and its development alongside technological advances in society. The limitations of copyright, its international nuances and how to properly ensure yours is protected are all covered, and the stages of challenging or being challenged on legal uses of IP, as well as the many different types of IP that creators might have copyright over, are outlined.

Dr Bosher's background as a lawyer gives a great deal of credence to the approach she has taken in the book in respect of court cases around exploitation and protection of copyright and how they were handled; however, the tone remains accessible throughout. The book manages to effortlessly glide across an enormous timespan, between the first copyright in the early eighteenth century and the most up to date considerations about the use of music on platforms such as TikTok.

From licensing to sampling, fair use to AI, musicologists to blockchain and Pharrell Williams to *Stairway to Heaven*, there is so much of interest here, crammed into a concise, perfectly formed and enjoyable read. I expect that for many in our wonderful and often chaotic music industry, *Copyright in the Music Industry: A Practical Guide to Exploiting and Enforcing Rights* will become a well-thumbed guide as they navigate their way through a lifetime of contracts, royalty splits, licensing deals and hopefully not too many court cases.

David Martin
CEO, Featured Artists Coalition

Foreword II

Andrea Martin

While the music industry has evolved rapidly and beyond recognition since PRS came into being in 1914, the fundamental premise has not changed: there is no music industry without the songs, and there are no songs without the writers. And without copyright, writers cannot make a living or protect and control how their work is used. The primary purpose of copyright is to empower the creator.

While the views and analysis expressed in this book are entirely those of the author, we share a common view that everyone involved in the music industry benefits from a better understanding of their rights. Copyright is not something for someone else to care about, nor can decisions about its future be left purely to lawyers and academics.

In the digital marketplace, creators have greater opportunities than ever before to reach new audiences around the world, but those opportunities are accompanied by greater challenges in controlling and enforcing rights. Therefore, it is more important than ever to educate ourselves on the individual rights that arise from the creation of a work, how they can be used to create value and ultimately what can be done when those rights are infringed.

Copyright in the Music Industry is a very welcome addition to anyone's library. It deftly explains copyright in a simple and friendly tone, while imparting significant information. The author's experience of the music industry and in-depth knowledge and understanding of copyright and the wider legal framework are evident throughout.

Andrea Martin
CEO, PRS for Music

Foreword III

Scott Farrant

Music copyright, or more accurately intellectual property (IP), are not typically terms that strike most music creators as sexy. They're not part of the creative process; they don't help with finding the right sound or a killer lick, nor do they allow a creator to connect to their audience or great co-writers.

Overall there's a very good chance that the majority of creators, especially those in the early part of their careers, will not want to pay any attention whatsoever to this subject; they'd rather be in the studio writing or recording, or out performing to their fans. But let's be honest here, put purely and simply: this is a big mistake.

Having worked in the music industry for more than 30 years, I have to say that 'IP-blindness' is one of the biggest avoidable causes of grief and trouble that a creator will experience as their career develops. IP is the bedrock of a creator's bread and butter: without IP creators would receive a mere fraction of what they do today. Imagine a world where Spotify, Apple Music, YouTube, Netflix, Network television companies, radio stations and many many more didn't have an obligation to pay royalties. It's IP that forces these entities to pay royalties and it is the contracts around IP that govern who gets paid what from this income. Importantly, IP is the framework under which publishing, recording and commissioning contracts are signed. A bad contract can be devastating to a creator's career through potential loss of ownership, loss of revenue, or loss of control over how they work, who they work with or even how they look and what they can and can't say or endorse. Think of it akin to going to work but never asking what your wages are, whether you get a lunch break, who you'll be working with and what you have to wear.

But IP pops up in other ways, too – for example, in sampling or interpolating other creators' songs. You may be inspired by someone else's song but is the chord progression or riff you've used plagiarism, leaving you exposed to legal action? Typically, clearing samples or interpolations after the fact is far more costly than clearing them up front.

So, whether the issue is not paying sufficient attention to a publishing or recording contract, or failing to clear a sample, or not being aware of what obligations you might have to a fellow band member, IP is and should be treated as a central tenant of a creator's working life.

This book sets out to simplify and demystify copyright in all its guises, using many real-life examples that help explain often complex situations. This book should appeal to both those who already understand some of the elements of copyright and want to delve deeper and, importantly, to everyone who hasn't ever had exposure to the ideas and principles of copyright. Drawing on real-life examples of how copyright is used and keeping the language at a comprehensible level allows both the substance and the deeply interesting nature of the subject matter to be brought across. This book is an engaging, interesting and well-paced read and Hayleigh even allows some of her good humour to shine through. Hayleigh keeps the language clear and understandable and thankfully avoids that persistent habit lawyers have of dressing things up in Latin.

Scott Farrant
Head of Global Publishing Operations, Kobalt

Preface

I really enjoyed writing this book, despite doing most of it amidst a global pandemic, and some of it with a broken elbow following the uptake of a new pandemic pastime (roller skating, if you were wondering!). While writing, I fully nerded out on the music, playing the songs as I told their stories. As I was doing so, I hoped to myself that the people reading this book might do the same thing, so to make that dream a little more plausible I created a playlist for your convenience. Please enjoy this immersive experience by searching for the playlist on Apple Music or Spotify: it's called Copyright in the Music Industry by Hayleigh Bosher.

The other reason I enjoyed writing this book is because I was allowed to write like an actual human being instead of a robot lawyer, which is mostly required for the usual academic research I do. I took so many liberties in that respect, but I hope it makes the book a more entertaining read. I have two main philosophies when I am attempting to help people understand more about copyright, particularly those who might be reluctant to engage with the idea: relevance and storytelling. This translates into two expectations for this book: at best you will find it directly relevant and beneficial for you, and at the least, particularly if you have any interest in music, the music industry or copyright in music, you will find the stories entertaining!

In addition to my gratitude to the experts who provided useful feedback for me on the content of this book, I would also like to thank my friends, my family and my therapist for helping to maintain my sanity during this time – in particular, Keren MacLennan for both encouraging and accompanying me on unconventional adventures (including, but not limited to, the roller-skating incident); Lana Hunt for the 3am espresso martinis; Beth Lloyd, Kate Warner and Liz for jokes that last for decades; Ally Meier for being a relentless cheerleader; and Dr Pamela Nika and Dr

Sevil Yesiloglu, who skip with me hand in hand against the grain of the stereotypical academic – who can in fact be cry-laughing in offices and singing in corridors, dressed in red, wearing lipstick, and still be badass researchers!

Acknowledgements

I would like to thank the following experts for their helpful comments and feedback on the book:

Alex Cole is a solicitor at the West End law firm Russells, advising music and entertainment industry clients on a wide range of commercial, intellectual property and company law matters: https://www.russells.co.uk/people/alex-cole.html

Austin Jacobs, a music industry accountant who specialises in royalty administration, royalty auditing and copyright valuations at Prager Metis. He is also a Fellow of the Institute of Chartered Accountants in England and Wales: https://www.pragermetis.com/about-us/our-team/austin-jacobs-fca-2

Charlotte O'Mara, a partner at gunnercooke LLP specialising in the creative industries and in particular music, media and entertainment. Charlotte advises on, drafts and negotiates contracts in all areas of the music, media, broadcast and entertainment & creative industries and related intellectual property rights. She regularly lectures on and hold tutorials on music and media law throughout the UK: https://gunnercooke.com/people/charlotte-omara/.

Key terms

Copyright	A type of intellectual property right that protects things such as original literary, artistic, and dramatic works, as well as sound recordings and films.
Defendant	The one being sued in a case.
EU	The European Union. At the time of writing, it seems the UK is apparently officially leaving the EU single market and customs union in December 2020.
EU Directive	Laws that are agreed at EU level but are implemented by each Member State into their own law by making their own legislation, using their own words, with some flexibility, but adhering to the minimum or maximum standards set in the Directive.
EU Regulation	Laws that are agreed at EU level and which apply directly in the Member State countries.
Intellectual property	An umbrella term that refers to all the different rights that protect creations. Copyright is a type of intellectual property right that protects things such as lyrics, music and sound recordings, as well as photographs, film and broadcasts. Other types of intellectual property rights include a trade mark (which protects things such as a logo and brand name), a patent (which protects inventions) and design rights (which protects what a product looks like).

IPO	The Intellectual Property Office is the government body responsible for intellectual property rights.
Jurisdiction	The system of laws in a country and the power to make legal decisions over a certain issue within that country's rules.
Licence	A type of contract that sets out the terms agreed for the use of a copyright work.
Litigation	Arguing in court.
Parties	Sadly, not a rave; this means the different sides in a legal dispute, or different sides of a contract, agreement, or negotiation.
Royalty	The payment for use of a copyright-protected work.
TRIPS	An international agreement called the Trade-Related Aspects of Intellectual Property Rights.

Copyright in the Music Industry playlist

PART I

Music and copyright

This book is presented in five parts. The first part is all about what copyright is and how it works. It introduces copyright and helps you to understand why it is so important, then explains the way that it works and what protection it does and does not provide.

Chapter 1 sets out why copyright is important and why you should care about it as a creator, artist, musician, producer or someone working in the music industry. This includes looking at the different justifications for copyright, plus addressing some of the common misconceptions around copyright and highlighting the benefits of having some copyright knowledge.

Chapter 2 explains what copyright is and how it works. It covers the way that law is made and applied, including how the copyright rules are different around the world. It clarifies what it means for a copyright work to be an original expression of an idea and when something can be protected by copyright. It also covers registration of copyright.

Chapter 3 gives more details on how music copyright works by explaining how it is split up into different elements that are protected with their own layers of copyright, such as lyrics as a literary work, melody as a musical work and the master as a sound recording. It also mentions protection in visual art in the context of album artwork.

Chapter 4 goes into more detail on what rights copyright gives you, such as the right to copy, distribute, rent and lend, perform, communicate and adapt the song. This chapter also discusses additional rights from which a creator can benefit alongside copyright, including performers' rights, moral rights and image rights.

Chapter 5 then covers what copyright does not give you; these are the exceptions and limitations to those rights explained in Chapter 4. The limitations are the ways in which the aforementioned rights are limited, such as in time and scope. The exceptions are circumstances where the work can be used without permission, such as under fair use in the US, or fair dealing for the purpose of parody or quotation, criticism or review in the UK.

1 Why copyright matters in music

This chapter first addresses the question of why copyright matters in music and why it is so important for any musician, any artist or any other person working in the music industry to care about copyright. Once we are all on the same page (pun intended) with the 'why', we can get into the 'what' – in Chapter 2, which provides an introduction to what exactly copyright is.

1.1   Why copyright matters in music

Having worked with many artists and musicians, I know that the first step in this conversation is to highlight why you should even care about copyright at all. Some musicians and artists believe that copyright is either something for someone else to be concerned with, or something that is just plain boring. Others perceive copyright as too complicated or as an obstacle to their creativity, and avoid it for those reasons. These are just some of the common misconceptions that give copyright a bad reputation. This chapter addresses these concerns, clarifies what copyright is for and how it can benefit you, and explains how just a little understanding of copyright can go a long way to help you avoid making unnecessary mistakes.

So, without further ado, here are my reasons to let go of any of the aforementioned misconceptions and carry on reading this book about copyright in the music industry.

1.2   Copyright is *for* creators

Copyright is not a natural phenomenon; it is human made – which is great, because this means that in places where it is not working, it can be changed! In fact, it has to change all the time, to keep up to date with new technologies and consumption behaviours in society. The law is not fixed or static; it is a constant work in progress. There are certainly copyright rules which do not work and need updating, but that does not necessarily mean that the entire idea of copyright is broken. It is useful to think of copyright as a concept, or big idea, that was invented to enable and support the creation and distribution of creative works. The concept of copyright is then written into law – these are simply the rules, or you could say policy, which are decided on by the government or judiciary to determine how the big idea of the copyright game will be played on their field, or in their country. The rules are different in different countries, because each has their own entire legal system, culture and way of doing things. There are international agreements signed between many countries that set minimum standards as to what the rules should say, but beyond that the specifics of the rules are tailor made. These rules can – and should – be changed and updated from time to time. This section will talk more about the idea and concept of copyright. The specific rules are explained in further detail in the subsequent chapters.

The main point here is that humans made copyright – and did you ever wonder why? Not to make your life more difficult, but for the benefit of creators, creativity and the spread of culture and knowledge.

Copyright regulation as we know it came about after the printing press was invented in the fifteenth and sixteenth centuries – essentially because, before printing, manual copying was pretty laborious and so not such a threat to writers. The first copyright law was created in the UK in 1709 and was called 'An Act for the Encouragement of Learning, by Vesting the Copies of Printed Books in the Authors or Purchasers of such Copies, during the Times therein mentioned'. Seriously. But at least it was self-explanatory; the law was made to encourage learning by granting copyright to authors. It does this by giving the author the exclusive right over their work, which enables them to licence it, disseminate it and receive remuneration in return, which then enables them to continue to create. Copyright has come a long way since then, and the rules are different, but the principal purpose is the same. Copyright helps musicians protect their creativity, get paid for their work and control the use of their music. It also enables the production of the work to be published and shared. In that sense, copyright is a win–win. Society gets music and musicians get remunerated for their creativity.

There are a number of different ways to justify why we have copyright. Not everyone agrees on which is the most suitable and, as explained below, different countries tend to lean towards one or the other. Regardless of which you find the most compelling, they all clearly emphasise that copyright is for creativity and, therefore, for the creator. Knowing why we have copyright can help to understand why it is useful for you. There are two main rationales for why we have copyright: the Anglo-American economic approach and the Continental Europe author perspective. The two justifications are briefly explained below.

Broadly speaking, the Anglo-American approach emphasises the economic role of copyright as a system that compensates creators for their work, which would otherwise be a freely accessible commodity with no market value, because it is easy to duplicate. So, copyright steps in to ensure that creators get paid for their work, which enables them to continue to create, and rightsholders can disseminate that creativity, knowledge and culture – thus benefiting society as a whole. The economic justifications of copyright focus on different elements of this transaction. For example, some argue that copyright is granted because it is fair to reward the creator for their efforts and for giving it to the public, making copyright a form of legal gratitude. Another related perspective is that the sharing of creativity and innovation is good for society as a whole, and therefore copyright acts as an incentive for creators. This perspective presupposes that without copyright creators would not be motivated, or able, to create and disseminate their work.

A different perspective, often taken in Continental Europe and referred to as personality or author rights, argues that when you create something it is an extension of yourself and your personality, and therefore you should own and control it. This justification takes the view that copyright is granted because it is the right thing to do, not because society will benefit from the work. Under this umbrella of author rights, there are also a number of different justifications for copyright that focus on a slightly different emphasis. Some believe that copyright is a way for the author to ensure that no one speaks in their name without their authority; for example, copyright allows you to stop an organisation that you do not support from using your song in their advertising campaign.

At the heart of copyright and all these justifications and different rationales is the motivation to protect the creation and dissemination of creative works, balanced with the public interest. The take-home message here is that copyright is meant to help creativity, not hinder it!

1.3   Copyright is how music makes money

The music business is fundamentally a copyright industry, as copyright exploitation is the central mechanism for revenue generation within it. For example, the music industry generated $43 billion in revenue in the USA[1] and contributed more than £5.2 billion to the UK economy in 2018,[2] through music creators, music retail, recorded music, music representatives, music publishing and live music. All these activities are made possible through the exploitation of music copyright, the musical composition, the recording of the music, music performances and the branding of the artist.

From the economic perspective, as explained above, it could be said that all these ways of making money from music are made possible by the copyright laws that provide the creator with the rights in the music, which are then licensed to allow for its dissemination. Of course, copyright is not the only required factor – the music, business models, people and consumers are also essential elements in the way that the music industry makes money – but copyright does play a fundamental role. Understanding copyright can therefore help to monetise your music from global revenue streams.

In my experience of working with creators and musicians, especially early on in their careers, I have come across somewhat of a trend in response to talking about making money from creative work. There is a romanticised notion of the struggling artist: the idea that a good creator, or a real

---

[1]   Citi GPS, *Putting the Band Back Together: Remastering the World of Music* (Citi GPS: Global Perspectives & Solutions, August 2018) 3.

[2]   UK Music, *Music by Numbers 2019* (UK Music, 2019) 6.

creator, is focused only on their creativity and is utterly unconcerned with matters of financial success. For some creators with whom I have spoken, it seemed as if talking about copyright and money in relation to their work was an insult to their creativity. They wanted me, and the world, to know that their craft was about creativity and their creative output was about communicating something meaningful to them and had absolutely nothing to do with money or financial gain. Money was a dirty word. If you can relate to this idea of the creator, you may wish to consider the following perspectives.

If you are uncomfortable thinking about making money from your music, try this: consider all the time and energy you put into your work, into learning and perfecting your craft and into creating your music. Think of money as just another form of energy (bear with me), and making money from your creativity therefore as simply a fair exchange. Just as in the reward rationale for copyright explained above, it is legal gratitude for the effort you have put into creating and sharing your work. Another way to look at it, from the incentive perspective, is that copyright enables you to be remunerated for your efforts so that you can take what might otherwise be a hobby and turn it into a career. You are then financially supported to continue to create.

A few years ago, I was part of a project that involved creating a copyright education platform called copyrightuser.org. As part of this project, we interviewed a host of different creators about their thoughts and feelings on copyright, in order to better understand the creators' perspective and inform the material we provided on the website. We filmed the interviews and you can watch the videos on the website. When we interviewed the musicians, one of the questions that we asked them was: 'What motivates you to create?' One of the interviewees replied: 'Money motivates me because DJing isn't a hobby for me, it's my actual career.'[3] If you think about it from a big picture perspective, you are not the only one who benefits from your creativity. You are able to create, and society is able to benefit from your creativity being shared. And copyright facilitates this exchange.

There is another recurring theme that crops up when talking to early career creatives, which you may recognise. It is that at one point or

---

[3]   www.copyrightuser.org/create/creators-discuss/musician/ accessed 6 November 2020.

another someone has told them that they cannot possibly make any money from their music – that this is a pipe dream. Especially in the age of the internet and online infringement, the music industry is different from what it was when CD sales, or cassettes, or vinyl, or the radio held it all together – and so on and so forth with the pessimism.

Of course, it is true that things are different now than in those times. However, please consider that everyone speaks from their own experience. If you asked Elton John or Stormzy or Beyoncé, do you think they would agree that there is no money to be made in music? I didn't think so. All right, so not everyone is going to be as successful as Beyoncé, but you can say that about every industry. The point is that people do make money from music and the music industry continues to thrive. Music is part of who we are. It has been part of humanity since humanity. Musicians and artists have been making money from music for literally hundreds of years. While the way the money is made might shift, business models will adapt to changes in technology and society; it is still possible to make a career in music, and I personally believe that it always will be.

In Western culture, there is a stereotype of the struggling artist; one who lives on low or little income, working irregular hours and willing to suffer this lifestyle for the sake of their art. While there is of course some basis for this preconception in that the majority of artists tend to be on a low income, and do work all hours, this does not mean it is impossible to cultivate enough revenue to make music your career – particularly when you have a working knowledge of copyright in your toolbox! Moreover, as Section 1.4 discusses, copyright is not just about the money; it is also about owning and controlling your work.

1.4   It's not just about the money

The question of why we create music itself in the first place is more complex than asking why we have copyright! Research has shown how music can change your mood or help you run faster. Music is used as a therapy technique for people with dementia. Darwin said 'music is our greatest mystery'. It has also been described as an evolutionary adaptation that helps us to navigate the world and deal with change.[4] One of the musicians we interviewed for copyrightuser.org answered the question 'What motivates you to create?' by saying: 'I don't think that you can be solely motivated by money in this industry … you just have to love what you do, love the music.' In fact, the love of music was a recurring theme in many of the musicians' answers to this question of what motivates them to create.

Love and passion for music, as well as other non-monetary rewards from creating music and working in the music industry, have been demonstrated to be reasons for motivation and job satisfaction in research about musicians. For instance, one research study found that artists have different criteria and conceptualisations of what is considered a good job and a good income. Moreover, in looking at predictors of income and income satisfaction, the study found that artists derive value from their work in a variety of ways in addition to monetary income. In particular, the study identified that artistic activities associated with reputational rewards and altruistic behaviours were also important to the artists' job satisfaction.[5]

In that case, you might think copyright is actually less important if creators are motivated by their love for the music and not the financial incentive. However, we also asked the musicians in the copyright interviews: 'What does copyright mean to you?' In response, they noted that it is 'a way of people knowing who's written the song'. Another theme that came up in the interviews was that copyright was used as a way to control the spread of their music; where, when and how it was used. Most of the artists said that if someone else wanted to use their music, they would want the person to ask for their permission first. Copyright is what allows the musicians to have this control. Having copyright in their music grants them the sole right to copy and use their work, and so if someone else wants to use it they need the permission of the rightsholder first. (Unless they benefit from a copyright exception, explained in Chapter 5.)

---

[4]   Leonid P, 'How Music Helps Resolve Our Deepest Inner Conflicts' (*The Conversation*, 24 March 2015)   https://theconversation.com/how-music-helps-resolve-our-deepest-inner-conflicts-38531 accessed 14 June 2020.

[5]   Miller A and Cuntz A, *Unpacking Predictors of Income and Income Satisfaction for Artists*, WIPO Economic Research WIPO Working Paper No. 50 (WIPO, December 2018).

Copyright, and related rights such as moral rights (discussed in Chapter 4), is a way to control the use of your creativity. It allows you to own your work and control how and where it is shared, as well as how it is used or edited. Whether to use the song as it is, or to make a remix of a song, or to use it in an advertising campaign – copyright owners are empowered to make these decisions about their work.

Copyright also enables people to know who created the work, as it recognises the creator and copyright owner. This is significant for the creator and also for the public. It is important for the public to know who created a song because, if they like it, they might want to find other songs by the same artist, for example. This is not to mention our tireless curiosity as humans to discover more and more about an artist, as evidenced in the documentary *Searching for Sugar Man*. The documentary film tells the story of two superfans from Cape Town who go in search of Rodrigues, an American musician whose music failed to take off in the US but became incredibly popular in South Africa – unbeknown to Rodrigues himself.

Fans and fan communities are another layer to the magic that music creates. They are also another reason why control of where and how your music is used is important. Consumers today, more than ever before, take into consideration broader factors in deciding where their loyalty lies. This is shown, for example, by the case of R. Kelly. Following the sexual assault allegations addressed in the *Surviving R. Kelly* documentary, there was a #MuteRKelly protest outside Kelly's studio in Chicago, calling for a boycott of his music. As Laura Gillespie, Ethics Fellow at Stanford University, explains: 'The idea is that in listening to the songs of a person who has failed to respect some value I claim to hold, then perhaps I am failing in some way to respect that value.'[6] Copyright allows you to control the use of your music, and decide if it can be used for and by causes, campaigns and people or organisations that align with your values, and therefore your listeners, fans or followers. For example, you may remember a Nescafé coffee advert in 2003 that featured Muse's cover of the Nina Simone song *Feeling Good*. Nescafé, owned by Nestlé, did not have permission to use the song, as Muse reportedly did not want their music used in support of this product. The band took legal action to enforce

6   Jaya S, 'The Ethics of Pressing Play: Navigating Popular Music When Alleged Misconduct Is Seemingly Everywhere' (*Billboard*, 21 December 2018) www.billboard.com/articles/columns/pop/8491160/ethics-of-pressing-play-in-music accessed 14 June 2020.

their copyright and were paid £500,000 in a settlement deal, which they donated to the charity Oxfam.

1.5   You do not need to be a lawyer

As mentioned at the beginning of this chapter, some of the misconceptions about copyright include things such as 'this isn't for me to worry about, I am the talent' or 'it's too confusing for me'. Granted, some aspects of copyright regulation and policy can be complicated, but the good news is that you do not need to be a legal expert – that is what lawyers are for. So, to some extent there are details about copyright that you do not need to worry about, and there will be times when you will need to seek legal advice from a lawyer or legal expert who does understand all the layers and complexities of copyright. *However*, in the meantime, the basics are much easier to grasp than you might think. *And*, when it comes to copyright, a little bit of knowledge can go a long way.

Understanding the copyright basics now can help to inform early decisions that avoid bigger problems down the line. It will also give you enough of an understanding to know *when* it is time to find a legal expert. Moreover, when you do speak to that expert, you will actually know what on earth they are talking about, rather than being totally lost and feeling out of your depth.

This book is primarily written for musicians, artists, producers, performers and those working in the music industry. It aims to give you a basic overview of copyright, how it applies to music and how it works in the music industry, in a way that is easy to understand – so that you will be able to make informed decisions, one of which is knowing when it is time to find a legal expert! (See more details on finding a legal expert in Chapter 7.)

1.6   It can help your creativity and your business

Understanding copyright and its role in the music industry is central to understanding the music business and how it works. Moreover, copyright is a law that is based on policy, which means that it is political and can

– and does – change dramatically and frequently. The changes made in copyright policy will have direct impact on creators, music and the music industry. It is therefore imperative to have a working knowledge of the regulations that affect the big picture of the music industry, and you as someone working within it.

Likewise, if you are engaged at some level in understanding copyright law and its impact on your industry, you can then get involved and participate in discussions around that change. When copyright rules and policy are made, or changed, it is a response to a new technology, or a development in society, and policymakers and lawmakers require information from those on the ground in order to make those decisions in an effective way. All over the world there are organisations and unions that campaign and lobby[7] for music and artists' rights, conduct research, write responses to government proposals, and engage in all sorts of other initiatives that you can engage with on a deeper level if you understand what copyright is and what it means for yourself and the industry. (More information about these organisations is provided in Chapter 7.)

Equally, understanding copyright can have direct benefits by helping you with your creativity and creative process. This is because knowing more about the difference between taking inspiration and copyright infringement, for example, can help you to better mitigate the risks of infringement (explained in Part III of this book). Moreover, it will enable you to take advantage of, and build on, freely available ideas and works either in the public domain or benefiting from the exceptions under copyright where permission is not needed (see Chapter 5).

Knowing how copyright works can also help you make informed creative and business decisions. This could be, for example, in relation to avoiding infringement claims, by taking steps in advance to enable you to prove your own independent creativity. Copyright knowledge can

---

[7] I always wondered why it is called 'lobbying the government' when an organisation or group tries to influence law, policy or decisions of government. So, just in case you were also wondering, here is a short side story: I was at the UK Houses of Parliament, stood in the *lobby*, outside where the members of parliament sit … and that's literally it! Before the days of email, in order to persuade your MP of your cause, you simply met them in the lobby. Technically, you can still go to the reception desk in the lobby and ask to see your MP, although these days you'd be better off making an appointment.

also empower you to understand how to maximise the benefit from your music, for example by utilising different licences.

1.7   It can help you avoid making mistakes

Understanding copyright can help you avoid making regrettable mistakes. Not in life, but at least in relation to accidentally signing your soul away, or not signing something and losing your investment in a project – a couple of things people tend to want to avoid.

A very common mistake that I have dealt with for clients in music, and in all areas of creativity in fact, is: 'Oh no, we didn't sign a contract because we were friends.' Emphasis on the word *were*! (*Lawyers simultaneously facepalm*.) This can, and does, create all kinds of issues later on. To be totally frank, the fact that you are friends, or partners, is even more of a reason to have a contract! Without a contract it is difficult to know where you stand, who owns what or what can be done with the work. Once you know about copyright and all that comes with it, you will see why it is much better to have a written agreement in place (contracts are discussed in Chapter 8).

Another problem for those less versed in copyright jargon is that they might sign something they did not fully understand. If nothing else, please ask an expert to help you with your contracts before signing. It might seem straightforward, but one little misunderstood word can mean the world of difference. For example, the difference between the word 'licence' or 'assignment' of copyright in a contract can be the difference between letting someone use your work for a limited time or giving it to them forever. (Licences are explained in Chapter 9.)

It is easy to make a mistake when it comes to copyright because there are so many misconceptions and common misunderstandings about what it is, what it does and how it works. When I was working on the copyrightuser.org project, I created a Frequently Asked Questions section on the website. I did this by looking at the most commonly asked copyright questions on an internet forum.[8] What struck me as more interesting than

---

[8]   www.copyrightuser.org/faqs/ accessed 6 November 2020.

the questions asked, however, was not the questions themselves but the answers provided by other users. The reason this was intriguing to me is because, when someone asks a question, they understand that they do not know what the answer is: that is, evidentially, why they ask the question in the first place. On the other hand, when someone voluntarily *answers* a question on an online forum, they clearly believe that they know the correct answer. However, to my horror and amazement, what I found was that *all* of the answers – to the hundreds of questions I looked at – were either wholly or particularly incorrect. All of them. Hundreds of incorrect answers. Hundreds of people so confidently advocating their misunderstandings about copyright. I used this data to come up with eight common myths about copyright that we turned into myth/reality cards on the copyrightuser.org website.[9]

This is not the only research to have demonstrated the same point. For example, one asked students: 'Do you know what copyright means?' In all, 84 per cent responded yes. The participants who said they knew what copyright was were then asked to explain what copyright means. Again, *all* of their descriptions were either wholly or partially incorrect.[10] Likewise, the Kantar Media Online Copyright Infringement Tracker shows annually that awareness and understanding of copyright infringement remains lacking for users.[11]

But! Fear not, because this here book will bust those myths and give you a clear understanding about what copyright is, how it works in the music industry and how to exploit your copyright and enforce it to protect your work.

---

[9]   www.copyrightuser.org/educate/enjoy/myth-reality-cards/ accessed 6 November 2020.

[10]   Palfrey J, Gasse U, Simun M and Barns RF, 'Youth, Creativity and Copyright in the Digital Age' (2009) 1(2) International Journal of Learning and Media 79.

[11]   Kantar Media, *Online Copyright Infringement Tracker Wave 8* (UK Intellectual Property Office, 2018) 53.

2   What is copyright?

Before we go any further, it is time to get acquainted with what exactly copyright is and how it works. In the last chapter we looked at why copyright matters and the different rationales for why we have it. This chapter explains what copyright is and what the regulations say. In particular, it addresses three key areas. First, is what copyright is and what it protects; this includes a tiny bit of legal background on how law is made and applied, how copyright works around the world and what it means for a copyright work to be an original expression of an idea. Second, the chapter explains when something can be protected by copyright; third, it discusses whether or not you need to register your copyright.

2.1   What is copyright and what does it protect?

This first section will explain what copyright is. As part of that explanation, it then moves on to look at the criteria for copyright to subsist. This threshold for copyright includes that the work needs to be original, and the expression of an idea, rather than just the idea itself. These criteria are explained in more detail below.

So, to begin: what is copyright? Well, copyright is essentially a legal recognition of creative output as a commodity. It is all the legal rules that protect music, lyrics, sound recordings, photographs and videos – among other things. In the law, these creative outputs are called 'works'. The law organises these works into categories, such as literary works (meaning writings), artistic works (such as a drawing), dramatic works (such as a dance), films and sound recordings. How exactly these different categories apply to a song is explained in detail in Chapter 3.

At its core, copyright is – big surprise – the right to copy. Hence copy-right. It is the right to exclude others from copying or using a protected work. The right to copy the work is held entirely by the copyright holder. That said, copyright is not a monopoly right, like other types of intellectual property rights such as a trade mark. This means that while copyright can enable rightsholders to stop others from copying their work, it does not prevent someone from independently coming up with a work that is similar to or the same as it. The full extent of the rights that copyright provides for the copyright holder, such as copying, distributing, performing and editing, are explained in detail in Chapter 4.

When copyright law was first made in 1709, it was intended to prevent the copying of literature by granting the copyright holder the exclusive right to copy their work. As we know, this right has expanded over time to now include a broader range of creative outputs, for a longer period of time. In its infancy, copyright lasted a mere 28 years.[1] Nowadays, copyright generally lasts for 70 years after the death of the creator. As will be explained in Chapter 3, different elements of a song have their own copyright that can be owned by different people and may even have a different duration of copyright. This can also mean that each element of the song's copyright lasts for 70 years after the death of the corresponding creator. This does not apply if the different parts of the song were specifically written for the same song: this moves into joint-ownership (explained in Chapter 6) and then means that the copyright will last 70 years after the death of the last surviving creator.[2]

Since copyright is all about preventing copying, it is not concerned with how good or bad the quality of a work is; it is not based on any merit or excellence. However, works such as musical works, as well as literary, dramatic and artistic works, do have to be original. Originality in copyright law does not necessarily mean the same as originality in everyday language. The meaning of originality in copyright terms is discussed in more detail in Section 2.4.

Just quickly, before that, in order for the explanations about originality (and essentially this entire book) to make more sense it is helpful to get a little insider information about how law is made and applied around the world. The next two sections talk about the differences between civil law and common law countries and their impact on the way that the law can

---

[1]   Under the UK Statute of Anne 1710, copyright lasted 14 years and could be renewed for an additional 14 years of protection.

[2]   For example, under the UK Copyright and Duration of Rights in Performances Regulations 2013.

change around your circumstances. Subsequently, the territorial nature of copyright is explained, which is extremely important to consider as it enables you to ensure you are considering the laws that are relevant for you.

2.2   How is law made?

This section will be as quick and painless as possible. Hold tight. So, there are two main types of legal system, this being the ways in which law can be made and applied in a country; they are called either a civil law jurisdiction or a common law jurisdiction. These two different systems dictate how the law is set out in that country, and how it is applied.

In a civil law jurisdiction, the primary source of law is a written code of core principles that is usually general and broad, which is supplemented with articles that deal with specific issues. The idea is that the code sets out all the principles of law and rights in one place which citizens can access. Law codes are laws enacted by a legislature and are considered superior to case law, so judges refer to and apply the code directly to the case in court before them. Civil law countries include all European Union Member States (except Ireland and Cyprus), all of continental South and Middle America (except Guyana and Belize), Quebec in Canada, all of East Asia (except Hong Kong), all of North Africa, Francophone and Lusophone Africa, Azerbaijan, Kuwait, Iraq, Russia, Turkey, Egypt, Madagascar, Lebanon, Indonesia, Vietnam, Thailand and the state of Louisiana in the US.

In contrast, there is the common law system which originated in medieval England. This system is not based on a codified set of laws but historically on judge-made law, where a judge takes into consideration previous cases with similar circumstances in order to decide like cases alike. This is called precedent and means that, in common law countries, the way that a case is decided can be relevant to others in similar circumstances. Common law countries still have some written laws, called statutes, which set out the key principles of the law, decided by the government and written by the legislator. What this means in practice is that we look to the statute to know the principle of law, for example that a work must be original in order for copyright to subsist in that work. However, we then look to the judge's decisions in the case law to understand what exactly the term originality means in that context. Common law countries include England and Wales, Ireland, Australia, New Zealand, Israel, India, Cyprus, Nigeria, Singapore, Malaysia, Hong Kong, the United States (except Louisiana), Canada (except Quebec), Pakistan and Bangladesh.

It is helpful to know which type of legal system you are dealing with because it can help you understand the ways in which the law is made, applied and changes within any particular country. More importantly, perhaps, it can help you to understand the impact of the law or a legal decision on your own situation. Speaking of different systems of law in different countries, it is also important to know that copyright law itself is not the same everywhere in the world. In fact, every country has its own copyright law, and Section 2.3 will explain a little about how that works.

2.3   How does copyright work around the world?

It is important to know that copyright is territorial, which means that the laws and rules about copyright are different in different countries. In other words, every country has its own copyright, which includes having its own variations of the rules and regulations on what copyright looks like in that jurisdiction.

This can create somewhat of a challenge when we think about the global nature of music, the music industry, the internet and online technologies. There are, however, a number of different international agreements in place that try to make life a little easier in that respect. They are sometimes called agreements, treaties or conventions.

The first and most important international copyright agreement is called the Berne Convention, and is signed by 188 countries around the world.[3] This sets out the minimum standards of copyright regulation for all those countries, meaning that 188 countries around the world have in place the same basic rules of copyright relating to literary and artistic works, including films. For example, all countries that are signatories to the

[3]   The Berne Convention for the Protection of Literary and Artistic Works 1886, last updated 1971 (Paris).

Berne Convention agree that copyright does not require registration in order to arise, and that it will last at least 50 years after the death of the creator.

This might not seem like such a huge deal, but the Berne Convention is actually the basis for international copyright relations and the starting point for copyright laws around the world. It also provides that all signing countries will give the same national protection to copyright works that were created in any of the other signing countries. This is called national treatment, and means that, for example, your work will be treated the same in France as it would if you were a French citizen, and vice versa in all the signatory countries.

A second important international agreement that is particularly relevant for the music industry is called the Rome Convention.[4] It provides a similar basis as the Berne Convention, but this one secures protection in performances for performers (actors, singers, musicians, dancers), in sound recordings (phonograms as they are called in these legal documents) and in broadcasts for broadcasting organisations. As of 2020, 95 countries were signed up to the Rome Convention.[5]

These rights in sound recordings are also supplemented by the Phonograms Convention 1971 and the WIPO Performances and Phonograms Treaty 1996. The Beijing Treaty on Audio-visual Performances 2012 also grants further recognition of rights in performances. It provides the performer with rights, in fixed audio-visual performances – such as in films – to reproduction, distribution, rental and making the performance available. It also provides the rights of broadcasting, communicating and fixation to the performer in non-fixed audio-visual performances such as live performances.

A third important international agreement is the Agreement on Trade-Related Aspects of Intellectual Property Rights (otherwise known as the TRIPS agreement).[6] This agreement is between the 164 member states of the World Trade Organization (WTO). Countries also sign

---

4   Rome Convention for the Protection of Performers, Producers of Phonograms and Broadcasting Organizations 1961.

5   www.wipo.int/treaties/en/ShowResults.jsp?treaty_id=17 accessed 6 November 2020.

6   The Agreement on Trade-Related Aspects of Intellectual Property Rights (TRIPS) 1995.

agreements between themselves about how copyright is dealt with. In the EU there are Directives and Regulations that attempt to harmonise the laws of copyright across Member States in some ways. There are also other agreements, such as the Marrakesh Treaty[7] which sets out mandatory exceptions and limitations to copyright, and the WIPO Copyright Treaty[8] which introduced legal protection against circumvention of technical protection measures.

This book provides an overview of copyright principles which are relevant in many countries, with specific details on the laws throughout the world, particularly the UK, US, and EU, but also with mention of other jurisdictions such as Australia, Canada and others. Throughout this book, some of the international agreements mentioned here will be referred to where relevant. The key thing to remember is that copyright law is territorial and so the laws are slightly different in different countries, although these international agreements facilitate trade and harmonise minimum standards within signatory countries.

Now that you are up to speed on the different legal systems and how copyright works around the world, Section 2.4 explains in more depth the threshold requirements for copyright. In other words, what are the criteria for copyright to subsist, for example, in your lyrics or song? The first of the sections that follow looks at the requirement of originality, which includes a consideration of the fact that copyright only protects the expression of ideas and not ideas in themselves, as discussed in Section 2.5.

2.4   Copyright protects original works

For copyright protection to subsist in a literary, dramatic, musical or artistic work, it must be original.[9] Note that this criteria for originality does not apply to a sound recording. This is because a sound recording can never be truly original, since the fixation of a musical work requires

---

[7]   Marrakesh Treaty to Facilitate Access to Published Works for Persons Who Are Blind, Visually Impaired or Otherwise Print Disabled 2013.

[8]   WIPO Copyright Treaty (WCT) 1996.

[9]   In UK copyright law this is set out in Copyright, Designs and Patents Act 1988 (CDPA 1988), section 1.

that, technically, the song is copied in the recording of it. The requirement is therefore slightly different in relation to a sound recording, in the sense that it cannot be a copy of another sound recording.

As a starting point, the work should originate from the creator and not be copied. But when is a work that has not been copied original or unoriginal for the purposes of copyright? The statutory law and international agreements set out that a work must be original in order for copyright to protect it, but they do not define what originality is. As described above, in common law jurisdictions we look to the judge's interpretation and application of this word to the cases, in order to have a greater understanding of what is meant by original.

In the UK, originality has been explained by the courts as when a creator adds their own 'skill, labour and judgement' to the work.[10] This was the UK threshold for originality for a long time, but more recently the EU court phrased this criterion in a different way. It said that originality is when the creator uses their own 'intellectual creation'.[11] At first there was some concern about what this meant for UK law, but subsequently we have seen that UK decisions have adopted both the 'skill, labour and judgement' and 'own intellectual creation' wording when deciding if a work is original.[12]

To understand more about what these requirements mean, we can look at some key case examples. The UK courts have said that it refers to 'the expression of original or inventive thought'.[13] The nature of the work is also a factor that will be considered, as was the case in the matter involving copyright protection of the Lego brick.[14] In the Lego case, the modified design of the Lego brick was said to have taken skill and effort, but since

---

[10] *Walter v Lane* [1990] AC 539, 552; *University of London Press v University Tutorial Press* [1916] 2 Ch 60; now read in light of the relevant EU Directives and *Infopaq International v Danske Dagblades Forening* (C-05/08) ECLI:EU:C:2009:465, as shown in the case of *Newspaper Licensing Agency Ltd v Meltwater Holding BV* [2011] EWCA Civ 890 (CA) 20.

[11] *Infopaq International v Danske Dagblades Forening* (C-05/08) ECLI:EU:C:2009:465.

[12] Such as in the cases of *Temple Island Collections Ltd v New English Teas Ltd* [2012] FSR 9; *Martin v Kogan* [2017] EWHC 2927 (IPEC); see also Rose D and O'Sullivan N, 'Football Dataco v Yahoo! Implications of the ECJ Judgment' [2012] 7(11) JIPLP 792.

[13] *University of London Press v University Tutorial Press* [1916] 2 Ch 601, as per Peterson J.

[14] *Interlego AG v Tyco Industries* [1989] AC 217.

it lacked artistic or visual character, it was not enough for copyright to subsist.

In relation to the meaning of own intellectual creation, the EU courts explained this in more detail in the *Infopaq*[15] case, which was about whether there was copyright in 11-word extracts of news articles. The EU court said that originality required the creator to exercise free and creative choices, and express their personal creativity; in other words, that the creator should stamp their personal touch on the work.

As such, when deciding if something is original or not, there is no general test, and the courts decide on a case-by-case basis. In the EU and UK, the judges will likely consider the extent to which the arrangement or configuration of the work is dictated by its function, since the more limited the choices available to the creator, the less likely it is that they are able to express independent intellectual creation.[16] Likewise, in the US a work has to be not copied, and of sufficient creativity to constitute a copyright protected work.

An interesting example to consider is that of John Cage's most famous work, 4'33" (four minutes, thirty-three seconds), recorded in 1952, for which – plot twist – he instructed the performers *not* to play their instruments for the entirety of the piece. So, the sounds heard on the track come from the environment in which the performance occurs, such as a creaking door, a cough and a bird chirping. Amazingly, in readiness for the first ever UK performance of the piece, BBC Radio 3's controllers reportedly had to switch off their emergency back-up system, which was designed to kick in when it detected unexpected silence on air! Be that as it may, many would argue that the piece lacks the necessary skill, labour and effort to qualify for copyright protection as a musical work. Moreover, since nobody did anything on purpose during the recording there would be no creative choices. Although it might be said that Cage made the creative choice *not* to make a choice, and the piece is original in the sense that it is unusual, this would not likely constitute originality in the copyright sense. Having said that, sound recordings don't need to be original and therefore the sound recording of the track could have been protectable.

---

[15]   *Infopaq v Danske Dagblades Forening* (C-5/08) ECLI:EU:C:2009:465.

[16]   *SAS Institute Inc v World Programming Ltd* [2014] RPC 8, 31.

So far, this section has explained that for copyright to subsist in a literary, dramatic, musical or artistic work, it must be original. Originality is determined on a case-by-case basis, requiring the creator to put their own intellectual creativity into the work, and taking into account factors such as making free and creative choices. For copyright to apply to your musical work, you cannot copy it from another musical work, and you need to exert your own skill and effort, with your own personal touch.

The originality threshold for copyright is considered to be relatively low. Original does not mean completely unique in that sense. Despite not protecting silence, copyright has been known to protect short jingles and short tunes: for example, 'Fourscore' by Lord David Dundas, which was the signature interval music used by the UK TV channel Channel 4, is copyright protected even though it includes only four different notes. Originality becomes more of an important issue when discussing infringement of copyright (see Part III). The next section moves on to clarify another requirement of copyright – that it protects the expression of an idea, not an idea itself. This criteria is linked to the principles discussed above, because the difference between the idea and an expression of an idea is found in the originality of the work.

2.5   Copyright protects the expression of ideas

Copyright does not protect ideas; it only protects the expression of ideas. We call this whimsical phrase the idea–expression dichotomy. What it essentially means is that copyright does not protect a general idea – say, for example, the idea of a song about celebrating birthdays. The Hill Sisters, Patty and Mildred, wrote the most popular song in the entire world – *Happy Birthday to You* – which would be an example of a creative expression of the idea of a song about birthdays. Other expressions of that same idea are *Happy Birthday* by Stevie Wonder, *Happy Birthday* by Kygo featuring John Legend, *Birthday* by Anne-Marie, *Birthday* by Will.i.am featuring Cody Wise, *Birthday* by Katy Perry, *Birthday* by JP Cooper, *Birthday* by The Beatles, and so on!

This concept is recognised at international level by the TRIPS agreement and the WIPO Copyright Treaty. It is globally accepted that ideas are freely available for everyone to use, and this also relates back to the rationales discussed in Chapter 1. This is because it is important that copyright is not a monopoly right, in order that it can promote creativity. Certain aspects of a song are considered to be simply ideas that no one can own – the genre or theme, for example. If it were possible to copyright an idea, then we would only have one birthday song, and the rest would be an infringement of the first.

The exact point at which an idea becomes an expression of an idea is not defined. This is discussed in more detail later in relation to the infringement section (Part III) because this crucial point is often the crux of an infringement argument: if the copied part is simply the idea, there can be no infringement because there is no copyright.

2.6   When is something protected by copyright?

This section summarises the criteria for when a work can be protected by copyright and whether you need to register that copyright or not.

As mentioned, copyright arises automatically, as long as the creative output reaches the threshold criteria for copyright. That threshold can be summarised as:

1. It is a type of work that copyright protects – such as a literacy work (lyrics), musical work (melody), artistic work (visuals or album artwork) and sound recording (master).
2. The literary, artistic, dramatic and musical work is original and not copied; this includes that the work constitutes the individual expression of an idea. Likewise, the sound recording is not a copy of another sound recording.
3. In some countries, such as the UK and US, it is required that the work is fixed in permanent form – so written down or recorded. Broadly speaking, it is generally the common law systems that require the work to be fixed, whereas the civil law systems do not.

Once the work reaches these three criteria, copyright arises automatically. Section 2.7 explains if and when you need to register your copyright.

2.7   Do you need to register your copyright?

In the US, while it is true that copyright arises automatically and you do not need to register it to obtain copyright, you do need to register it in order to enforce your copyright. This means that you need to register your copyright if you want to bring an infringement claim in the US. To bring a claim for copyright infringement in the US, the rightsholder is required to register the copyright before making the claim and provide evidence of the ownership with registration as part of the action. As such, it is much more common practice to register copyright in the US, because registration gives the copyright holder certain rights and enables legal action to proceed.

However, in the UK, and elsewhere in the world, you do not need to register your copyright; it arises automatically once the above described threshold is met. The important thing to remember here is that an idea for a song in your mind is not copyright protected: you need to write it down or record it.

The good news is that copyright is free and automatic: ta-dah!

But wait, before you go rushing off to the ball, there is one thing you should know. The fact that copyright is free and automatic means that you do not have a certificate of ownership to prove you are the rightful owner of the copyright, as you might have with other types of intellectual property, such as a trade mark. You may have heard that one way to copyright something is to send it to yourself in the post. Well, now you know that you do not need to do that in order for copyright to arise, since it is automatic, but there is some sense in the scheme. If you compose a song and post a copy of it to yourself, for example, it would arrive back to you with a date stamp on the envelope from the post office. So, the sealed delivery can be used as evidence to show that the song existed on that date. Since it's the 2020s, you do not need to post it to yourself – an email would also suffice, and even a voice note on your phone includes a digital date stamp.

Either way, it is important to understand that the date-stamped recording alone does not necessarily prove that you created the work, because you could just as easily post yourself something that someone else created. But the recording shows that the work existed on that date. This can still be very helpful: if someone claimed you had copied their song that they wrote in 2018, but you could show that your song existed in 2016, then the claim is immediately dropped.

However, if you did want to provide evidence that you created the song, it is much more compelling to be able to show a record of your whole creative process, rather than just the finished song. Remember, copyright is not a monopoly like other intellectual property rights, as it only gives the rightsholder the right to not have their work copied. It is perfectly possible, and legal, for two people to independently come up with the same expression of an idea. (This is discussed in more detail in Chapter 13, where we look at the difference between taking inspiration and copying.)

For now, in terms of how you obtain your own copyright, the key thing to remember is that copyright arises automatically, and you do not need to register it. However, this comes with the responsibility of keeping and maintaining a paper trail which can be used as evidence of your creativity and the existence of your work at the time you created it. If you are in the US, it is common practice to register your copyright, although it arises automatically, as this enables enforcement of the rights.

The next chapter explains how a song can have more than one copyright attached to it, giving more details about the different types of works that apply, such as literary and musical works, sound recordings and even the imagery of the album artwork.

3   Copyright in a song

Copyright law organises the creative works that it protects into categories, such as literary, artistic, dramatic, musical, film and sound recording. This means that a work, or a song, can have more than one copyright attached to it. This chapter will explain in more detail the different copyrights that can be attached to a song, including the sheet music, lyrics, melody, sound recording and album artwork. (There are also additional rights that can be attached to music, such as performers' rights, moral rights and image rights of the artist, and these are discussed in Chapter 4.)

Knowing how different elements of a song have their own separate rights is essential when it comes to understanding ownership of the rights in music, as well as in order to be able to manage the relationships between the stakeholders in the rights, and the revenue streams, discussed in Part II of this book.

3.1   Protecting sheet music: copyright in literary works

Section 3.1 begins by looking at how copyright developed over time to protect the different elements of a song, as it now does. You may notice that historical context is a running theme throughout this book so far, and that is because the way that copyright rules appear is a direct result of key developments in history. Copyright is always a product of its time, so in order to make any sense of it we need to understand the context within which it was made.

As was introduced in the previous chapters, the first copyright law was made in 1709 in the UK – the one with the long title about encouraging learning, also known as the Statute of Anne.[1] Initially, this law was quite narrow in that it only granted authors the exclusive right to copy their own literary work for 14 years, with the possibility to renew it for an additional 14 years. This meant that the only type of creative work recognised by the law at that time was books and writings, not music in any form.

The reasons for this are mostly due to the fact that the copyright law for the protection of writing came about after book publishers lobbied the government for these statutory rights. At that time the music publishers cared less about legal protection than the booksellers did, because they made most of their income from selling contemporary works, for which lead time was more important than exclusive rights for appropriating the value of new music.[2] The music publishers started to come to the copyright party in 1735. When the copyright term granted by the original Statute of Anne in the works owned by the book publishers came close to falling out of copyright, they decided to get together and lobby the government for a new law that extended how long copyright could last. (This pattern of behaviour is seen at the juncture of every copyright term extension – to life of the creator plus 50 years, and now life of the creator plus 70 years.)

Back to 1735. The draft law (known as a bill) was imaginatively titled the 'Bill for the Better Encouragement of Learning' and included a clause to extend copyright protection and encompass music. It suggested that the new law would say: 'This Act shall extend, and be construed and taken to extend to the Author or Authors of any Book or Books of Musick, or any Composition in Musick whatsoever, whether printed or engrave.'[3] Sadly, the bill failed. The book sellers tried again in 1737, but again failed to get the bill through Parliament. Feeling defeated, no doubt, after a good cry, the book sellers picked themselves up, brushed themselves off and decided to turn to the common law instead. (I did say that the 'how law is made' section in Chapter 2 would come in handy.) The book sellers

---

[1]   Officially titled: An Act for the Encouragement of Learning, by Vesting the Copies of Printed Books in the Authors or Purchasers of such Copies, during the Times therein mentioned 1710.

[2]   Carroll M, 'The Struggle for Music Copyright' (2005) 57 Florida Law Review 907–61, 931.

[3]   Bill for the better Encouragement of Learning and for the more effectual securing the Copies of Printed Books to the Authors or Purchasers of such Copies, during the Times therein mentioned, 6 May 1735, clause 12.

brought a series of cases to the courts in a period known as 'the battle of the booksellers'.[4]

Following suit, albeit a trifle late – by 65 years – Bach decided to take one for the music team. In 1777, Composers Johann Christian Bach and Karl Friedrich Abel sued publisher James Longman for copyright infringement of their music in London.[5] The judge in this case, the legendary Lord Mansfield, declared that the wording of the law was to be interpreted broadly; as such, the term 'books and other writings' in the Statute of Anne did, in fact, encompass printed music.

Some have argued that the consequences of this case were far-reaching, as it standardised the means for obtaining and enforcing rights within the music publishing sphere.[6] Others have suggested that at that time the law was not considered particularly useful for enforcing copyright against illegal copying of sheet music. Luckily, in 1842 a new copyright law specifically extended protection to musical works, codifying what had been achieved in the courts. However, the law was limited in that it did not provide a procedure for claiming damages, and cases tended to fail.[7] In 1881, the Music Publishers Association (MPA) was formed and pursued illegal copying of sheet music on behalf of members. But it wasn't until 1906, when the Musical Copyright Act came into force, that music publishers really began to succeed in enforcement against large-scale infringement of sheet music.

In the US, musical compositions – which were understood to be a printed form of the music – were not explicitly subject to copyright until 1831, when Congress added the words 'musical composition' to the list of statutorily protected works under the Copyright Act of 1831.[8]

However, the plot thickens … just as the publishers had begun to achieve their aims in the protection of sheet music, a new challenge emerged! Musical mechanical devices arrived between 1831 and the early

---

[4]   Deazley R, 'Commentary on Bach v. Longman (1777)' in Bently L and Kretschmer M (eds), *Primary Sources on Copyright (1450–1900)* (2008, www.copyrighthistory.org).

[5]   *Bach v Longman* 2 Cowper 623 (1777).

[6]   Carroll M, 'The Struggle for Music Copyright' (2005) 57 Florida Law Review 907–61, 954.

[7]   Towse R, 'Economics of Music Publishing: Copyright and the Market' (2017) 41 Journal of Cultural Economics 403–20, 405.

[8]   US Copyright Act of 1831, chapter 16, section 1, 4 Stat. 436, 436 (repealed 1909).

1900s, in the form first of player pianos (which played pre-programmed music from perforated paper rolls), then gramophones and subsequently records. As a result, the concept of copyright in music expanded from just the sheet music to include music reproduced by mechanical means. Enter stage left; the UK Copyright Act 1911. This act of law is widely regarded as the basis for the modern music industry. It provided copyright holders with the rights in their music, including reproduction by mechanical means as well as by the printing of the sheet music. In addition, the UK law created a new right in the recording itself, which we now refer to as the sound recording, explained in more detail below.

However, this was not the case everywhere: these rights were not recognised in the US until much later. At the time, the US Supreme Court found that the copyright statute provided for the unauthorised copying of a musical composition 'in intelligible notation', but that this did not extend to infringement by a player piano in the US at that time.[9] The US Copyright Act of 1909 significantly updated copyright law in America and did include the protection of mechanically reproduced musical compositions, such as those played on player pianos and phonograph players, as 'copies' of the original composition.[10] However, as recently as March 2020 the US courts confirmed that this legislation did not extend copyright protection beyond sheet music,[11] stating: 'Although the 1909 Act extended copyright protection against infringement beyond the mere reproduction of the sheet music, Congress did not provide that copyrighted works could be anything other than sheet music or ... the musical composition transcribed in the deposit copy.' In other words, only sheet music was protected by copyright. The deposit copy is the copy of the sheet music that was filed with the US Copyright Office and sets out the extent of the protection for that rightsholder. The judges are saying that the copyright was there only in the sheet music filed in the US Copyright Office, not in the sound of the music itself. When they say that the 1909 Act extended copyright protection against infringement beyond sheet music, that means that you could infringe the sheet music by playing or recording the music contained in the sheet music. The rights were not limited to, for example, copying out the sheet music onto another piece of staff paper. Therefore, under the 1909 Act, copyright only subsisted in the

---

[9]   *White-Smith Music Publ'g Co. v. Apollo Co.*, 209 U.S. 1, 17–18 (1908).

[10]   US Copyright Act 1909 Act, chapter 320, section 1(e), 35 Stat. 1075, 1075 (1909) (repealed 1976).

[11]   *Skidmore v Led Zeppelin* DC No 2:15-cv-03462-RGK-AGR, 9 March 2020.

sheet music itself and the piano rolls were to be considered as 'copies' of the original composition because they copied the sheet music. The Act did not protect the sound of the original music or expand to the sound made by the player piano.[12] This becomes an important distinction when trying to argue copyright infringement, and is still relevant in modern cases that refer to music made during this time, such as the *Stairway to Heaven* case discussed in more detail in Chapter 12.

3.2   Protecting song lyrics as literary works

This section looks at the copyright protection in the lyrics of a song. Song lyrics are protected as literary works when they are written down. Literary work does not just mean books or literature; it means the work is expressed in print or writing.[13] Literary work is just the name of the category into which copyright organises different works. This can be significant because different types of works can have different legal rules attached to them.

As explained in detail in Chapter 2, literary works need to be original in order to be protected by copyright. Original does not mean wholly unique, but does mean that the lyrics cannot be copied, and that you have put your own personal touch on the lyrics. As Billie Holiday famously said: 'If you copy, it means you're working without any real feeling. No two people on Earth are alike, and it's got to be that way in music, or it isn't music.'[14]

In relation to the amount of writing you need to do, it has been decided by the courts that a single word would not qualify as a 'work' for the purposes of fulfilling the requirement of a literary work. Likewise, names and invented words are not protected.[15] (An artist's name or a band name can be protected by a different type of intellectual property called a trade mark, which has its own set of legal rules.) However, in a significant European case the EU court found that, while words in isolation are not

---

12 *Goldstein v California* 412 U.S. 546, 564 (1973).

13 *University of London Press Ltd v University Tutorial Press Ltd* [1916] 2 Ch 601.

14 www.goodreads.com/author/quotes/53334.Billie_Holiday accessed 6 November 2020.

15 *Exxon Corp v Exxon Insurance Consultants International Ltd* [1982] RPC 69.

considered to be an intellectual creation and are therefore unprotectable by copyright, 12 words formulating a news headline were found to be capable of copyright protection.[16]

In general, courts around the world give a broad interpretation to the meaning of a literary work. For instance, the UK law defines a literary work as 'any work, other than a dramatic or musical work, which is written, spoken or sung'. The US law is similar, stating: 'other than audio-visual works, expressed in words'. The WIPO Guide to the Berne Convention[17] offers examples such as novels, news, poems, recitations, stories, irrespective of their content, their length, their purpose (meaning entertainment, education, information, discussion, advertisement and so on) and their form (meaning manuscript, print or scribbled on a napkin).

As such, we can confidently say that lyrics are protectable by copyright, as long as they are original. The question of whether the lyrics are original is particularly consequential when considering if a song is infringing the copyright of another song with similar or the same lyrics. This is covered in Part III, looking at all the details on copyright infringement.

3.3   Protecting melody: copyright in musical works

Turning now to the melody in a song, this is protected by copyright as a musical work. There is no internationally recognised legal definition of musical works. As mentioned, in the UK a song is separated into different copyright-protected parts, such as the melody as a musical work and the lyrics as a literary work. The UK law says that a musical work consists of music, exclusive of any words or action intended to be sung, spoken or performed with the music. That is because those elements would be protected under different types of copyright, such as literary or dramatic work. The consequence of this approach is that these different types of copyright could be owned by different people.

---

[16]   *Infopaq International A/S v Danske Dagblades Forening* (C-5/08) ECLI:EU:C:2009:465.
[17]   WIPO Guide to the Berne Convention for the Protection of Literary and Artistic Works (Paris Act, 1971).

An exemplary case that demonstrates the impact of defining a musical work and who owns it came before the UK court in 2005.[18] Hyperion Records hired, and paid a fee to, Dr Lionel Sawkins, who researched and created new performing editions of Lalande (whose work is out of copyright). In 2002 Hyperion Records released an album of Lalande's work which featured performances of four performing editions. Sawkins claimed that he had copyright in these editions, but Hyperion Records argued that the 'figuring of the bass' and 'added ornamentation' was not music. The courts sided with Sawkins, saying that the effort, skill and time spent in making the performing editions was sufficient to satisfy the originality requirement for copyright protection. The court did state, however, that

> the essence of music is combining sounds for listening to. Music is not the same as mere noise. The sound of music is intended to produce effects of some kind on the listener's emotions and intellect. The sounds may be produced by an organised performance on instruments played from a musical score, though that is not essential for the existence of the music or of copyright in it.

Thereby noise was excluded from copyright protection. (It would be interesting to consider whether this could be argued any differently in light of the growing popularity of café noise, background noise or even ambient rainforest noise tracks, since they may be considered as a combination of sounds for listening to!)

In other countries, such as Italy, the music and the words are considered as a whole. France and the US both define a musical work as including any accompanying words. This means that the length of copyright would depend on the life of the lyricist and the composer even if they did not co-create both parts. However, there is an EU law, called the Term of Protection Directive, which means that the length of copyright is unified for co-writers of musical works in the EU, whether or not the composer and lyricists are co-authors under national law. At international level, the Berne Convention says that a musical work is a musical composition, with or without words, and encompasses music in its widest form – including everything from symphonies to jingles.

---

[18] *Sawkins v Hyperion Records Ltd* [2005] EWCA Civ 565.

3.4   Protecting the master: copyright in sound recordings

A master is the first recording of the song, now usually made on a computer. Each instrument and voice-part is recorded onto a separate track, hence the name multi-track recording. The multi-track recordings are mixed and edited down into a two-track stereophonic, monaural or Surround Sound master which creates a published song in a playable format. So technically, there are two masters: the multi-track recordings and the final two-track record. In general, the term master is used to refer to the recording of the song, in copyright this is referred to as the sound recording or phonogram.[19]

The sound recording, or phonogram, has its own copyright. The copyright holder of the sound recording is usually the producer of the sound recording, or the record company, agreed within the terms of the contract. The producer is the person, or legal entity (company), who first fixes the sounds, so the person who makes the recording. As explained in Chapter 2, the sound recording does not need to be original in the same sense as a literary or musical work, but it cannot be copied from another sound recording.

Sound recordings are protected under national laws that also comply with international agreements, including the Rome Convention, the Phonograms Convention and the TRIPS Agreement. The WIPO Performances and Phonograms Treaty defines a sound recording as 'any exclusively aural fixation of sound of a performance or of other sounds'.[20] A soundtrack to a film is also considered a sound recording for these purposes in some countries, such as the UK, but not in the US. In that country a sound recording is defined as 'the fixation of a series of musical,

---

[19] This terminology has discriminatory roots, which should not be tolerated. If your contract uses offensive wording, you can, and more importantly should, ask them to change it, as Pharrell Williams and others have, hopefully we won't be seeing this in future contracts: Halperin S and Helligar J, The Big Payback: How Pharrell Williams Is Breaking the Chains of the Music Industry's Troubled Past (2020) https://variety.com/2020/music/news/pharrell-williams-master-slave-industry-contracts-1234729237/ accessed 18 December 2020.

[20] WIPO Performances and Phonograms Treaty (WPPT) (1996), Article 2.

spoken or other sounds, but not including the sounds accompanying a motion picture or audio-visual work'.[21]

In Canada, sound recordings are defined as 'a recording, fixed in permanent form, consisting of sounds ... but excludes any soundtrack of a cinematographic work where it accompanies the cinematographic work'.[22] The UK definition is a recording of sounds, from which the sound may be reproduced, or a recording of a literary, dramatic or musical work, regardless of the medium or method. The difference is that the UK and Canada recognise the soundtrack of a film as its own sound recording with its own copyright when it is not accompanying the film, whereas the US does not.

In the UK this gives copyright a slightly different scope, and the copyright in a sound recording lasts for 70 years from the release of the work (rather than 70 years after the death of the creator, as with musical and literary works). This is similar to the way in which the UK separates lyrics and musical works, as explained above, but the US includes them together.

The copyright in a sound recording is of that recording. This means that if you made a cover of a song, you may not be infringing the rights in the sound recording – although you would still have to contend with the derivative right in the recording, as well as any rights in the lyrics, melody, performance and so on. In fact, songs are sometimes re-mastered as a way to give a new copyright term to a sound recording. (This is sometimes the motivation behind a 50-year celebratory re-mastered collection of works!)

As discussed, copyright law broadened and adapted alongside the development of technologies such as phonographs. This is a fundamental part of copyright, to adapt and keep up with new technologies. Moving into the era of home taping now ... to the boombox! (For those too young to know, this was a large portable cassette player with two cassette tape slots that allowed you to record from one tape to another – first developed by Philips 'Radiorecorder' in 1969. For those of us who had one of these as a kid, I know I am not the only one who used it to create my own radio station!) A study in 1987 showed that 73 per cent of adults had home recording equipment, and 59 per cent of those people borrowed

[21]   US 1977 Copyright Act, section 101.
[22]   Canada Copyright Act, section 2.

other people's tapes to record onto blank tapes at home.[23] In 1988 the British Phonographic Industry (BFI) took a manufacturer of a double cassette-deck to court, arguing that the manufacturer was authorising the infringement of copyright, but the law at the time was unable to reach that far and the case failed.[24] (These days this would be called secondary copyright infringement, explained in Chapter 11.) After much debate and lobbying of government, a levy system was introduced to include a cost to compensate for the fact that the device prejudiced the interests of copyright holders. In the US, sound recordings were not given their own protection until 1972, when the unauthorised reproduction and distribution of a sound recording made after 15 February 1972 was prohibited.[25]

When the US passed the 1972 laws that gave protection to sound recordings, they held back from giving rights in public performances because Congress did not want to force radio stations to pay for music. At that time, radio was accustomed to using music for free, other than the music publishing payments. It wasn't until some years later – in 1995, when Congress passed the Digital Performance Rights in Sound Recording Act – that public performance rights were given to sound recordings in the US.[26] This law was not retrospective, but after a falling out between the music industry and streaming services the US included protection for pre-1972 sound recordings under the Music Modernization Act in 2018, which gives some of these sound recordings copyright protection until 2067!

The 1976 Copyright Act dramatically changed the status of music copyright in the US, particularly since it stated that public distribution of a sound recording qualified as publication of a musical composition. This meant that after this law came into force, composers could submit a recording of their music rather than just the sheet music. The impact of this on the scope of protection is huge – explained in the section on sheet music above and the *Stairway to Heaven* case discussed in Chapter 12.

---

[23]   British Market Research Bureau study, HC Official Report Standing Committee E, 24 May 1988, Col 293 and 322.

[24]   *CBS Songs Limited & Others v Amstrad Consumer Electronics Plc* [1988] UKHL, 15.

[25]   17 US Copyright Act, § 301(c).

[26]   Although, the act still did not extend public performance rights in sound recordings to terrestrial broadcasts.

3.5   Protecting album artwork: copyright in artistic works

The artwork for a song or album can be protected by copyright as an artistic work; this includes a graphic work, photograph or collage. As discussed in Chapter 2, the work needs to be original in the same way as a literary or musical work. As long as the artwork is original it would meet the threshold for copyright, irrespective of artistic quality.

One of the issues that can arise in determining whether something is protected by copyright or not is the question of whether it fits within the list of categories discussed above, such as a literary work, musical work or sound recording. A relevant example of this issue is the case involving the cover of English rock band Oasis' 1997 album *Be Here Now*. Noel Gallagher arranged a selection of props for the album cover, with a Rolls-Royce in a swimming pool surrounded with other objects such as a motorbike and a clock. The scene was photographed and used as the *Be Here Now* album cover. However, a photographer from a newspaper was also present at the scene and took a photograph which was then published in the newspaper, alongside an offer to sell posters of the image. The record company sued the newspaper, but the case failed because they could not show that the scene fell within any of the copyright-protected categories. The arrangement of the objects was neither an artistic work nor a dramatic work. The newspaper had not copied the album photograph but had instead used its own image.[27]

When comparing this to the case of Sawkins and Hyperion, discussed above in the musical work section, it is curious to note that the courts recognise, in essence, that organising sounds makes music that is capable of copyright protection as an original music work. On the other hand, the arrangement of objects does not equate to a dramatic or artistic work in the case of the Oasis album cover. So, what does that mean for theatre set designs, where props are arranged in a similar fashion, such as the elaborate set design by Julie Taymor for *The Lion King* or the revolving stage for *Les Misérables* by John Napier? Parts of the staging might be protected as a literary work – for instance, the drawing design and certain elements might be protected under other types of intellectual property rights, such

---

[27]   *Creation Records v News Group* [1977] EMLR 444.

as design or patent. In the US, one court has recognised copyright for a scenic design.[28] Nevertheless, it is by no means clear where the line is drawn between protectable and unprotectable elements of copyright outside the traditional forms mentioned in the statutory laws.

The importance of album artwork nowadays has shifted, in that the attractiveness of the cover of a CD or vinyl record might have played a bigger role in the decision-making process of a customer browsing in a shop. That said, artwork is still a relevant factor in the online presentation of music, and for many artists it is a visual extension of the creativity, emotion or theme of their music. Moreover, the artwork continues to be a huge part of a successful campaign in terms of getting music out there as well as creating additional revenue streams, such as through merchandise. As such, it is still relevant to know that this artwork is protected by copyright. Likewise, it is imperative to know who owns and controls the copyright in the artwork in order that it can be utilised. Ownership of copyright is discussed in more detail in Chapter 6; managing that ownership through contracts is discussed in Chapter 8, and through licences in Chapter 9.

Now that this chapter has set out for you the different rights that can be attached to a song, including the sheet music, lyrics, melody, sound recording and album artwork, Chapter 4 will explain what exactly these rights provide.

---

[28] *Arcenas v Hall*, No. 97-8388, slip op. at 6–7 (S.D. Fla. 7 October 1997); see also Womack J, 'Big Shop of Horrors: Ownership in Theatrical Design' (2007) 18 Fordham Intellectual Property, Media & Entertainment Law Journal 225.

4   What copyright gives you

Chapter 2 covered what copyright is, Chapter 3 set out how it applies to the different elements of a song, and this chapter explains what copyright provides for the rightsholder. Chapter 5 will cover what is not included in copyright protection. This chapter first sets out what rights copyright gives the copyright owner. Second, it explains the additional associated rights of performers' rights, moral rights and image rights. These next two chapters will empower you to know where you stand with regard to the extent of your own rights in your work, as well as your ability to use others' work, and vice-versa.

4.1   What does copyright give you?

Copyright is structured to balance the interests of the different stakeholders (such as the creator, the distributor and the public). As discussed in Chapter 1, the aim of copyright is to balance the rights of the creator with those of the public interest, in order that the creator be remunerated for their work and that the public may access that work. Whether the regulation strikes this balance fairly is a question that we should ask frequently, because the context of creativity and access to creativity is always evolving, and in response so should the regulation.

The way in which copyright balances the interests of the stakeholders is by granting rights to the copyright holder and at the same time putting some limitations on those rights. The rights granted are discussed in this section and the limitations and exceptions to these rights are discussed in Chapter 5.

As a copyright holder, the law gives you the exclusive right to copy your work. This means that you have the ability to stop others from using your work without your permission, giving you control over the use of your work – how it is used and by whom. The law provides a list of things that only the copyright holder can do, and these are referred to as the restricted acts, since they are the restricted uses of the work. These restricted acts are: to copy the work; issue copies of the work to the public; rent or lend the work to the public; perform, show or play the work in public; communicate the work to the public; or make an adaptation of the work.[1] The meaning of each restricted act is explained in more detail in the following sub-sections.

4.1.1   Copying: the right to reproduce the work

Restricting copying is the essence of the power of the copyright holder. The law enables the rightsholder to stop other people from copying or reproducing their work. This means that if you own the copyright in a song, no one else can take that song and copy it without your permission. There are two ways to look at this: first, it means that a person cannot literally copy your whole song without your permission, for example for an advertising campaign, film soundtrack, political party election campaign or political rally. Artists have been seen to enforce their rights against political parties that use their music without consent, on the basis of copyright. For example, in 2014 New Zealand's National Party used a song called *Eminem Esque*, which was basically a version of Eminem's *Lose Yourself*, in its election campaign. The High Court found the songs to be substantially similar and Eminem was awarded NZ$600,000 in damages for copyright infringement.[2] Similarly, at the time of writing, Neil Young is suing Donald Trump for using his songs *Rockin' in the Free World* and *Devil's Sidewalk*. Young is using his copyright to control the use of his work in a political campaign that he does not support, stating in the complaint that he '[i]n good conscience cannot allow his music to be used as a theme song for a divisive, un-American campaign of ignorance and hate'.[3]

Second, restricted copying means that someone cannot listen to your song and create their own version by copying it to make another song that is exactly the same as, or substantially similar to, yours. Doing either of

---

[1]   UK Copyright, Designs and Patents Act 1988, section 17; US Copyright Act, section 106.
[2]   *Eight Mile Style v National Party* [2017] NZHC 2603.
[3]   *Neil Young bda Silver Fiddle Music v Donald Trump For President Inc*, complaint filed SDNY August 2020.

these things would constitute copyright infringement, which is explained in detail in Part III of this book.

In relation to the first type of copying, taking the whole song, this includes digital copies stored by electronic means – so on a computer, whether saved or streaming. Most countries have a broad and encompassing definition of copying. The UK,[4] Australia[5] and Canada[6] say that copying can be in any material form. German law says copying can be by whatever method and in whatever quantity.[7] The US defines copies as a work fixed by any method from which the work can be perceived, reproduced or otherwise communicated.

In relation to what is meant by the second kind of copying, and especially what is meant by a substantial part as opposed to an insubstantial part, this is not defined in the statutory or codified law. This means that we look to the case law to better understand where the line between the two rests. But, spoiler alert: there is no line! It is not quite that simple, but it is the crux of any decision on whether infringement of this kind has taken place. As such, this is discussed in detail in Part III.

4.1.2   Issue or distribute copies of the work to the public

A copyright holder also has the exclusive right to issue copies of their work to the public and distribute copies of their work to the public. In other words, the copyright owner has the right to stop other people from issuing or distributing their work to the public. This means that no one can take your song and circulate or share it without your permission; only the copyright holder can put it on the market. As an example, in the UK there was a case, known as CD-WOW, in which the judges found that a company had issued copies to the public when it sent infringing copies of CDs in the post from Hong Kong to customers in the UK, who had ordered them from the company's website.[8]

---

⁴   UK Copyright, Designs and Patents Act 1988, section 17.

⁵   Australia Copyright Act, section 21(1).

⁶   Canada Copyright Act, section 3(1).

⁷   Germany Copyright Act, Article 16(1).

⁸   *Independiente Ltd v Music Trading On-line (HK) Ltd* [2007] FSR 1 (Ch).

The distribution right is robust and similar across countries such as the UK, US, France and Germany. In the EU the right is interpreted broadly to include advertising and offering for sale.[9] The international agreements that set out the minimum standards of protection, such as the WIPO Treaty 1996, say that the distribution right only applies to hardcopies that can be physically put into circulation, and therefore does not apply to online sharing (as this is covered by a different restricted act called communication to the public – explained below).

However, cases in the US and Hong Kong have been seen to take a much broader interpretation that has applied this right to online sharing. The US courts have included peer-to-peer file sharing of songs as instances of having illegally distributed the sound recordings in those songs. For example, in the well-known case involving the peer-to-peer sharing website Napster, the court stated that the users of Napster had violated the copyright holder's distribution rights.[10] However, in more recent cases, the US courts have said that publication and distribution are not the same thing, as was seen in the case brought by US record companies against university students using a peer-to-peer filesharing software to download and disseminate music without paying for it.[11] In another case the US courts held that actual dissemination was required, rather than simply making available for the distribution right to be infringed. This is difficult to establish in the circumstances of online infringement, since it would need to be demonstrated, with evidence, not only that the website had made the copyright material available, but that it had been transmitted and received.[12] Cases in Hong Kong have also been seen to include transmission of copies online as an infringement of the distribution right.[13]

The distribution right is specifically limited by the exhaustion principle in all EEA countries, which is explained in the next chapter. Likewise, this only applies to tangible copies of works, not digital or online versions.

---

[9]   *Dimensione Direct Sales Srl, Michele Labianca v Knoll International SpA* (C-516/13) ECLI:EU:C:2015: 315; *Titus Alexander Jochen Donner* (C-5/11) ECLI:EU:C:2012:370.

[10]   *A & M Records Inc v Napster Inc* 239 F.3d 1004 (2001) at 1014.

[11]   *London-Sire Records Inc v Doe* 1 542 F. Supp. 2d (D. Mass 2008) 153.

[12]   *Capitol Records Inc v Thomas* 579 F. Supp. 2d 1210 (D. Minn 2008).

[13]   *Chan Nai Ming v HKSAR Court of Final Appeal of the Hong Kong Special Administrative Region* FACC No 3 [2007] 3 HKC C 225.

4.1.3   Rent or lend the work to the public

A copyright holder has the exclusive right to rent or lend copies of their work to the public. As such, the copyright owner can stop others from renting or lending their work to the public. Renting means making a copy available for use, on the condition that it will be returned, or used for a limited amount of time, for direct or indirect commercial advantage. Lending is the same but without the commercial advantage, such as in the case of a free library. What this means is that if a person buys a copy of your song, they cannot rent or lend it to the public without a licence. This includes digital copies as well as physical copies of the work.

In the case of commercial rental of sound recordings and films, EU law gives remuneration to authors and performers which cannot be given to anyone else or surrendered, even after transferring the rental rights to a producer or distributor. This means that as the author of a song, you will receive royalties from any rental of your song, even if you have transferred your copyright to a record label or publisher. These royalties are organised and distributed through collecting societies, discussed in Chapter 7.

Rental rights have been established at international level through the TRIPS Agreement and WIPO Treaty. In the US the rental rights cover only phonorecords (a physical object that embodies sounds, such as a CD) and not copies, so they do not include the music accompanying a film or audio-visual work.

In relation to non-commercial lending, such as when a library provides copies of works freely to members of the public on a short-term basis, this is recognised in EU Member States,[14] the UK[15] and various other countries, such as Australia.[16] The lending of these works is also remunerated through collecting societies, but the funds come from the government. There is no public lending right available in the US.

---

[14] EC Directive on Rental Right and Lending Right and on Certain Rights Related to Copyright in The Field of Intellectual Property 2006/115/EC.

[15] UK Public Lending Right Scheme 1982.

[16] Australian Public Lending Act 1985.

4.1.4 Perform, show or play the work in public

The copyright holder has the exclusive right to perform, show or play their work in public, and as such is able to prohibit others from performing, showing or playing their work in public without permission. The 'public' aspect requires that there be an audience.

In general, the legal meaning of performing a work is to represent the work by sight or sound, such as by way of a live performance of actors, singers or musicians. The right to perform the work to the public initially only concerned dramatic works, since simply excluding the right to reproduction would not have been much help in the case of protecting against the unauthorised performance of a play, for example.[17] However, this right now also includes the performance of a musical work, literary work and the playing or showing of a sound recording, film or broadcast. This is recognised at international level in the Berne Convention, which states that rightsholders have the exclusive right to public performance of their dramatic or musical work and the recital of their literary work.

In the UK,[18] the meaning of performance is any mode of visual or acoustic presentation of a work, including lectures, addresses and speeches, where there is an audience present at the time of the performance. The meaning of the public in this context has included people attending a concert, but also people in a shop[19] and in a hotel lounge.[20] This is much the same under US law, which grants the copyright holder the right to publicly perform their work, across all types of copyright works other than sound recordings or sculptures.[21] The US definition of perform is also broad and encompassing, to include recital, rendering, playing, dancing, acting and so on.

If the performance is recorded and that recording is broadcast to an audience, this is called communication to the public. Under EU law this is an aspect of the public performance right. In the UK this is a separate right, explained in more detail below.

---

[17] First introduced in the UK in 1833.
[18] UK CDPA 1988, section 19.
[19] *PRS v Harlequin* [1979] 2 All ER 828.
[20] *PRS v Hawthorns Hotel (Bournemouth)* [1933] Ch 855.
[21] US Copyright Act s 106 (4)–(5).

4.1.5   Communicate the work to the public

Communication to the public is a more recent type of copyright protection. It was an extension of the performance right, explained above, to apply to modern communication systems. It furthers the performance right in the sense that, under communication to the public, the performance does not need to be live in front of an audience. Instead, it accounts for an audience that is not present at the time of the performance, but nevertheless is an audience member at another time.

The communication to the public right is recognised at international level and was established in the Berne Convention, with a view to enhancing protection for rightsholders in the digital age.[22] At the time of creating this particular law, the technology that was specifically in the mind of the legislators was on-demand television broadcasts, which could be accessed by the user at a different time or place than the original performance or broadcast. Some countries, such as the UK, have a specific right for communication to the public; others have included this type of protection within existing public performance rights.

In the EU the right to communication to the public has been used to restrict the transmission of films over hotel networks,[23] when a hotel provides CDs and CD players to guests,[24] in a pub,[25] and in a spa,[26] but not in a dentist's waiting room[27] that was playing soothing music for patients – go figure. As you can imagine, this series of case law has been super controversial and communication to the public is certainly one of the more confusing areas of copyright law. Nevertheless, it has been very helpful in protecting the copyright interests in music that is illegally shared online. Courts have found that peer-to-peer filesharing and illegal online streaming services are communicating to the public. This includes websites that act as a search engine for users to find and access illegal works by pro-

---

[22]   The Berne Convention 1886, as amended, Article 11*bis* (1).

[23]   *Sociedad General de Autores y Editores de España (SGAE) v Rafael Hoteles SA* (C-306/05) ECLI:EU:C: 2006:764.

[24]   *Phonographic Performance (Ireland) Limited v Ireland and Attorney General* (C-162/10) ECLI:EU:C: 2012:141.

[25]   *Football Association Premier League v Karen Murphy* (C-403/08 and C-429/08) ECLI:EU:C:2011:631.

[26]   *OSA Ochranný svaz autorský pro práva k dílům hudebním o.s. v Léčebné lázně Mariánské Lázně a.s.* (C-351/12) ECLI:EU:C:2014:110.

[27]   *SCF v Marco Del Corso* (C-135/10) ECLI:EU:C:2012:140.

viding hyperlinks to illegal content. Essentially, since only the copyright holder has the right to transmit their work over the internet, both the creators and the users of websites that provide unauthorised content, or even links to unauthorised content, are considered to be infringing copyright.

The US includes broadcasting and recitation in its public performance rights and has an additional right to public display. The US approach to the legal meaning of 'public' in this context includes any place open to the public, or where a substantial number of persons outside of a family circle is gathered.[28] In Canada, communication to the public is considered to be any transmission of signs, signals, writings, images or sounds by wire, radio, visual or optical or other electromagnetic system.[29]

4.1.6   Make an adaptation of the work

The copyright holder has the exclusive right to adapt their work, meaning that they can prohibit others from making adaptations to their work without permission. This right is recognised at international level through international agreements such as the Berne Convention, which states that, as a minimum, creators have the exclusive right to authorise adaptations, arrangements and alterations to their work.

The right to make an adaptation means that the copyright holder has control over the transformation of their work into another type of presentation, such as transcribing a musical work for piano into one for a full orchestra. This includes cinematographic adaptations, for instance from a book into a film or by translating the work into another language. Moreover, changing the arrangement of a work refers to adaptations made within the work, such as creating an orchestral version of a popular song. This right is broad and encompassing, and includes other alterations such as editing the work. However, this right is not harmonised and is therefore slightly different in different countries; it is also found in different parts of the law, in that sense. For example, France and the Netherlands include adaptation as part of their copying right. On the other hand, countries such as the UK and Japan provide for adaptation as a separate right. The US also has a separate right but it is worded differently, stating that the rightsholder has the exclusive right to create

---

[28]   *Columbia Pictures Indus Inc v Aveco Inc* 800 F 2d 59 (3rd Circ 1986).
[29]   Canada Copyright Act, section 3(1)(f).

derivative works based on their copyright-protected work. Derivative simply means a work based on a previous work, such as translations, musical arrangements, dramatisations, fictionalisations or adaptations, and therefore the effect is the same.

This first part of this chapter has set out the principal rights that copyright provides for the rightsholder, essentially letting you know what copyright gives you. This second part of this chapter now turns to the additional rights that form part of copyright or come alongside it. These are often referred to as neighbouring rights, and include performers' rights, moral rights and image rights. These are rights that come in addition to copyright or alongside it and provide additional areas of protection. Therefore, it is important to be aware of these rights in order to fully understand the scope of your protection.

4.2   Performers' rights

At the heart of the performer's right is the ability of the performer to be remunerated for the exploitation of the work in which they performed. It also provides the performer with the ability to prevent the use of the work without their permission through means such as broadcasting, communicating to the public and reproduction. Moreover, the right of fixation also remains with the performer, meaning that the performer's permission is required to record their performance. In fact, the original motivation for this right was about trying to prevent 'bootlegging' – the recording and exploiting of live performances.

Performers' rights are recognised at international level through agreements such as the Rome Convention, the TRIPS agreement, the WIPO Performances and Phonograms Treaty[30] and the Beijing Treaty on Audio-visual Performances.[31] A performer is defined as an actor, singer, musician, dancer or other person who acts, sings, delivers, plays in or otherwise performs a literary or artistic work. Examples include actors in films, voice-over artists featured in adverts and backing vocalists singing

---

[30]   WIPO Performances and Phonograms Treaty (WPPT) (1996).
[31]   Beijing Treaty on Audiovisual Performances (2012).

on a record. An aspect of the sound recording is the performance of the song on the master.

Performers can licence, assign or waiver their rights to third parties. Under EU law, the performer retains, and cannot waiver, their right to equitable remuneration for the rental of the work.[32] Performers' rights last for 50 years after the performance; or, if it is fixed as a sound recording, 70 years after the release; or, if it is recorded but not as a sound recording, for 50 years from the publication of the recording.[33] In reality, performers routinely transfer most of their rights to a record company when they sign a recording contract. Although they may transfer control of these rights to the record company, by law they will still retain some economic rights in their performances. This means that when the sound recordings are broadcast or performed in a public place, a collecting society (see Chapter 7) will collect royalties and distribute them directly to the producers and performers on a shared basis.

This includes sessional musicians, who also often transfer their performers' rights to the producer of the sound recording, usually in exchange for a one-off payment. For that reason, this type of performer is called a 'non-featured artist'. The producer of a recording sets aside the revenue for the session fund, which is paid to a licensing body and distributed back to the non-featured artist through a collecting society.

Performers can assign their rights to producers in return for royalties, the terms of which are set out in the contract, which usually includes a deduction of the royalties taken by the producer. After the 50th year of protection has passed, the clean slate provision becomes enforceable. The clean slate provision obliges producers to start paying royalties in full. This ensures that performers can benefit from the extension of the duration period.

A performer who has transferred their rights to the producer of a sound recording can reclaim their rights if the producer is not exploiting the recording. To do this, the performer notifies the producer, who then has

---

[32] EC Directive on Rental Right and Lending Right and on Certain Rights Related to Copyright in The Field of Intellectual Property 2006/115/EC, Article 5(1), (2).

[33] Directive 2011/77/EU of the European Parliament and of the Council of 27 September 2011 amending Directive 2006/116/EC on the Term of Protection of Copyright and Certain Related Rights.

a year to attempt to distribute the work; if they cannot do that within the time frame, the rights in the performance revert back to the performer.

The Performance and Phonograms Treaty and the Beijing Treaty[34] both made it compulsory for signatory countries to provide moral rights protection for performers. Moral rights are another type of additional or neighbouring right to copyright, and are explained in the next section.

4.3   Moral rights

Moral rights are rights that connect a creator or author to their work. These rights were originally developed in Continental Europe and are now recognised at international level through the Berne Convention.[35] They are actually also reinforced as a human right under the Universal Declaration of Human Rights 1948, which states that 'everyone has the right to the protection of the moral and material interests resulting from any scientific, literary or artistic production of which [t]he[y] are the author'.[36]

The US, however, has resisted the literal implementation of these provisions, using derivatives in different parts of their laws in order to comply with the international agreements, although the reach of these rights is considered extremely restricted compared to other countries. The UK, Australia and Canada have all transposed these laws into their national copyright legislation. These rights are considered to be especially strong throughout Continental Europe, as they sit more comfortably with the rationale for authors' rights. As explained in Chapter 1, this perspective is referred to as personality or author rights; it takes the view that when you create something it is an extension of yourself and your personality and therefore you should own and control it.

These are not economic rights because they cannot be sold or licensed in the same way as the rights provided by the restricted acts discussed earlier in this chapter. This means that they cannot be transferred, and always

---

[34]   WPPT (1996), Article 5 and Beijing Treaty on Audiovisual Performances (2012), Article 5.

[35]   The Berne Convention, Article 6*bis* of the Paris Act 1971.

[36]   Universal Declaration of Human Rights 1948.

remain with the creator, unless – as happens in certain circumstances – the creator decides to waiver or surrender these rights. Moral rights provide the creator with different types of rights in their work. These can be summarised into two main categories: (1) the right of attribution and (2) the right of integrity in the work. These rights are explained below.

1. The right of attribution – also called the right to paternity – means the right to be identified as the author or creator of a work which you created.[37] Likewise, this includes the right to object against any false attribution,[38] meaning not to be incorrectly cited as the creator of something that you did not make. In civil law countries these rights are non-waiverable; in other words, you cannot give them up. In the UK these rights are subject to exceptions and conditions. For example, in order to benefit from the right of attribution in the UK you must assert your right.[39] That is why you see authors' rights asserted in their work, such as at the beginning of this book. In the UK, the right of attribution lasts for the same length of time as the copyright in the work and the right not to be falsely attributed lasts for 20 years after the death of the creator. In some countries, such as France and Spain, these rights last forever.

2. The right of integrity means the right to object to derogatory treatment of a work, or any part of it. The Berne Convention describes this as the right to object to any distortion, mutilation or other modification of, or other derogatory action in relation to, the work, that would be prejudicial to the honour or reputation of the creator.[40] In the UK, this right lasts for the same length of time as the copyright in the work. Again, this right is recognised broadly in civil law countries such as France, Germany and Japan. In France and Spain, this right is perpetual. Although these rights are less rigorous in common law countries such as the UK, Canada and the US, they do still exist in one form or another.

As mentioned, performers also have moral rights in their performances. As such, performers have the right to be identified as the performer and the right to object to derogatory treatment of their performance. The derogatory treatment right enables performers to object to alterations

---

[37] UK CDPA 1988, sections 77–79.
[38] CDPA 1988, section 84.
[39] UK CDPA 1988, sections 78–79.
[40] The Berne Convention, The Paris Act 1971 6*bis*(1).

made to their work, which is particularly relevant if the changes intended to be made risk damaging the performer's reputation.

4.4   Image and publicity rights

Well-known artists, musicians and producers often utilise benefits from their so-called image or publicity rights. These are rights in your own image, as well as branding and marketing, which are important for building your reputation and growing your fan base, your market and essentially your record sales. Successful artists are successful brands. Most of what is required to build a successful brand is outside the remit of a book about copyright, as much of it comes down to a different type of intellectual property right called trade mark. (A trade mark is essentially a name, logo or slogan that is registered against a product or service in the countries in which you are operating. It is an asset that can then be licensed for sponsorship and merchandise.)

It is essential that you are aware of the existence of additional rights such as publicity rights in building your brand, particularly as they are being exploited more by artists and are growing in relevance in the social media era.

In the US these types of rights are specifically recognised in the law as publicity rights. This is unsurprising since there is quite the celebrity culture in the US. For example, New York Civil Rights Law prevents the use of a 'name, portrait, picture or voice ... for advertising purposes or for the purposes of trade without ... written consent.'[41] This is the law that Lindsay Lohan used to sue Grand Theft Auto for creating a character called 'Lacey Jonas' that looked like her.[42] Incidentally, she also tried to use this right to sue Pitbull for his lyrics 'I got it locked up like Lindsay Lohan' in his song *Give Me Everything*, but was unsuccessful.[43]

[41]   New York Civil Rights Law §§50-51.
[42]   http://ipkitten.blogspot.com/2014/08/lindsay-lohan-and-new-york-right-of.html
[43]   *Lohan v Perez*, 924 F. Supp. 2d 447 (E.D.N.Y. 2013).

Another example of an artist using their publicity rights around the use of their music was the dispute between 50 Cent and Rick Ross.[44] The copyright in 50 Cent's song *In Da Club* is owned by his then record label, Shady/Aftermath Records. However, the contract only transferred his publicity rights to the label for the duration of his recording contract, which ended in 2014. So, while he does not have the copyright in the song, he can enforce his publicity rights. Rick Ross released a mixtape, *Renzel Remixes*, where he raps over sampled songs, including *In Da Club*. He raps over the original instrumental, ending with the original hook and outro from 50 Cent. Rick Ross would only have needed permission from the label, the copyright holder. So 50 Cent brought a publicity claim instead, for the use of his voice and stage name, claiming that the remix misappropriated his name, performance and likeness. However, the US court decided Rick Ross' use of 50 Cent's voice was an inevitable result of his use of the song and the use of his stage name served to accurately identify the source. The remix did not imply an endorsement, was not derogatory and did not invade 50 Cent's privacy; the claim failed.

In other countries, such as the UK, celebrities have been able to benefit from other laws, including passing-off, to protect their image. For example, when Topshop decided to sell a T-shirt with a picture of Rihanna on the front, she successfully sued them in the UK under the law of passing-off.[45] In this case, the judges said that while there are no image rights which allow a celebrity to control the use of their name or image in the UK, they can rely on other laws such as passing-off, breach of contract or breach of confidence. In the case of Topshop, Rihanna was successful because, by selling the T-shirt, Topshop represented to customers that it was in some way connected or associated with Rihanna, which it was not. In other words, it seemed as if Topshop and Rihanna were in some kind of agreement, sponsorship or endorsement deal but they were not; this is illegal under the laws of passing-off in the UK.

---

[44]   *Jackson v Roberts*, No. 19-0480 (2d Cir. 2020).
[45]   *Fenty & Ors v Arcadia Group Brands Ltd & Anor* [2015] EWCA Civ 3 (22 January 2015), 29–33.

5 What copyright does not give you

The previous chapter explained what copyright provides for the rightsholder, and now this chapter sets out the limitations and exceptions to those rights. The limitations define the scope of your rights. It is important to be aware of the exceptions to copyright so that you understand when and how others can use your work without your permission, and likewise when and how you can legitimately use other people's copyright-protected work without their permission.

5.1   Limitations to copyright

The purpose of putting limitations on the rights provided to the copyright owner is to balance the interest of the stakeholders. One way in which the rights are limited is through length: they do not last forever. The international agreements that set out the minimum arrangements for copyright stipulate that for literary and artistic works (which includes musical and dramatic works), protection must last for at least 50 years after the death of the creator.[1] There are a few nuances: for example, for cinematographic works the term can be 50 years after the work has been made available to the public with the consent of the author, or 50 years after the making of an unpublished work. Photographic works and works of applied art have a shorter minimum term of at least until the end of 25 years from the making of the work.

These are the minimum lengths of the rights; countries can extend beyond them but cannot reduce the length of protection to less than is specified by the Berne Convention. Generally, in many countries, copyright lasts 70 years after the death of the creator. As explained in Chapter

---

[1]   The Berne Convention 1886 (as amended 28 September 1979), Article 2(1).

1, this was not always the case and the term has been continually extended over time. The snag is that the new laws which provide longer protection are not usually retrospective! This means that in order to figure out how long the copyright on a particular piece of protected work lasts, you need to know when the piece was created or published, in what country and by whom, including the year of their death and the copyright law at the time it was created! This can be quite the task. When a work has fallen out of copyright, it is deemed to be freely available in the public domain. A work is in the public domain when there is no copyright attached to it, for example because the copyright has expired. When a work is in the public domain it is freely available for anyone to use without permission. There are a number of services and websites that make public domain material available. However, when deciding to use public domain material, such as a sound clip for a sample in your song, it is worth undertaking the due diligence to confirm that the work really is in the public domain. This is particularly necessary if the work is being disseminated through a publisher or record label, who will expect you to have done so – and by expect, what I really mean is contractually oblige you to.

For performers' rights, the duration is different. Performers' rights in unreleased performances last for 50 years. This 50-year period begins from the year in which the performance occurred. A recording of a performance is considered to have been released when it is first published, played or shown to the public. If during this 50-year period a recording of the performance is released, then the duration depends on the type of work that the recording is. If the recording of the performance is a sound recording, the term of protection extends to 70 years from the date of release. This duration for performers' rights was extended in November 2013. To ensure that all performers can benefit from this change, further protections were created, and so these new protections become applicable following the 50th year since the release of the recording. If the recording of the performance is not a sound recording, the term of protection extends to 50 years from the date of release.

Another way in which copyright is limited is by scope, in that it does not protect ideas, only the individual expression of an idea, as discussed in detail in Chapter 2. There is also a limitation to the monopoly of the copyright holder, called a compulsory licence; this means that a licence must be issued when requested and cannot be refused. These issues are discussed in Chapter 9, which covers licensing. Section 5.2 turns to discuss the exceptions to copyright.

5.2   Exceptions to copyright

The copyright exceptions apply in specific circumstances in which a copyright-protected work – that is still within its copyright term – can be used without the permission of the copyright holder. In some countries these exceptions are provided in a closed list, such as in the UK. In others, such as the US, there is not a closed list but instead they have a system called fair use. The closed list of the copyright exceptions is explained below, followed by an overview of fair use. It is really important to understand that these systems of exceptions are different, and to grasp what is legally allowed under each one – particularly as there is often confusion between the two systems which can lead people to do something which they believed was legal, but turned out to be illegal under the system of the country they were in. In my experience, people tend to have heard of fair use, although not necessarily to understand exactly what it allows them to do, but the main misconception is that fair use is relevant in countries outside of the US, such as the UK. It does not help that in the UK a group of the copyright exceptions are known as fair dealing, so it is easy to get them mixed up! However, as mentioned, these laws are territorial and not harmonised, so they are diverse in each country. This means that a piece of creative work that might fall under a copyright exception in one territory, and so be perfectly legal there, might not fall within the copyright exceptions of another country, and may therefore be considered copyright infringement.

At international level, certain exceptions are provided for by the Berne Convention, while some are mandatory, such as the allowance of quotation. There is also a specific international agreement called the Marrakesh Treaty that requires countries to provide an exception for the purpose of enabling access to copyright-protected works for visually impaired people. However, most of the copyright exceptions are discretionary. Accordingly, countries can decide if they want to implement these exceptions in their national law, and on what terms they apply. Some countries choose to do so and others do not, meaning that the law is varied across the world. Also, it is worth noting that when I say 'choose to', that is a massive over-simplification of the process of policy change and lawmaking that is involved. An example of the carnage that can be caused as a result of this is given below when discussing the private copying exception in the UK.

For the closed list of copyright exceptions, each one has its own specific set of circumstances to which it can apply. These will be briefly explained below. The aim here is to give you an idea of the different exceptions that exist and what the circumstances for their legitimate use might be. However, if you are planning to benefit from one of these exceptions or wish to consider if someone else's use of your work falls within these circumstances, I strongly suggest that you look in more detail at the specific criteria for that exception within the relevant country. In practice, the use of copyright exceptions is a process of evaluating both the circumstances and risk, because it is not often a clear-cut matter as to whether the exception would apply in that particular circumstance, or if the use of the work complies with the criteria of that exception. The general perception is that the UK has narrow and specific exceptions and as a result many people take a risk-averse approach. This is sometimes a shame because they do not utilise exceptions where they clearly exist. In contrast, there is a general perception that the US fair use system is much broader and encompassing. However, while it is certainly more flexible, a range of factors need to be considered in order to benefit from fair use. Strangely enough, I have often seen the opposite approach to risk in relation to fair use, where people assume that what they are doing falls within the exception when in fact it does not. In both circumstances, knowledge is power. These are copyright defences and not rights, which require the users to fulfil certain criteria in order to claim them. As such, knowing the difference and the requirements can sort the legal uses from the illegal uses and enable you to make informed decisions regarding the risk.

The most relevant exceptions for the music industry are quotation and parody. These are set out in more detail below and we will come back to them when discussing music sampling in Chapter 14.

5.2.1   Quotation, criticism and review

As mentioned, quotation is a mandatory copyright exception under the Berne Convention, which states that all signatory countries must make it legal for quotation of a work to be made so long as the work was already lawfully made available to the public and the extent of the quotation is fair, in that the amount used does not exceed what is justified by the purpose. Although the exception itself is compulsory each country is free to make its own rules and conditions about when and how it can apply, for example, with regard to what that country considers to be fair.

Under the UK fair dealing exceptions, quotation is provided together with an exception for criticism and review.[2] (Well, backstory: before 2014, the UK did not actually have a specified quotation exception; it formed part of the criticism and review exception. In 2014, new exceptions were introduced into UK law which included the expansion of this exception to specifically include quotation.) The exception for quotation, criticism and review applies to all types of copyright material in the UK, but watch out because this is not the case for all of the exceptions! The purpose of this exception is to enable the critique and review of a creator's work without having to get the creator's permission first – this is important because otherwise a creator would be able to censor reviews they did not like. The reviewer can use examples of the creator's work to demonstrate to their audience the point they are trying to make. Similarly, extracts of copyright works can be used without permission for quotation in other contexts, such as using a short quote in a history book, an academic article – or a book about music and copyright! Without these exceptions it would be an infringement of copyright to do these things.

However, in order to benefit from these exceptions, the reviewer or person using the quote must meet the following criteria, under UK law. Both the quotation and the criticism exceptions require that: (1) the purpose is really for quotation, criticism or review; (2) the material used is available to the public; (3) the use of the material is fair; (4) where practical, the use is accompanied by a sufficient acknowledgement. In relation to fair dealing for the purpose of quotation, on top of the four criteria mentioned above there is one additional requirement: that the use of the quotation must extend no further than is required to achieve the purpose. These rules are explained in a little more detail below.[3]

---

2   UK CDPA 1988, section 30.
3   See also www.copyrightuser.org/understand/exceptions/quotation/ accessed 6 November 2020.

5.2.1.1   *The reason is genuinely for the purpose of quotation, criticism or review*

This means that the purpose of the use is really criticism, review or quotation and not something else. A review can consider not only the merit and particulars of another work, but also the philosophy of the work, or its moral or social implications. However, you cannot simply reproduce the material without accompanying it with genuine critique or putting it into context, by way of discussion or assessment. For example, showing a whole film and simply commenting at the end that you liked it would not be acceptable.

5.2.1.2   *The material used is already available to the public*

This means that the copyright work was already made available to the public, such as by being legally published or distributed, or if there has been a performance, exhibition or communication of the work to the public. However, it does not include work that has only been made available confidentially, no matter how many people this confidential information was shared with. So, for example, if someone were to share a private letter, the material in the letter is not understood as being available to the public and therefore cannot be used, such as is being argued at the time of writing in the case brought against a British newspaper by the Duchess of Sussex, Meghan Markle.[4]

5.2.1.3   *The use of the material is fair*

When quoting a work any specific aspect of the material can be used, even if these parts are not representative of the whole work. The review can be positive or negative, or even an unbalanced or hostile critique, without infringing the copyright of the creator of the work (although defamation laws can prevent outright lying if it detriments the reputation of a person).

There is no legal definition of what exactly is a fair or unfair amount of the work that can be used; it is at the courts' discretion based on the individual facts of the case and the purpose for which the material was

---

[4]   Bosher H, 'Meghan Markle Letter: What the Law Says About the Press, Privacy and the Public's Right to Know' (The Conversation, 2019) https://theconversation.com/meghan-markle-letter-what-the-law-says-about-the-press-privacy-and-the-publics-right-to-know-124619 accessed 19 July 2020.

used. There may even be circumstances where it is fair to use the whole of a piece of work – for example, a short poem or a photograph. Essentially, for use of someone else's copyright-protected work to be fair, it should not conflict with the way in which they normally exploit their work. So, it is helpful to think about whether the use of the copyright material is, or could be, in commercial competition with the copyright owner.

5.2.1.4   *Where practical, sufficient acknowledgement is provided*

Any use of another's work for the purpose of quotation, criticism or review should include an acknowledgement that identifies the creator, or the work and the title of the material used. It is the author who should be identified and not the owner of the copyright (these are not always the same person, as explained in Chapter 6). For example, when referencing a song in this context, the name of the artist and the song title need to be acknowledged, rather than the record label or publisher.

If you are making use of the work online, it is not enough to just link to the original material. It is a common misconception that simply crediting the creator or writing 'no copyright infringement intended' under a YouTube video somehow means that that use falls outside of copyright infringement. Oops! This is incorrect, although the acknowledgement part is necessary if the person is intending to benefit from a copyright exception.

5.2.1.5   *The quotation must be no more than is required to achieve the purpose*

This standard only applies to the exception for general quotation, and not to criticism and review. The relationship between this requirement and the requirement that your use is fair is obviously an important one. In theory, while your use might be regarded as fair, it could still be more than is required to meet your purpose. Therefore, while the new exception for quotation provides greater freedom to quote the works of others for purposes other than criticism and review, the scope for relying on this new exception is narrower because there are more criteria. What is considered to be 'no more than is required' is not defined in the legislation. This would be resolved by the courts on a case-by-case basis, so we cannot say for sure what this would be.

5.2.2   Parody

A parody is a new creative work that uses or references an existing work for humour or mockery, often as a form of critique or comment on society. Parody is vital for free speech (and the lols); that is why it must be enabled through a copyright exception.

At European level, use of a copyright work is permitted for the purpose of caricature, parody or pastiche.[5] The UK introduced a parody exception in 2014, although it has been criticised as being fairly narrow, vague and ill-defined,[6] since there is little explanation as to its scope and no case law to determine more information. As a general rule, the exception requires that the user seeks permission from the rightsholder. (Which totally defeats the point of it being an exception, because if they say yes then it is being used *with* permission!) This does include if the rightsholder says no. (Which is also absolute nonsense, as the point of this requirement is defeated if it doesn't actually matter what the rightsholders' response is?!) But still, permission must be at least sought – and for that purpose, remember to keep a record of the request and reply. The amount used will also be a factor, likely similar to that of the other exceptions. The parody needs to add some creative layer to the work, since the new work only needs to evoke the previous work, rather than be a whole and direct copy of it. In fact, it needs to do more than re-working or altering a copyright-protected work; it should communicate a new message distinct from the earlier work. Lastly, the courts are likely to consider whether the use causes any commercial harm to the original rightsholder, for example if the parody is in direct competition with the original work.[7] However, research suggests that parodies tend to be of commercial benefit to the work, rather than causing any financial damage.[8]

---

[5]   The Information Society Directive, Article 5(3)(k).

[6]   See Jacques S, *The Parody Exception in Copyright Law* (OUP 2019).

[7]   UK CDPA 1988, section 30A and schedule 2(2A); see also www.copyrightuser.org/understand/exceptions/parody-pastiche accessed 6 November 2020.

[8]   See Erikson K, 'Evaluating the Impact of Parody on the Exploitation of Copyright Works: An Empirical Study of Music Video Content on YouTube' (UK IPO 2013).

5.2.3   Other exceptions

There are a number of other copyright exceptions, such as news reporting, educational institutions and private study, and others relating to libraries and archiving. These are briefly mentioned in this section.

Many countries offer a copyright exception for the purpose of news reporting, since it would inhibit the ability of the press to have to secure copyright permission in order to publish breaking news. This exception is provided for in EU law and so can be found in one form or another in all European countries.[9] In the UK,[10] similar criteria apply for this exception as for the criticism and review one (the purpose is really for reporting current events, the use of the material is fair, and it is accompanied by sufficient acknowledgement). However, there is no need for the information to already be made available – hence news! (Finally, a copyright rule that really does make sense.) There is a fourth criteria, though, which is that this exception does not apply to photographs – a small but significant sentence in the law, from which delicately hangs the careers of the paparazzi and many photographers.

Educational establishments benefit from some copyright exceptions, such as for the purpose of instruction by the teacher. In the UK this exception is extremely narrow and most educational establishments actually pay a blanket licence for their use of textbooks for students, and other such activities.[11] Likewise in the UK, there are exceptions for research and private study, text and data mining, libraries, museums and galleries, archives and preservation.[12]

Some EU countries also have a private copying exception, which allows for a person to make a reproduction of a copyright-protected work for their own private use, as long as there is no direct or indirect commercial gain and the rightsholder is fairly compensated. One way in which the rightsholders can be compensated is through a levy system. This means,

---

[9]   Directive 2001/29/EC of the European Parliament and of the Council of 22 May 2001 on the Harmonisation of Certain Aspects of Copyright and Related Rights in the Information Society (the Information Society Directive), Article 5(3).

[10]   UK CDPA 1988, section 30(2),(3); see also www.copyrightuser.org/understand/exceptions/news -reporting/ accessed 6 November 2020.

[11]   www.copyrightuser.org/understand/exceptions/education accessed 6 November 2020.

[12]   www.copyrightuser.org/understand/exceptions/ accessed 6 November 2020.

for example, that some of the costs of equipment that allows reproduction of copyright-protected material, such as a photocopier, revert back to the authors of the work that will be copied by the machine. (This makes it sound as if machines are taking over the world to copy rightsholders' work. More on robots in Part V.)

In the UK, in October 2014, the government ambitiously introduced a private copying exception permitting individuals to make personal copies of copyright work for private use (such as format shifting CDs to MP3 files). However, the Musicians' Union; UK Music; the British Academy of Songwriters, Composers and Authors; and the Society of Musicians took legal action against the UK government claiming that the exception was illegal since they were not fairly compensated, as is required by EU law.[13] They were correct, and as a result, in July 2015 the exception was quashed by the courts. Slam dunk. Any acts of private copying which would have fallen under the exception in the UK now revert back to being acts of infringement.

5.2.4   Fair use

As mentioned, the US copyright exception system is called fair use. Fair use sets out the principles, to be applied on a case-by-case basis, in which copyright-protected material can be used without the rightsholders' permission in America. The US law[14] provides that fair use of a copyright-protected work for purposes such as criticism, comment, news reporting, teaching (including multiple copies for classroom use), scholarship or research is not an infringement of copyright. However, when deciding if the particular use made of a work in any specific circumstance is a fair use, the factors to be considered will include the following:

1. The purpose and character of the use (which includes whether the use of the work is transformative), and whether such use is of a commercial nature or is for non-profit educational purposes.
2. The nature of the copyright-protected work, meaning the type of work that was copied. This is because the US courts give more protection to creative works, such as songs, novels and artworks, than they do to factual works such as non-fiction books.

---

[13] www.bailii.org/cgi-bin/markup.cgi?doc=/ew/cases/EWHC/Admin/2015/2041.html&query= EWHC+and+2041&method=boolean accessed 6 November 2020.
[14] 17 US Code, section 107.

3. The amount and substantiality of the portion used in relation to the copyright-protected work as a whole; the general principle is that the more of the work used, the less likely it is to be fair use.
4. The effect of the use upon the potential market for, or value of, the copyright-protected work; in other words, the damage caused to the copyright holder by the use of their work.

An example of a successful fair use claim involved Drake's 2013 song *Pound Cake/Paris Morton Music 2*, which used a previous spoken-word recording titled *Jimmy Smith Rap* by jazz musician James Oscar Smith. In 2017, a New York judge decided that Drake's use of the spoken-word recording was transformative. The crucial point in the case was that Drake's song transformed the message of the original work, 'adding something new, with a further purpose or different character, altering the first with new expression, meaning or message'.[15] Therefore, Drake was successful in claiming fair use and his use of the spoken-word recording in his song was not copyright infringement.

5.3   Exhaustion of rights (first sale doctrine)

One more limitation worth mentioning is called the exhaustion of rights. The rights of distribution are said to be 'exhausted' in the particular copy of the work once it has been sold. This means that your rights in the physical CD or vinyl end after it has been lawfully sold. Therefore, if someone legally purchases your CD, they are able to sell it on eBay, or give it to someone else as a gift. Your rights in the song and the sound recording on the CD remain; it is only in the physical copy of that CD that the rights are exhausted.

In general, these principles only apply to physical copies and not digital copies.[16] Most countries also specify that the exhaustion of rights only applies within the country, so that copies cannot be imported without the rightsholder's consent. In the EU, when the copyright is exhausted in one Member State it is exhausted in all Member States.

---

[15] *Estate of James Oscar Smith v Cash Money Records* 1:14-cv-02703-WHP (30/5/2017).
[16] Except in special cases such as computer programs, as in *UsedSoft GmbH v Oracle International Corp* (C-128/11) 3 July 2012.

In the US this is called the first sale doctrine. It provides that the owner of a lawful copy or phonorecord[17] is entitled to sell or dispose of possession of the copy, without the copyright holder's permission. This has the same meaning: that the copyright holder's rights on the physical record end at the point of sale. The focus of this provision is on the owner of the lawful copy and does not apply to someone who merely has a licence to use the copy.[18] In the US the doctrine also applies to copies lawfully made abroad.[19]

This chapter concludes Part I of this book, which covered what copyright is, how it works, why it is so important, what it protects, and what exceptions and limitations there are to that protection. Part II looks at managing these rights – who owns them, the different people involved and the contracts and licences that manage those relationships – as well as taking a look at how copyright works on social media.

---

[17]   Meaning the tangible physical thing that the song is recorded on to, such as cassette tape, vinyl or CD.

[18]   *Vernor v Autodesk Inc* 621 F 3d 1102 (9th Circ 2010).

[19]   *Kirtsaeng v John Wiley & Sons Inc* 568 US 519 (2013).

PART II

MANAGING MUSIC COPYRIGHT

Part II looks at how copyright is managed in music. This gives you an insight into the way that rights are allocated, the different players involved and what their roles are, and then how the contracts and licences between you and them operate.

Chapter 6 covers ownership of copyright. It explains initial ownership, joint ownership and what happens if you make a work as a freelancer or in the course of employment. It also clarifies the situation if the creator is unknown or has died, and it concludes with a summary on the ownership breakdown of a song.

Chapter 7 sets out the roles and relationships within the music industry, introducing the different people that artists might work with, such as band members, lawyers, publishers, record labels, managers and collecting societies. It also provides information about some of the relevant organisations, lobby groups and communities that represent those within the music industry.

Chapter 8 builds on the roles set out in the previous chapter, to explain the key aspects of the contracts that manage the copyright in those relationships. It includes a basic introduction to contracts and covers collaborator agreements, management contracts, recording contracts and publishing contracts, as well as sponsorship, influencer and merchandising agreements.

Chapter 9 covers licensing; it explains the difference between an assignment and a licence of copyright, and what limitations there are on the terms of a licence. It then looks at some of the types of copyright licences that operate in the music industry.

Chapter 10 considers managing copyright on social media. It explores ownership and infringement of content uploaded to social media platforms and takes a closer look at the use of music on TikTok and YouTube.

6   Who owns the copyright?

Part II of this book covers managing the copyright in music, including how the rights are allocated and can be utilised. The first step in this process is to understand who owns the copyright and consequently who can make the decisions about what happens with it. Therefore, the first chapter in Part II looks at copyright ownership. It explains initial ownership, along with what happens if there are more people involved in the creation of the work, in joint or collective ownership situations. Second, it explains what happens if you create a work for hire – as a freelancer or session musician, for example – as well as what happens if you are creating works as part of your job or employment. Third, this chapter sets out what happens if the creator is unknown or has died. The chapter concludes with a summary of who owns the different parts of a song. Chapter 7 goes into more detail on the different people involved in the making and distributing of music.

6.1   First ownership

Usually the first owner of the copyright is the creator. (Since copyright was originally concerned with the protection of literary works, as explained in Part I, often the creator is called the author even when referring to creative works other than writings.) However, in the music industry this will depend entirely on how the music was recorded and under what circumstances. If you make a studio deal, for example, the studio owner might want a stake in the copyright. If you are in an agreement with a record company, they usually expect to own the copyright in the recording, otherwise known as the master. If you have a publishing deal, the publishing company will often own the composition. The roles, relationships and agreements with record and publishing companies, as well as other stakeholders in your music, is discussed in more detail in Chapter 7. For now, what you need to know is that technically you are the first owner of the music as the creator, but it will likely be licensed under agreements with a record label and/or publisher.

At international level, the issue of authorship is not defined, and it is left to each country to decide in their national laws how exactly it is determined. In general, these laws recognise that the natural person who conceived of and executed the work is the creator, or author, and therefore the first owner of the copyright.

Australia, Canada and India vest the ownership of copyright in the creator of the work, excluding in the circumstances of employment discussed below. In the UK the law states, for literary, dramatic, musical and artistic works, that the copyright owner is the creator of the work. However, in the case of a sound recording, the initial copyright owner is the producer. (The producer does not mean a music producer but rather the person who made the arrangements necessary for making the sound recording, unless of course that person was also a music producer. Often the record company qualifies as the producer.) In the case of a film, the copyright owners are the producer and the principal director. For a broadcast, it is the person making the broadcast and in the case of a typographical arrangement of a published edition, it is the publisher.[1] For a literary, dramatic, musical or artistic work which is computer-generated, the author is taken to be the person who made the necessary arrangements for the creation of the work.[2] (This is discussed in more detail in Part V of this book, relating to AI-created works.)

The German copyright law also vests the exclusive right to reproduce and distribute a sound recording in the producer. If the producer is an enterprise, then the owner of the enterprise is the copyright owner.[3] Likewise, French law also provides that the producer of a sound recording is the copyright owner, and that is deemed to be the person who takes the initiative and responsibility for the initial fixation of a sequence of sounds. In this instance a person can be a natural person or a legal person, meaning it can be an individual or a company.[4] This is the same under Canadian law. In the US the copyright vests in the author, including in the case of a sound recording.[5] In most circumstances the producer will be contracted under a work for hire, meaning that the copyright holder becomes

---

[1] UK CDPA 1988, section 9.
[2] UK CDPA 1988, section 9(3).
[3] Germany, Copyright Act, Article 85(1).
[4] French Intellectual Property Code, Article L.213-1.
[5] US Copyright Act 1976, s 201(a).

the company or person that made the hire. Work for hire circumstances are discussed in more detail below.

The ownership can also be joint, since different people might contribute to the song. This is explained in section 6.2.

6.2   Joint ownership

More than one person can contribute to the creation of a song. For instance, one person may write the lyrics and another the melody, or two people could write lyrics together and a third and fourth person develop the melody. Then, of course, someone else may produce the record.

If one person writes the lyrics and another creates the melody, they could have separate copyright in each part of the song. In such a case, if someone wanted to use, for instance, just the melody, they would only need the permission of the melody creator. More often, in practice, co-writers agree to joint ownership of the song. In this scenario, the co-writers both have copyright in the song regardless of how much or how little they contributed to it – unless otherwise agreed – and then the copyright lasts for 70 years after the death of the last surviving creator.

Either way, it is imperative that when you are working with other people to create your music, you agree, in writing, who owns what part and what portion of the copyright in the music. This is the case even, and especially, if you are friendly with your co-writer. Try not to think of this agreement as a formal or awkward thing that you must do, but rather as a way to make sure that everyone knows where they stand. It is a way to safeguard all the contributors against disputes arising later from any misunderstandings or disagreements about who owns what and who can make decisions about what happens with the song.

The contract should be clearly written and unambiguous, and for the avoidance of doubt, all the rights of those involved in the song making and recording should be specified – including writers, collaborators, band members and even session musicians. You also need to be clear on this when completing the Joint Registration Form – either yourself with PRS, or via your publisher, for the purposes of allocating royalty payments.

(PRS is a collecting society, explained in Chapter 7; royalty payments are explained in Chapter 9.)

There have been many copyright disputes that come down to arguments about ownership of the work. For example, in a case involving Spandau Ballet,[6] a five-member pop group, Mr Kemp was the song writer and composer, as well as the guitarist/keyboard player and singer. Three of the band members sued Mr Kemp for shares in the copyright of the songs, arguing that they had contributed to the songs during rehearsals. The court decided that Mr Kemp's songs existed as literary and musical works before being reproduced in material form by the band in rehearsals, and that he was therefore the copyright author and owner. Moreover, it was specified that a drummer adding a short drum loop that does not make any material difference to the song does not qualify as co-writing.

However, this was not the case in relation to *Whiter Shade of Pale*,[7] one of the most successful popular songs of the late 1960s, recorded by the band Procol Harum. The musicians on the recording were Gary Brooker (voice and piano), Matthew Fisher (Hammond organ), David Knights (bass), Ray Royer (guitar) and Bill Eyden (session drummer). The producer was Denny Cordell and the sound engineer Keith Grant. The writers of the song credited on the record label were Keith Reid (lyrics) and Mr Brooker (music). The song is four minutes long and features an organ solo by Matthew Fisher, which was considered to be distinctive, memorable and the most identifiable part of the song. Matthew Fisher brought an action in court claiming that his contribution to the song entitled him to joint authorship, and therefore a stake in the copyright. The courts agreed with Fisher and granted him a 40 per cent share in the musical copyright.

In general, the concept of joint authorship is that two or more creators work together on inseparable or interdependent parts of a unitary whole. However, contributions must be original material expressions, not just ideas or non-copyrightable materials. In the US it has been recognised that contributions do not have to be equal, but adding ideas, directing changes and giving approval would not be enough.[8] However, a Dutch court did allow joint authorship in a photograph between the photogra-

---

[6] *Hadley and Others v Kemp and Another* [1999] Chancery Division.

[7] *Matthew Fisher v Gary Brooker* [2006] EWHC 3238 and [2009] UKHL 41.

[8] *Aitken, Hazen, Hoffman, Miller PC. v Empire Construction Company*, 542 F. Supp. 252 (D. Neb. 1982).

pher and the stylist, where the stylist had creatively arranged needlework pieces for the photograph to be taken.[9]

The concept of joint authorship was considered in a recent UK case between a Ms Kogan and a Mr Martin,[10] concerning the authorship of the screenplay of the film *Florence Foster Jenkins*. Mr Martin claimed that he was the sole copyright owner and argued that Ms Kogan was simply an encouraging sounding-board and proofreader, who also provided minor suggestions and background information based upon her musical expertise. On the other hand, Ms Kogan claimed joint authorship with Mr Martin. She said that while Mr Martin was the main writer and contributed considerably more, she had input creative collaboration and that they had been bouncing ideas off each other at speed. In this case the court confirmed that, under UK law, joint authorship involved four elements: (1) collaboration; (2) authorship; (3) contribution; and (4) non-distinctness of contribution.[11] It explained these points in detail as follows:

1. For joint authorship, the collaboration must be for a common design. In other words, joint authorship only arises when the work is created as a result of a collaboration between contributors pursuant to a common concept, idea, goal or plan. This means more than a critique and involves looking at the nature of the interactions between the contributors, as well as the nature of the work itself.
2. For literary, artistic, dramatic and musical works, the owner is not necessarily the person who makes the fixation – in other words, the question is not: 'who did the writing?'
3. The contribution of a joint author must be authorial, and this depends on the type of work. In the present case example, the screenplay was a dramatic work where devising aspects such as the characters, the plot and dramatic incidents could, in principle, amount to a contribution of an authorial kind. This relates back to the discussion on originality in Chapter 2: it is about whether the author expressed their own intellectual creation by making free and expressive choices.

---

[9]   *Kluwer v Lamoth*, Dutch Supreme Court, 1 June 1990, NJ 1991.

[10]   *Kogan v Martin* [2019] EWCA Civ 1645; see commentary http://ipkitten.blogspot.com/2019/10/guest -post-martin-v-kogan-court-of.html accessed 6 November 2020.

[11]   UK CDPA 1988, section 10(1).

4. Joint authorship depends on the individual contributions being
    non-distinct, meaning that the contribution of each person is not
    separate from that of the other. There is no further requirement that
    the authors must have subjectively intended to jointly author a work.

In the US, there are two different forms of joint authorship, inseparable
(similar to non-distinct explained above) and interdependent, meaning
separate music and separate lyrics but meant to be part of a single work.
Under US law, no joint author can non-exclusively license the work
without the other's permission and can even sell their own undivided
interest. There was a recent US case on joint authorship between Lizzo
and two brothers, Justin and Jeremiah Raisen,[12] about the song *Truth
Hurts*. The Raisen brothers claimed they were involved in an early
writing session with Lizzo where they created a song titled *Healthy* which
included a quote from a tweet: 'I just took a DNA test, turns out I'm 100
percent that bitch.' Later, Lizzo created a derivative work of *Healthy*,
called *Truth Hurts*, which included the iconic lyrics. Lizzo argued that
joint authorship does not apply when a derivative work has been created
using a joint creation, where the joint author had no hand in creating the
second work. The courts agreed that joint authorship in a prior work is
insufficient to make one a joint author of a derivative work and therefore,
even if the Raisen brothers were co-authors of *Healthy*, they did not allege
any ownership interest in *Truth Hurts*, so the claim failed. However, it has
been reported that the brothers intend to amend the details of their claim
and continue to pursue the issue.

Overall, the judges stated that the contributions of joint authors do not
need to be equal. Just because one of the creators had the final say, or
contributed more, does not mean that there was not joint authorship
(although this may affect the share of copyright).

6.3   Works made in the course of employment

The previous sections set out who is the initial owner of the copyright
and what happens when there is more than one creator. However, there

---

[12] *Melissa Jefferson v Justin Raisen, et al.* Case 2:19-cv-09107-DMG-MAA, Document 57 (filed 14
    August 2020).

are some nuances to the above-mentioned rules, such as when the work is created as part of employment or by a freelancer as a work for hire.

In the UK, when a work is created in the course of employment, it is the employer – not the employee – who owns the copyright in that work.[13] This is the same in the Netherlands.[14] In France, ownership of copyright by a corporation is only provided for in the case of collective works and of computer programs created in the course of employment. Australia, Canada and India also vest ownership in the employer when the work was created in the course of employment.

The key thing to remember here is to check the terms of your employment contract, and potentially negotiate them if appropriate. In the absence of an explicit clause stating otherwise in your employment contract, the work you create during the course of your employment belongs to your employer. The employer is therefore the copyright holder and you do not have the rights (set out in Chapter 4) in the work. You may still retain some other rights, such as moral rights and performers' rights, depending on the contract and the law of the country that you are in. Often, in permitting countries, the contracts require the waiver of such rights, which means that they are surrendered. It is also worth noting that the words 'in the course of employment' have a broader meaning than 'while at work'. Other factors can be taken into consideration when deciding if the work was created in the course of employment, such as the remit of the employment contract and the job role, or if company equipment was used to create the work.

6.4   Works made for hire

When a work is made for hire or by a freelancer, the situation is not necessarily the same as it would be during the course of employment. In fact, it is usually the freelancer who is the initial copyright owner of the work. Again, this is subject to contract. This means that if you are hired to write lyrics or a musical work you should make sure there is a contract in place

---

[13]   UK CDPA 1988, section 11(2).
[14]   Netherlands, Copyright Act, Article 7.

that sets out who is the owner of the copyright and associated rights, and how you will be remunerated accordingly.

In the US the law does not distinguish between employee and freelancer in the same way. The US law states that the copyright owner is the person for whom the work was prepared – so the hirer or employer, not the freelancer – unless a contract says otherwise. In these circumstances, a work for hire includes work commissioned.[15] A freelancers' contributions can only be a work for hire if the work fits within one of the enumerated categories, and whilst employee work for hire status is automatic, there must be a signed agreement in place for freelancers.

6.5   Unknown authorship: orphan works

When there is a copyright-protected work but the copyright owner is unknown, this is called an orphan work. Some countries have made specific arrangements for enabling the use of orphan works under certain conditions. For example, Canada allows compulsory licensing on the condition that the user has made a reasonable effort to find the copyright holder.[16] EU law permits cultural heritage institutions, such as public libraries, to digitise works in their collections if none of the rightsholders can be identified after a diligent search.[17] The UK operates an orphan works scheme whereby if the copyright owner cannot be located after a diligent search, a licence can be obtained through the UK Intellectual Property Office.[18]

6.6   After the death of the creator

Copyright generally lasts 70 years after the death of the creator. So, when the creator dies, the copyright still lasts for 70 more years. For sound

---

[15]   US Copyright Act 1976, s 101.

[16]   Canada Copyright Act, Art 77.

[17]   Directive 2012/28/EU of the European Parliament and of the Council of 25 October 2012 on Certain Permitted Uses of Orphan Works.

[18]   UK CDPA 1988, section 116. See also www.copyrightuser.org/understand/exceptions/orphan-works/ accessed 6 November 2020.

recordings, copyright expires 70 years after publication, or 50 years after it was made if it was not published.

Ownership of copyright can be inherited through a will. Copyright is an asset that forms part of the owner's estate if they have made a will to that effect. As such, copyright devolves in accordance with the will. The person who inherits the copyright is then able to manage and enforce the rights in the same way as the creator would have been able to.

An issue that arises more often than you might expect is a copyright owner passing away intestate, meaning either that they had no will or that the will did not include allocation of the copyright. In such cases, the copyright passes in accordance with the intestate or inheritance laws of the country in which they died. Some of the most famous people in music to have died intestate include Aretha Franklin, Prince, Jimi Hendrix, Bob Marley, Sonny Bono, Amy Winehouse and Kurt Cobain.

6.7   Who owns my song?

As a basic summary of what has been covered in reference to the creation of a song, we can say the following:

1. The musical composition or melody, as a musical work, would initially be owned by the creator of that melody.
2. The lyrics, as a literary work, would initially be owned by the lyricist, except where the lyrics are part of a joint work with the music as discussed above.
3. The master, as a sound recording, is usually owned by the producer (meaning the person or company that made the arrangements – often the record label; not always the music producer).
4. The album artwork can be protected as artistic work and would initially be owned by the creator of that work.
5. There could also be performers' rights involved in the performance of the song.
6. If you make a music video, this would be considered a film for copyright purposes and the copyright owners would be the producer and the principal director.
7. Moral rights are relevant to all the above-mentioned parts of the song. Moral rights can apply to lyrics, composition or melody,

performance and artwork. This includes when they are used in the sound recording or film. Moral rights cannot be licensed but they can be waivered, meaning that they are surrendered and cannot be enforced.

Copyright ownership rights are subject to contract, discussed in Chapter 8. For instance, if the work is made for hire then the contract between the creator and hirer would determine who takes ownership of the work. Usually, the hirer takes ownership of the copyright in exchange for a one-off fee payment. Likewise, if the creation was made in the course of employment, it is usually the employer that owns the work. In the case of a song, the rights are usually licensed or assigned to the publisher and the sound recording to the record label, alongside collecting societies.

The roles of the record label, publisher and collecting societies are explained in the next chapter, as well as those of lawyers, managers and other key people and organisations.

7   Roles and relationships

If it's not the music and the copyright that make the industry go round, it's the people. This chapter looks at the different people you may be working with, what their roles are, and how that affects your copyright and control of your work. It covers band members, lawyers, publishers, record labels, managers and collecting societies. The chapter concludes by providing information about some of the relevant organisations, lobby groups and communities that you can engage with. This chapter sets the scene for the subsequent chapters on contracts and licensing, which explain the legal agreements between yourself and these key people.

7.1   Group members and band contributors

If you are a duo, part of a group or in a band, or even working in collaboration with others, it is important to bear in mind that these other people may have a stake in the copyright of the music. They may also have other rights attached to the work, such as moral rights or performers' rights.

The contracts that groups sign will have different clauses than is the case for solo artists. This is because the contract needs to set out what happens if the group splits up, if someone decides to leave or if there are disagreements between band members. It also sets out who is responsible if there is a breach of contract, how the profits are shared and who bears the costs of expenses. Members of a band or group can be key members or non-key members, on a salary or given a profit-share. Therefore, the people collaborating or contributing to the creation of your work need to be considered and contracts need to be put in place to manage these arrangements. Not having a contract in place can cause all sorts of problems down the line. Without a contract in place, it is not clear who owns or controls the copyright in the work. This means that should there be a falling out, for example, one band member could prohibit the others from using the music the band have created together, or even the band name, depending on the circumstances. This can result in long, expensive arguments that are completely avoidable with the clarity of a good contract. (Contracts are covered in Chapter 8, including the band agreement between the members and the contracts that the band sign with third parties.)

7.2   Lawyers, attorneys and legal experts

When considering signing any contract, you should take legal advice. Maybe you are thinking 'of course she would say that – she's a lawyer'. But I didn't say you had to take my advice; any legitimate legal advice will do. The reason why lawyers are so keen on you taking legal advice on your contracts is that they have seen all the consequences of not doing so. Just as people don't go to see a doctor when they are healthy, most people come to see a lawyer when there's a problem. However, lawyers are not only able to help you solve legal problems. To extend the doctor/patient metaphor – we are also like a nutritionist, who can help prevent problems from arising later on!

It is essential that you are clear on what you are signing, and that you get a fair deal. Managers should insist that the artist receive legal advice about the terms of the contract before signing; likewise, it is normal practice for record labels and publishers to include a clause in their contracts that legal advice must have been taken. Some of them want you to take legal advice so much that they will even pay for it! This is because a number of cases were successfully taken to court where the contract was deemed to be unreasonable, and everyone wants to avoid falling down that rabbit hole.

One example of a dispute around the fairness of contracts was the case of Elton John and his lyricist Bernie Taupin, which they brought in relation to a series of publishing, recording and management agreements. The contracts signed by the parties essentially provided their manager, Mr James, with a loophole. This enabled Mr James to sub-publish Elton John's songs in order to receive substantial rates of commission. Mr James used affiliates in other countries to sub-publish compositions, and it was agreed that the artists were paid based on the UK receipts (after the sub-publisher had taken its 50 per cent cut) and not the at-source amount (whatever the sub-publisher received). This resulted in a 25/75 split rather than a 50/50 split. Mr James was able to substantially reduce his personal net earnings on paper, which in turn depleted Elton John and Bernie Taupin's gross revenues from their work. Although the arguments of undue influence failed against the manager, the claims in respect of the sub-publishing and licensing agreements succeeded (in part) against the recording and publishing companies owned by Mr James. The impact of this case was that the court specified that there was a fiduciary obligation on the part of the defendants to account properly for royalties received, and that those to whom royalties are payable should be able to have trust and confidence that the publishing and recording companies will treat them fairly.[1] Now, a properly negotiated publishing agreement will require a publisher to pay at source, to the extent that it uses its own group companies to sub-publish in other countries and, to the extent that it uses third party sub-publishers, cap the amount by which it can reduce the writer's royalty.

Seeking legal advice on the contract is therefore imperative to ensure that you are not signing something unreasonable. The lawyer will be able to explain the contract to you, and they can also negotiate the terms of the contract on your behalf.

Lawyers working in the industry also bring experience and connections. Particularly in the US, there is a growing trend for music lawyers, or attorneys, to also act in some of the roles traditionally performed by a manager. The essential role of the lawyer is acting on instructions, so you can define the breadth of their input.

There are also legal consultants, such as myself, who practise not as regulated solicitors but instead as business affairs consultants. There are different reasons why someone might decide to operate as a consultant rather than a regulated solicitor – in my case it's simply because I am also an academic and running my own consultancy allows me to be more flexible. The main difference between a consultant and a solicitor in the UK is that consultants are not regulated by the Solicitors Regulation Authority (SRA).[2] This means that consultants are not bound by the SRA rules,

---

[1]   *Elton John and Bernie Taupin and others v Richard Leon James, Dick James Music Ltd and This Record Company Ltd* [1991] F.S.R. 397. See more on this case, undue influence and restraint of trade in Chapter 9.

[2]   www.sra.org.uk/ accessed 6 November 2020.

which means they can be more flexible in some ways but are restricted in others. For example, consultants cannot get involved in litigation. (Although this is a specialist area for which specific solicitors and barristers are qualified, and so you could be referred to this type of expert by a consultant or lawyer in any event.) It also means you cannot complain about a consultant to the SRA in the way that you could complain about a solicitor.

When it does come to finding a legal expert, in the UK you can go to the Law Society website and search under 'media, IT and intellectual property', put in your postcode and be provided with a list of lawyers. This is simply a directory and so there is no ranking in that sense. Therefore, you should look further into the law firms and lawyers by researching on their websites. Many lawyers also offer a free short initial consultation, but do not expect them to provide you with free legal advice. This is not the purpose of an initial consultation; it is simply to enable you to make a decision on whether to hire them or not.

Additionally, the PRS legal referral service provides a list of qualified music business solicitors who have agreed to help PRS members with music business issues, for a time period of up to one hour. There are other resources that can help you with this mission, such as the Music Week Directory, and organisations which will support you as a member if you join them; some of these offer free legal advice or financial support towards legal fees.

7.3   Managers

Managers play an essential role in an artist or band's team. They help with the day-to-day running of everything and support the artists in making all their decisions, from what deals to take to negotiating those deals, deciding who to hire and liaising between all the other people and companies involved. Some provide creative input, but all generally act as the person to contact for the artist's attention, such as for sponsorship deals or appearances and so on. Managers might also run the social media channels (social media and copyright is discussed in Chapter 10).

There are two types of manager – personal and business – although in places such as the UK both types of work are usually undertaken by the same person, sometimes with the support of a personal assistant. In the US it is more common to have a personal manager and a separate business manager, who is often also an accountant or financial advisor. A personal manager takes care of the day-to-day needs of the artist, including organising their schedule and overseeing that everything goes to plan. They also liaise with the publishing company, the recording label and other relevant people. A business manager, meanwhile, focuses on business planning rather than the day-to-day. They will be more involved in things such as negotiating deals, changes to contracts, setting budgets and facilitating touring.

When looking for a manager, in the UK you could check out the Music Week Directory, which contains a list of contacts and resources within the UK music industry – from labels, publishers, live agents, promoters and press officers to booking agents, merchandisers, retailers, venues, studios, van hire and so on.[3] There is also a managers' community called Music Managers Forum (MMF), which is discussed in more detail along with other relevant organisations and communities in the final section of this chapter.

Managers operate in different ways and their depth of involvement with an artist or band varies depending on the agreement between them. Some managers get involved with creative decisions; others do not. In a recent study, MMF found that the roles and responsibilities of managers are expanding.[4] The scope of the manager's role needs to be agreed in a management contract. The legal contract between the manager and the artist sets out the rights and responsibilities of the parties, fees and payments, and what happens when the parties want to go their separate ways. (This is set out in more detail in the following chapter on contracts.)

7.4   Record labels

As the name suggests, the recording industry is about the recording, production and dissemination of sound recordings. As explained, in most

---

[3] www.musicweek.com/music-week-directory accessed 6 November 2020.

[4] MMF, *Managing Expectations: An Exploration into the Changing Role and Value of the Music Manager* (MMF 2019).

instances the record company will be the owner of the copyright in the recordings that they have paid for. The record companies offer creators access to support, specialist expertise and financial backing that might not otherwise be available to them. The payments and royalties that the artists receive from the music are set out in the recording contract, as explained in the following chapter. Usually the financial support or advance payments provided by the label, for the costs of recording and expenses, will be recouped by the record label before the artist will receive any royalty payments.

There are essentially three major record labels – Sony, Universal and Warner – all of which include a number of subsidiary companies. There are also independent record labels. The major record labels have big budgets and international distribution networks, while independent record labels tend to be more diverse in their artists. The limited reach of independent labels can mean that they only take on a certain territory rather than acting worldwide, as is the norm for the major labels. Having said that, AWAL[5] doesn't fit this traditional model of independent or major label, as it is a global independent label. AWAL operates on the basis that the artists retain their rights, taking only a limited licence of a period such as three years, after which time the rights can be taken back by the artist (thus avoiding any of the trouble Taylor Swift experienced when the rights to her first six albums were sold against her wishes).[6]

Recording companies not only enable the actual recording, production and release of the music, but can also work on the promotion and marketing of the record, such as by getting a song played on the radio or used in a film.

7.5   Music publishers

The music publishing industry is primarily engaged in the exploitation of the copyright in songs. Usually, songwriters transfer control of the rights in their song, or even all of the songs they write during an agreed period,

---

[5]   www.awal.com/ accessed 6 November 2020.

[6]   www.theguardian.com/music/2019/nov/23/taylor-swift-scooter-braun-amas-old-music-masters accessed 6 November 2020.

to the publisher. In return they receive a share in profits from the song in the form of royalties, and perhaps even an advance payment against future royalties. The copyright in the song will often revert back to the ownership of the writer after an agreed period of time that is stated in the contract.

The publisher's role includes copyright administration, meaning that they handle copyright registrations, agree licences, collect royalties and distribute payments to the songwriter. They also promote their songwriters and the use of their songs, for example in film, TV and advertising.

Music publishing is an old industry that has renewed itself and adapted to new technologies and changes in consumption behaviours. Music publishing started out concerned with sheet music – hence the name – but has moved with the times. The industry adjusted by focusing solely on CD and record sales, and now publishing companies have developed to cover the streaming market using rights management, taking a more proactive role in promoting songwriters, as well as engaging with lobbying and political policy. Modern developments in music consumption have challenged the music publishing industry, and some companies have addressed this by adopting roles traditionally undertaken by the record label.

Some publishers are also advancing their efficiency and reach to combat these challenges. For example, Kobalt[7] is an independent rights management and publishing company founded in 2000, which has developed new technologies with the aim of increasing the efficiency of tracking and collecting royalties on behalf of its members. Kobalt provides an app-based platform for creators that shows them their music usage across all their rights, in real time. This new technology puts the data directly into the hands of the creator, offering a level of transparency that can be utilised. The app utilises digital service provider reporting on song-specific date and territory play to let creators know exactly when and where their music is being consumed, helping them to understand where their audience is. This data has become more vital in the digital consumption age, as it can detail individual song plays rather than, for example, only knowing how many albums were sold, as was previously the case. All this information can help to inform decisions such as where to tour, push marketing and pitch for use of the song in TV and advertising, for example. Kobalt also

---

[7] www.kobaltmusic.com/ accessed 6 November 2020.

have an arrangement with YouTube, whereby Kobalt technologies (such as KORE, a digital collection tool, and its user-generated content matching suite, ProKlaim) operate to maximise income from user-generated content on YouTube. (More on YouTube in Chapter 10.)

7.6   Collecting societies

Collecting societies are a vital source of income for rightsholders. These are organisations that collect and distribute royalties to the rightsholders who have signed up as members. The collecting societies do this by issuing licences to places such as pubs, bars, restaurants and nightclubs as well as when the copyright work is performed, broadcast, streamed, downloaded, reproduced, played in public or used in film, TV or radio. In these circumstances, it is more effective for this to be done by a collective organisation, rather than every individual creator knocking on the door of every nightclub trying to get paid. Collecting societies do this work through issuing licences, which are explained in more detail in Chapter 9.

Most collecting society organisations are affiliated with international organisations, such as the International Confederation of Societies of Authors and Composers (CISAC),[8] which is a network of authors' societies with 232 member societies in 121 countries. CISAC is presided over by artists including Björn Ulvaeus (from ABBA), Yvonne Chaka Chaka, Arturo Márquez, Jia Zhang-ke and Miquel Barceló.

In the US, there are a number of performing rights organisations (PROs) that offer the same service for the performance rights in a song, meaning that when the song is performed to the public, either on the radio or in a bar, for example, the venue pays the PRO and the PRO shares those payments with the songwriters and publishers. (Weirdly, PROs are not able to collect money for music used in films in the US, unlike in other countries.) The share of these royalties is set out in the publishing contract. The main PROs in the US are the American Society of Composers, Authors and Publishers (ASCAP), Broadcast Music Incorporated (BMI) and smaller boutique PROs such as SESAC and Global Music Rights (GMR).

---

[8]   www.cisac.org/ accessed 6 November 2020.

In the UK there are various different collecting societies for different rights. The ones most relevant for songwriters, artists and musicians are PRS[9] and the Mechanical Copyright Protection Society (MCPS) – the rights of PRS and MCPS are administered by PRS for Music[10] – and there is also PPL.[11]

PRS pays royalties to its members when their music is used for broadcast on TV or radio, performed, or played in public, whether live or through a recording, streamed or downloaded. PRS has more than 5.5 million musical works in its repertoire, assigned to it by its members, which are used in films, television shows, games and other audio-visual works. MCPS pays royalties to its members when their music is copied as physical products, such as CDs and DVDs, streamed or downloaded, used in TV, film or radio. (This is called a mechanical licence, explained in Chapter 9.)

PPL licenses performers' and recording rights in music to radio stations, TV channels and some online services to include recorded music in their broadcasts. PPL works together with PRS to licence UK businesses and organisations to play music in public.

The French equivalent is the Society of Authors, Composers and Publishers of Music (SACEM),[12] and in Germany the collecting society is the Gesellschaft für musikalische Aufführungs- und mechanische Vervielfältigungsrechte (GEMA).[13] Not all countries have a collecting society, but this does not stop your national collecting society seeking royalties on your behalf in those countries anyway!

This is what has happened in the case between PRS and Qatar Airways. Qatar Airways is the national passenger airline for Qatar, with 206 commercial passenger aircraft which fly to 160 destinations in 80 different countries. It offers an inflight entertainment system that allows passengers access to audio and audio-visual content via onboard screens and headphones, or a downloadable app. Airlines are generally granted licences

---

[9]   www.prsformusic.com/ accessed 6 November 2020.

[10] www.prsformusic.com/what-we-do/prs-and-mcps accessed 6 November 2020.

[11] www.ppluk.com/ accessed 6 November 2020.

[12] www.sacem.fr/en accessed 6 November 2020.

[13] www.gema.de/en/ accessed 6 November 2020.

by copyright collecting societies that are based in the same country as the airline. Collecting societies also tend to have reciprocal agreements that allow them to grant licences in respect of rights assigned to foreign collecting societies. At present, PRS does not directly licence any airline based outside of the UK, but there is no collecting society in Qatar and so this case could change that. PRS wants to license Qatar Airways in respect of its repertoire works on a worldwide or territory-by-territory basis. It also believes that it can obtain an extension to its reciprocal agreements with other collecting societies, which would enable PRS to license works beyond its own repertoire. This is an ongoing case: in the first instance the parties were arguing about which country the case could be brought in – the UK or Qatar – and in a UK High Court decision the judge dismissed an appeal by Qatar Airways, finding that the copyright infringement case brought by PRS will be heard in the English courts and not in Qatar.[14] The copyright dispute in the case will now proceed to trial, unless Qatar Airways decides to accept the PRS licence … watch this (air)space!

7.7   Organisations, lobby groups and communities

So far, this chapter has explained a little about what lawyers, managers, record labels, publishers and collecting societies do. This final section is here to let you know about some of the organisations, lobby groups and communities that you might like to get involved with. This is by no means an exhaustive list – in fact, it barely touches the surface; it is just to get you started. You should take a look into the organisations relevant to you in your country. As Chapter 1 described, engaging with organisations, charities and communities such as these, which are relevant to your area of practice in the music industry, enables you to be part of the influence and change within and for your industry.

As mentioned, there is a managers' community called Music Managers Forum (MMF). This organisation was set up in 1992 and as of July 2020 has more than 850 managers based in the UK with global businesses, and a wider network of more than 2700 managers in the USA. MMF provides

---

[14]   *Performing Right Society Ltd v Qatar Airways Group QCS* [2020] EWHC 1872 (Ch) (17 July 2020); see http://ipkitten.blogspot.com/2020/07/prs-for-music-off-to-flying-start-in.html accessed 6 November 2020.

managers with professional development support, as well as being a lobby group that advocates on behalf of its members for change in the music industry and the relevant laws and policies.[15] MMF is also a member of the Council of Music Makers (CMM),[16] together with the Ivors Academy, FAC, MMF, MPG and the MU; through the CMM, the organisations jointly campaign for protections in law for the UK music industry's creative talent, to ensure they can thrive in the digital age.

The Ivors Academy is an independent charity that aims to advance the education of the general public in music and associated subjects by providing educational and training services about composition and songwriting, as well as scholarships, awards and grants to talented musicians in need of financial assistance.[17]

The Featured Artists Coalition (FAC) is a UK not-for-profit organisation representing the specific rights and interests of music artists.[18] The FAC prides itself on being created by artists, for artists.[19] It advocates on behalf of its members, lobbying the government in the interest of artists as well as working on education and research.

The Music Producers Guild (MPG)[20] is a community that was founded by producers, mixers, recording engineers, re-mixers and programmers who are passionate about making and recording music. The MPG has no political agenda as such, but it does still represent the community's views to government.

The British Phonographic Industry (BPI)[21] is the British recorded music industry's trade association and champions the interests of its membership, which is made up of more than 400 independent music companies and the UK's major record companies – Universal Music UK, Sony Music UK and Warner Music UK. The BPI also organises the BRIT Awards, the Hyundai Mercury Prize for 'Album of the Year' and the Classic BRIT Awards show, and co-owns The Official Charts.

---

[15] https://themmf.net/ accessed 6 November 2020.

[16] http://councilmusicmakers.org/ accessed 6 November 2020.

[17] https://ivorsacademy.com/ accessed 6 November 2020.

[18] https://thefac.org/ accessed 6 November 2020.

[19] https://thefac.org/who-we-are accessed 6 November 2020.

[20] https://mpg.org.uk/ accessed 6 November 2020.

[21] www.bfi.org.uk/ accessed 6 November 2020.

The Musicians' Union (MU)[22] is the UK trade union for musicians, formed of more than 32,000 members. It works to protect members' rights and campaign on behalf of musicians' interests, such as by campaigning and negotiating for better pay as well as protection and improvement of working conditions. It also offers advice, support and legal assistance for its members.

UK Music[23] is an industry-funded body, formed to represent the collective interests of the recorded, published and live sectors of the British music industry. For example, as a result of the impact of the COVID-19 pandemic in 2020 on venues, concerts and festivals and the people who work in them, UK Music, together with members of the UK Live Music Group – alongside a coalition of live music businesses, including artists, venues, concerts, festivals, production companies and industry figures – launched a campaign called Let The Music Play. The campaign aimed to highlight the importance of the sector within the UK economy and included a direct call to government to help the music industry with the ongoing damage caused by the pandemic. Artists across the industry such as Ed Sheeran, Dua Lipa and Paul McCartney signed a letter to Culture Secretary Oliver Dowden calling for support.[24]

The Music Publishers Association (MPA)[25] is a community for UK music publishers. It provides a collective voice for music publishing, as well as training, education, representation and a host of other benefits.

The International Confederation of Music Publishers (ICMP)[26] is a world trade association representing the interests of the music publishing community internationally, with a mission to increase copyright protection internationally, encourage a better environment for our business and act as an industry forum for consolidating global positions.

The Music Publishers Association (MPA)[27] is a community for UK music publishers. It provides a collective voice for music publishing, as well as training, education, representation and a host of other benefits.

---

[22]   www.musiciansunion.org.uk/ accessed 6 November 2020.

[23]   www.ukmusic.org/ accessed 6 November 2020.

[24]   www.ukmusic.org/policy/let-the-music-play/ accessed 6 November 2020.

[25]   mpaonline.org.uk/ accessed 6 November 2020.

[26]   www.icmp-ciem.org/ accessed 6 November 2020.

[27]   mpaonline.org.uk/ accessed 6 November 2020.

The International Federation of the Phonographic Industry (IFPI)[28] is an international organisation that represents the interests of the recording industry worldwide. It promotes the value of recorded music, campaigns for the rights of record producers and aims to expand the commercial uses of recorded music.

The different roles in the music industry having been introduced in this chapter, Chapter 8 will explain the relevant contracts that manage these relationships, and Chapter 9 will specifically address licensing – which is really just another type of contract. Chapter 10, the final chapter in Part II on managing copyright, looks at copyright and social media.

---

[28]   www.ifpi.org/ accessed 6 November 2020.

8   Contracts

Chapter 7 explained the different roles and relationships of band members, lawyers, publishers, record labels, managers and collecting societies, plus relevant organisations, lobby groups and communities. This chapter explains how the contracts that you might have with these people work. It includes a basic introduction to what a contract is and how they work, and then provides some information on some of the relevant contracts that you will come across in the music industry: collaborator agreements, including band and group contracts, as well as contracts with individual contributors such as songwriters, vocalists, producers and session musicians. It then covers the main music deals: management contracts, recording contracts and publishing contracts. Lastly, it mentions sponsorship, product placement, influencer and merchandise agreements.

In Chapter 1, I specifically said that you do not need to be a legal expert for copyright information to be helpful to you. I stand by that comment. This chapter is not intended to make you a legal expert in contracts! It will simply inform you on the type of contracts that are relevant, some key aspects of the contracts and a few things to look out for. If you have a record label and/or publisher, they will provide the contracts for you. You should, of course, still hire a lawyer to review contracts for you, but at least this way you will have some idea of what they are on about!

8.1   Introduction to the idea of contracts

Similar to copyright, contracts have a terrible reputation for being boring and complicated. Personally, I find it fairly easy to get people excited about copyright, but contracts is admittedly a little more challenging in that respect. I will try to keep this chapter as short and sweet as possible, so bear with me.

At its core a contract is simply an agreement recognised by law. In the contract the parties agree the terms of their arrangement and then it can be enforced by law if either of them do not comply with the agreement as made. The key thing here is that it is just an agreement between two parties, which means that the parties decide the terms of the agreement.

It is normal practice to negotiate a contract. I would go so far as to say that it is good practice to negotiate a contract. I have worked with clients who are reluctant to negotiate the terms of a contract presented to them, particularly if they are just so grateful to be offered a contract in the first place. I am not suggesting you should kick up a fuss for no reason, but if the contract is drafted by one side then it is going to be written in a way that is favourable to them. When I write contracts for clients, the same type of contract will look different depending on which side I am working for. So, negotiation is important for ensuring a fair contract and a good deal.

As mentioned in the previous chapter, there are cases where contracts have been deemed unreasonable. This happens when the courts recognise that even though the contract has been signed by both parties, it is not enforceable because the terms were so unfair. As a result, it is common practice in the music industry for managers, record labels and publishers to insist that the artist take legal advice on a contract before signing.

It is true what they say: the devil is in the detail. A word or a comma can truly change the meaning of a sentence in a contract, with dramatic outcomes for the parties involved. That is why it is so important to get a lawyer to review a contract for you, because they know what to look out for. The following sections will indicate the types of contract you might come across and what you might expect to see in them, but it is by no means legal advice and does not substitute for having a legal expert go over the specific detail of a contract with you.

8.2   Collaborator agreements

If you are working together with someone else, or a number of people, on a project, it is a good idea to have a contract in place that sets out the terms of the arrangement. This includes who owns what, what the obligations of each person are, who bears the costs and risks, what happens when you want to go your separate ways and what happens if you fall out.

In my experience, people often avoid using a contract when they are working with people with whom they are close or friendly. They say perhaps that it is awkward to discuss the idea of a contract with their friend. As you might have guessed, these people I am talking about are clients who have fallen out and who did not have a contract in place, which is why they needed legal assistance. In these situations, not only would a contract have avoided confusion and costs, but there have even been times when the work that was created in the collaboration is lost as a result. Having a contract in place lets everyone know where they stand and if things do go wrong it provides a roadmap of how to deal with the situation, so that everyone can go their separate ways and hopefully someone can at least take the work forward.

The following sections cover the types of agreement that are required for a band or group, followed by a look at the agreements for individual contributors such as songwriters, vocalists, producers and session musicians.

8.2.1   Band, group and duo agreements

A contract is particularly necessary if the situation involves a band, group or duo. The band contract is the agreement between the band members; this is in addition to the contracts that a band might agree to with third parties such as a record label or publisher. The band agreement needs to set out the band constitution, including who owns the band name, who takes final decisions, how the income is distributed, who is responsible for what and what happens if that person does not perform their responsibilities.

These contracts might also include agreements on what else band or group members can do, which will depend on the nature of the group. For example, it is common for pop groups to be in an exclusive agreement to work only within the band and not be in more than one group or release solo work during the term of the contract. This is not always the case: for example, American music producer Diplo clearly does not have such exclusivity agreements since he is a member of Major Lazer, LSD, Jack Ü and Silk City. Busy guy!

It is also imperative to agree on what happens if a member is leaving the band, or if the band decides to split up. If your band signs a record deal or publishing contract there will be clauses in those contracts, called leaving member provisions, which give the label or publisher the choice of either terminating or continuing with the leaving and remaining members under new contracts on substantially the same terms. Often the record label and publishing companies will also want to have first dibs on any leaving member as a solo artist, as well as the remaining members of the band. This arrangement deals with what happens in practical terms, as well as financially sorting out how the band's assets are divided.

8.2.2 Songwriters, vocalists, producers and session musicians

When a songwriter sells their song for another artist to perform there is, or should be, a contract in place. The contract will set out the arrangements in terms of delivery of the song, and more importantly how the copyright ownership and income from the song will be split between the parties. The share will depend on who the songwriter and artists are, as well as whether the deal is made together with a publishing company, which is usually the case. Songwriter contracts can also include other clauses, such as a guarantee that the songwriter was the original creator of the song and that they did not copy it from someone else. Usually this is arranged as a mechanical licence through MCPS (discussed in Chapter 9).

There also needs to be a contract in place if a vocalist contributes to a song. This is common with DJs who produce songs with featured artists. The contract needs to set out the ownership and the share of profits, and can also include agreements on how the artist is named on the track, which is usually presented as DJ featuring vocalist.

Both of these contracts need to provide for the transfer of the relevant rights in order to allow the producer of the record to make edits and in order for the distribution of the song to be made without inadvertently infringing the copyright of the songwriter or vocalist.

There are also music producers who simply create tracks, without vocals, for use by other artists. They could sell the track for a fee, but more usually there is a royalty agreement in place so that the producer receives a portion of the income from the song. For example, American EDM record producer DJ Dillon Francis produced a track which he gave to

Meghan Trainor and together they made the song *Underwater*. In this scenario you see the artists listed in reverse: Meghan Trainor (feat. Dillon Francis).

A session musician, sometimes referred to as a non-featured artist, will usually be asked to sign a contract in which they sell and surrender their rights in the music in return for a one-off payment.

We now turn to consider the main contracts you will likely come across in your adventures through the music industry: the management contract, the record deal and the publishing contract.

8.3   Management contract

A management contract is necessary to set out the terms of the relationship between the artist and the manager. It should include what the manager's role and responsibilities are, including the remit of their management of the artists' work – for example, it may cover absolutely everything that the artist does within the creative and entertainment industries, or it may only be specifically in relation to music.

The contract also needs to set out what countries the agreement is in place for. The manager will usually want this to be world-wide, but sometimes different managers work in different territories because these are where their contacts and expertise are.

Other things you will find in a management contract are an exclusivity clause – meaning that you are not allowed to let anyone else manage you, including yourself; and the length of the contract – usually 3–5 years. If you are signing with a management company it is a good idea to get a key person clause, which means you are tied to a particular person within that management company and if that manager leaves the company, you are able to terminate your contract. (This section of the contract has historically been referred to as the 'key man clause', but since it's 2020 let us put that term straight in the bin.)[1]

---

[1]   Especially since the MMF study reported that 42 per cent of managers identified as female. Applause! MMF, *Managing Expectations: An Exploration into the Changing Role and Value of the Music Manager* (MMF, 2019).

Naturally, the contract will also set out how the manager is paid. Typically, managers receive 20 per cent commission from the gross earnings of the artists (before expenses are deducted). Some managers are challenging this in response to their growing list of responsibilities. In a study conducted by the Music Managers Forum (MMF) which surveyed 183 managers and interviewed 14 management companies, it was found that 76 per cent of respondents followed the 20 per cent model, with only 6 per cent receiving anything above that.[2] As to when these contracts are signed, the study found that 59 per cent of managers contracted with artists before they commenced work or within the first 12 months of the relationship, whereas 41 per cent only addressed making any contractual arrangements when rights were signed to third parties or when the artist reached a certain professional level.[3]

Lastly, the agreement should set out what happens at the end of the contract, such as what can happen if the parties want to end the agreement early, including dispute resolution, as well as any continued earnings that the manager can make after the termination of the contract. This is known as a 'sunset clause' and is common in the UK and US, but less so in places such as Australia. In some territories, such as the US, these clauses can mean that a manager receives 3–5 years' commission on recording and publishing projects that they helped set up. In the UK, the commission is usually limited to work done and recordings made during the period of management of the artist. Sometimes this can be extended for longer. MMF suggests five years at full commission and five years at half commission, but Donald Passman suggests that you shouldn't settle for more than seven years in the US.[4] In the UK, five years at full rate and five years at half rate is standard. It really depends on the circumstances, and that is why it is so important to receive legal advice and help with negotiation of contracts.

[2] Ibid 34.
[3] Ibid 33.
[4] Passman D, *All You Need to Know About the Music Business* (Simon & Schuster, 2019) 41.

8.4   Recording contracts

As explained in Chapter 7, the record label is in the business of recording, production and dissemination of sound recordings. Additionally, as we learned in Chapter 6, the copyright in the sound recording is owned by the producer of the sound recording – usually the record label. This is particularly the case if it is an exclusive record deal. There are also some instances where the artist retains the copyright in the sound recording and then licenses it to the record label.

Before a record company will help you get your master recorded, you will sign a recording contract with them. The recording contract sets out what the artist will deliver and what responsibilities the record label will undertake. The record company's obligations are typically limited: the main things specified in the contract are usually that they will pay any advances and royalties; some sort of release commitment; and any artist approvals and audit rights that the artist's lawyer might negotiate. The record label might offer an advance payment but will recoup this before the artist receives any royalties. The amount of royalties received by the artist depends on their status within the industry and their negotiating powers, although there are general industry ballparks.

The contract will set out the 'term' of the agreement, meaning how long it will last for. It used to be that this was dealt with in the same way that most contracts refer to term, which is by time period, for example one or two years. However, after Dame Olivia Newton-John caused a ruckus by successfully suing her record label, this is no longer the case. Since Olivia was no doubt busy starring as Sandy in the musical *Grease*, she fell behind schedule on her record deal and her album *Making a Good Thing Better*, which was late. Her record deal with MCA was a two-year contract that required her to produce two records a year, and the label had the option to extend the contract for three more years (and six more records) if she didn't deliver on time. The judge decided in this case that the contract could not be automatically extended just because she had run over time.[5] As a result, record deals now conclude at the end of the marketing campaign, or six months after. This is sometimes referred to in the contract as the Impact Date. Alternatively, the contract may specify a set amount of

---

[5]   *MCA Records, Inc. v Newton-John* [90 Cal. App. 3d 21].

time after the record is released, usually 12 months and no more than 18. Recording contracts can also include an option-agreement. This basically means that the record label gets first choice on anything you create after the agreed number of records that you are obliged to make under the deal.

Lastly, the contract should set out what happens if things go pear-shaped. It is a good idea to have a clause in the contract which provides that if the record label does not release your record, you are able to get the rights back and terminate the agreement. How and when this can happen is set out in the contract: usually the artist has to give notice to the label 90 days after the record was supposed to be released, then the label has a set amount of time to either action the release or continue with the termination of the agreement.

8.5   Publishing contracts

As explained in Chapter 7, the publisher works on the exploitation of the musical composition. There are various types of publishing deals and each one has an impact on the ownership and management of the copyright. The three types explained below are the administration agreement, the single-song assignment and the exclusive agreement.

An administration agreement gives the publisher the right to administer your music on your behalf for a set period of time; this is called a licence, as explained in Chapter 9. Administering your copyright essentially means registering it with the relevant collecting societies as well as licensing out the songs on your behalf, collecting the payments from those licences and sending some money back your way. The publisher takes an admin fee for conducting your copyright affairs, usually somewhere between 10 and 25 per cent – meaning that you get 90 to 75 per cent. When the term of an administration agreement concludes, the rights in the songs revert back to the artist.

A single-song assignment, funnily enough, means that the songwriter assigns their rights in one song to the publisher. This is different from a licence because you do not necessarily get the rights back, and in a single-song assignment songwriters often retain 75–80 per cent.

The exclusive publishing deal means that for the period of the contract, the publisher owns and controls all the songs that you write during that time. The contract will typically last three years and sets out the requirements of the artist and the publisher. There are also minimum commitment deals, where each contract period revolves around the commercial release of an album with a sufficient portion of the writer's songs. This type of contract is usually an assignment rather than a licence, meaning that the rights in the songs are given to the publisher (apart from the performance rights granted to the collecting societies, explained in Chapter 7). As with the recording contract, publishers may provide an advance, and this is recouped by the publisher before you will receive any royalties. The publisher fee for a publishing contract is usually within the region of 20–30 per cent.

The final two sections of this chapter cover the agreements that need to be in place for sponsorship, product placement, influencers and merchandising.

8.6   Sponsorship, product placement and influencer deals

A sponsorship deal is when a company pays to be associated with an artist or band; this can be a deal specifically relating to a tour, or other types of sponsorship directly relating to the artist or band themselves. This might be a sponsorship deal, which tends to involve a marketing campaign, or an influencer agreement, which typically involves social media endorsement. For a sponsorship deal, a brand will pay for an artist or band to use their logo in association with their tour. The amount depends on numerous factors, such as who the artist is, the length and geographical reach of the tour and the scope of the association. In a sponsorship contract, usually no copyright or intellectual property rights are exchanged, but licences are used to enable use of the name, branding and music for the purpose of the association and marketing. In addition, your image rights (discussed in Chapter 4) will also form part of the agreement and may be on an exclusive or non-exclusive basis, depending on the negotiations between the parties.

Product placement is often used to support the financial cost of creating a music video. This is where companies pay to have their brand or products placed within the music video. There will be an agreement in place that specifies the placement or nature of the featuring of the product within the video. There are rules on the use of product placement, usually to the effect of informing the audience of its use.

Agreements to endorse products and services over social media are the most recent development in this area. We call these agreements influencer contracts and they set out what the influencer has to provide, usually in exchange for a fee or sometimes commission. In terms of copyright, the creator of the content would be the copyright owner, but of course the brand would want to be able to use the content themselves; therefore it is usually licensed or assigned in the agreement.

It is important to know that there are rules for online adverts and marketing on social media that apply to influencers, whether they are considered a celebrity or not. In the UK these rules are set out by the Advertising Standards Agency (ASA), which is the independent regulator of advertising across all media. The CAP code is the UK Code of Non-broadcast Advertising and Direct & Promotional Marketing, which is essentially the rule book for non-broadcast advertisements, sales promotions and direct marketing communications. The ASA reports that it now receives three times as many complaints about online adverts than it does about TV adverts and it has taken further action in many instances. For example, in 2018, *Made in Chelsea* star Louise Thompson and watchmaker Daniel Wellington were found to be in breach of a rule requiring adverts to be obvious, after Louise Thompson failed to use #ad in a sponsored Instagram post.

The ASA provides guidance specifically for influencers which sets out what content qualifies as an advert, when it is paid for and how to make sure that the posts are correctly labelled.[6] Adverts must clearly state when they are paid for, including payments by way of loan or reward; this includes monetary, or by gift, or otherwise. When offering discount codes, competitions or giveaways, influencers must be clear about their relationship with a brand or business, including past relationships. Essentially, you cannot mislead your followers or suggest that you are

---

[6] www.asa.org.uk/resource/influencers-guide.html accessed 6 November 2020.

simply a customer, or have used a product or services that you have not used. Influencer posts must be transparent, easy to understand, unambiguous, timely and prominent, without the need for people to click for more information, regardless of the device they are using to access the post. It is not enough to tag a brand or business in either the text, picture or video of a post without additional disclosure, or to provide a discount code without additional information. Influencers must avoid ambiguous language such as 'thank you', 'made possible by', 'in collaboration with' or 'thanks to…' without full disclosure. This also includes unclear hashtags such as #spon, #client or #collab.

The US equivalent of the ASA is the Federal Trade Commission, which provides that brands and influencers are required to clearly disclose the nature of their relationship. Social media posts must identify if they are sponsored, and video reviews must include both written and verbal disclosure of the partnership. Simply using the built-in tools on social media platforms is not adequate. Use of #ad and #sponsored is considered disclosure as long as the hashtags are highly visible and not just added to the end of a long string of tags. As with the UK rules, information must be clear, unambiguous and readily available to the user without further searching.

In Australia, influencer marketing is regulated by the Australian Association of National Advertisers (AANA) Code of Ethics, which states that advertising must be clearly distinguishable. These rules say that while there are no requirements that advertising or marketing communication must have a specific label, it does have to be clear to the relevant audience that the content is commercial in nature. As such, the Australian standards are more relaxed than those in the UK and US, where words such as 'friendship' would likely be considered ambiguous and posts that do not clearly state that they relate to an advertisement or partnership would be considered contrary to the codes of practice.

8.7   Merchandise

Merchandise usually becomes relevant when touring, but some artists get involved with merchandising before that. Depending on your fan base, this can range from posters, t-shirts and hoodies to branded phone and pencil cases.

A merchandise agreement will involve other types of intellectual property rights, such as a trade mark. A typical agreement will set out what the merchandise producing company creates for you, what territory it can operate in and how long the contract will last. In order to create the merchandise, the company will need to license your intellectual property rights and usually also your image rights to manufacture, produce and sell the products you agree on. There should also be a quality control clause. The company will likely want an exclusive licence and may even want to be able to sub-license to a third-party company for certain goods. Merchandise can be extremely lucrative, and the contract should set out the profit share.

It is perhaps outside the remit of copyright to mention the environment, but it is my book and I really like the planet so since we are here, I am going to do it anyway. Touring can be pretty brutal on the environment, as a result of artist and audience travel, catering, accommodation, venues, promotion and merchandise. However, in 2007 Radiohead commissioned the sustainability agency Best Foot Forward to help them assess the impact of their tours and implement solutions. It thought of everything, from encouraging fans to use public transport to switching all the lights to LED.[7] In recent years we have seen artists and the music industry move further towards more sustainable touring models to try and reduce the carbon impact, for example by reducing single-use plastic bottles, composting catering and carbon offsetting. The band The 1975 offered fans the opportunity to bring their own t-shirts to be printed with the band's branding, rather than purchasing new ones. And that was a good enough link to this section about merchandising to justify your public service announcement about green touring.

This concludes the chapter on contracts! The next chapter of Part II on managing copyright looks at licensing, which is secretly just another type of contract that has been mentioned already – but there is a little more to the story.

---

[7]   Giese J and ButzGreen J, *Touring Guide: A Guide for Musicians, Agents, Tour Managers, Promoters, Venues, and Booking Agencies* (Popakademie Baden-Württemberg) www.greentouring.net/downloads/GreenTouringGuide_EN.pdf accessed 6 November 2020.

9   Licensing

So far this part of the book on managing copyright has covered the people and their roles, then the key contracts that you will find in the music industry. Many of the contracts discussed in the previous chapter require that the artist licence or assign the copyright in their work. This chapter looks at licensing in more detail.

Licences are the way that rightsholders exploit their copyright and receive royalty payments in return when it is used. (Unless it is a Creative Commons licence which means that there are no royalties.) A licence differs from an assignment of rights. So, first, this chapter will explain what an assignment is, and then what a licence is and some of the types of licences that apply in the music industry.

9.1   Assignment

An assignment of rights is the full transfer of ownership of copyright from one party to another. Therefore, to assign your rights to someone essentially means to regard the copyright as belonging to them. As such, the person who the rights are assigned to becomes the owner of the copyright – as if they were the original creator of the work. As a result, the person assigning the rights loses all their entitlement to their work in respect of copyright.

An assignment can be whole or partial in terms of the rights assigned or the length of time. In terms of rights assigned, I refer you back to Chapter 4 on what copyright gives you, which covered the exclusive rights. These are the right to copy, perform, communicate the work to the public and so on. The wording of this type of assignment is often phrased around the things that the assignment permits rather than the restricted acts, just so it is absolutely clear what can and cannot be done without the copyright holders' permission. So, an artist may assign their rights in the performance of their work to one party and the right to copy and distribute the work to another.

An assignment can also be agreed for work that does not yet exist, usually seen in the recording and publishing contracts. This enables an agreement to be made where work is being commissioned – although in some countries, such as Spain, the partial assignment for specific purposes does not apply to modes of distribution not yet invented at the time of the agreement.[1]

There are rules in place to protect the creators and authors when signing these types of agreement; these rules set out the requirements for when a transfer of ownership has taken place. To be legally effective, an assignment must be in writing and signed by, or on behalf of, the rightsholder assigning their rights. An assignment is therefore a form of contract in that sense. Sometimes there is a whole contract specifically for the purpose of assigning rights; however, in most cases the assignment will appear as a clause within a long contract that includes a host of other things, such as in the case of a publishing deal.

The wording of an assignment does not need to be in any particular format, which can be considered both useful and unhelpful depending on the situation. If we had set language for an assignment, we would know what to look out for. On the other hand, having the freedom to use whatever words we like gives flexibility to the intended meaning of the parties and allows assignments to be made without the need to know the magic words! The courts have found that wording such as 'transfer all the assets' in the UK, the sale of 'all the right, title and interest' in Australia[2] and the sale of 'all other property to which the companies are entitled' in South Africa[3] equates to an assignment. Typically, a recording or publishing contract will actually use the word 'assign' but other types of contract may not.

As mentioned in Chapter 4, while you can assign your copyright, moral rights are not assignable. However, contracts can enable the waiver or

---

[1]   Spain Copyright Act, Article 43(5).
[2]   *Murray v King* (1983–85) 3 IPR 252.
[3]   *Kelp Valves (Pty) Ltd v Saunders Valve Co Ltd* 1987 (2) SA 1.

surrendering of moral rights, meaning that you give them up as part of the deal.

In the US, there is also a funky rule that enables creators to terminate a transfer or assignment of their copyright 35 years later.[4] For songs created on or after 1 January 1978, the creator can send a notice to the person or company that they assigned their rights to and terminate the agreement. This is a unique rule under US law and does not apply elsewhere.

In summary, essentially an assignment is the equivalent of selling the full ownership in your rights. A licence, on the other hand, is more akin to lending some of your rights. This is explained in the next section.

9.2   Licensing

The idea behind a licence is that, as the creator, you may wish to outsource the exploitation of your work. In order to do this, while you want to remain the copyright owner, a licence enables the distributor to legally use the work for the specific purpose agreed between you.

As such, a licence is an agreement whereby the licensee is able to use the copyright work for a specific purpose, for a specified amount of time. In exchange, the licensor receives royalty payments from the licensee. Therefore, a licence is a type of contract that sets out the terms of this agreement; it should set out what the parties are permitted to do, giving permission for the carrying out of certain activities, such as marketing a record.

In theory a licence of copyright may be more limited in scope than an assignment and does not equate to a full transfer of ownership. A licence can be exclusive or non-exclusive. An exclusive licence means that the company or person is the only one that has a licence for that work, including the creator themselves. A non-exclusive licence, meanwhile – as you might expect – means that the copyright can be licensed to multiple people. This means that the creator is able to license the same work to

---

4   US Copyright Act 1976 s 203.

as many other people as they like. Some licences are a mix between the two, meaning that they are exclusive but only in a certain country or for specific modes of exploitation.

9.3   Limitations on assignments and licences

For the most part, the terms of a licence or assignment come down to the agreement and negotiations between the parties, aside from two main limitations on the way that copyright can be transferred or exploited.

9.3.1   Undue influence

A court might set aside an agreement if there has been undue influence – where a person in a position of dominance has used that position to obtain an unfair advantage for themselves, and as a result caused damage, loss or injury to the person relying on their authority or aid. There are two parts to this assessment: the person must have influence over the other; and they must have used that influence to gain a transaction that was disadvantageous.

This is what happened in the case of Irish singer-songwriter Gilbert O'Sullivan, who was able to have his contracts with his manager set aside as a result of undue influence. O'Sullivan gave evidence that no actual pressure had been exerted upon him to sign the agreements, but the judge decided that undue influence was to be presumed because of the special relationship between the two, especially as O'Sullivan had trusted his manager and signed the agreements without taking legal advice.[5]

The Elton John case,[6] where the judges held that there was a presumed fiduciary duty between the manager and client, came after this. In this case there were other factors involved, such as the length of time it took the artists to bring the claim, which shows that these matters are decided on a case-by-case basis and are therefore not clear-cut. But in general we can say that the first part of the undue influence test is demonstrated in

---

[5]   *O'Sullivan v Management Agency & Music Limited & Others* [1985] Q.B. 428.

[6]   *Elton John and Bernie Taupin and others v Richard Leon James, Dick James Music Ltd and This Record Company Ltd* [1991] F.S.R. 397; see Chapter 7.

relationships between managers and artists, and that artists need to take independent legal advice before signing agreements with them.

9.3.2   Restraint of trade

The second way in which licensing agreements are limited to protect the artist is called restraint of trade. This is a general principle of contract law that means that people are allowed to practise their trade, and therefore any contract that restricts a person's right to practise their trade needs to be justified. In these situations, the terms of the agreements cannot restrict any more than is necessary.

Restraint of trade was found in the case *Macaulay v Schroeder*,[7] where a songwriter entered into an agreement with music publishers assigning his copyright to the publisher for five years, plus another five years if the royalties exceeded £5,000. However, the contract provided no obligation for the publisher to actually exploit the songs. The court held that the contract was one-sided and that this was in restraint of trade because it was unreasonable to tie the composer to the publisher for potentially ten years, during which his work could be sterilised if the publisher chose not to publish, without any opportunity to recover his copyright. Therefore, the contract was held to be invalid.

Another example of a successful restraint of trade case came after Holly Johnson left the 1980s group Frankie Goes to Hollywood. The group had a record deal with Zang Tumb Tuum for up to nine years, which included a clause stating that if a member left the group, they could not work for another record company. When Johnson decided to leave the band, the record label tried to enforce this contract, but the court said that the clause was in restraint of trade. The court set out that it is for record labels to be able to justify the length and one-sidedness of their contracts, which the label was not able to do in this case.[8]

However, in other cases it has been found that the restraint of trade was a reasonable one, such as when George Michael tried to get out of his contract with Sony Music Entertainment. After the band Wham! went their separate ways, the leaving member clause in the contract with Sony

---

[7]   *Schroeder Music Publishing v Macaulay (Formerly Instone)* [1974] 1 W.L.R. 1308.

[8]   *Zang Tumb Tuum v Holly Johnson* [1993] EMLR 61.

determined that George Michael would continue to be signed by Sony as an individual artist. The judge recognised that this clause was a necessary restraint of trade in order to protect the interest of the record label and their investment. Additionally, George Michael was duly compensated and the contracts were re-negotiated, providing a compromise that was freely entered into on legal advice.[9]

Now that this chapter has set out what an assignment and a licence are, and the two main limitations on both, in the following sections it will explain some of the different types of licences seen in the music industry.

9.4   Mechanical licensing

Back in the days of piano-rolls, songs were reproduced mechanically; this is why the licence to reproduce a song into a sound recording is referred to as a mechanical licence. The mechanical licence is obtained by the record label, to enable it to record the performance of a song or reproduce a sound recording. The fee of the mechanical royalty goes to the copyright holder, usually the publisher. The amount of this royalty is either negotiated between the record label and publisher, or – often – prescribed by law.

In the UK, MCPS, in alliance with PRS for Music, administers the mechanical licences of composers, lyricists and music publishers for the copying of music on a product such as CD, DVD or vinyl. The fee for the licence was set by the UK Copyright Tribunal at 8.5 per cent after a dispute arose between the British Phonographic Industry and MCPS, who were unable to come to an agreement on what the fee should be.[10] For a large digital service in the UK to offer music content for permanent download the fee is 8 per cent of gross revenue or minimum fee per download (whichever is greater).[11] For online streaming, tailored licence agreements are in place for certain platforms such as Facebook and YouTube, and small digital services offering streaming from their own

---

[9]   *Panayiotou v Sony Music Entertainment* [1994] EMLR 229.

[10]   *British Phonographic Industry Ltd v Mechanical Copyright Protection Society Ltd* (CT/13/92) issued 12 April 1994.

[11]   www.prsformusic.com/licences/using-music-online/music-download-licence accessed 6 November 2020.

service can also obtain a licence from PRS.[12] Publishers generally license mechanical rights for physical records on a collective basis, but for digital, in many cases, they have withdrawn the mechanical right from MCPS and license this directly.

Throughout Europe and in many other countries, the mechanical licence fee is set by the Bureau International de l'Edition Mécanique (BIEM), an organisation that represents 60 mechanical rights societies from 59 countries.[13] The royalty rate agreed between BIEM and the International Federation of the Phonographic Industry (IFPI) for mechanical reproduction is 11 per cent on the Published Price to Dealers (PPD – the highest price charged by a record producer to a retailer selling directly to consumers) for physical audio products only.

In the US, mechanical licences are compulsory in certain circumstances, meaning that once a song is recorded and released the copyright holder is obliged to license the song to anyone that wants to use it in an audio-only recording. The certain circumstances limit the situations in which rightsholders can be compelled to license and include things such as the song having previously been recorded and distributed – so not the first recording of the song. They do not apply to dramatical music such that used in musicals. The fee for this licence is also set by law and so is called a statutory fee, which is calculated at a cost per minute of the song. The rate is currently 9.1 cent per minute for a five-minute song, or 1.75 per minute of a song that is more than five minutes long. In 2018 the US introduced a new law called the Music Modernization Act, which updated the rules to include compulsory mechanical licences for streaming, although the certain circumstances part and the rates are slightly different.

9.5   Synchronisation licences

Synchronisation licences apply when music is synchronised with visual images, such as in films, adverts or computer games. This can be a lucrative licence for an artist and also boosts discovery. If you have signed

---

[12] www.prsformusic.com/licences/using-music-online/limited-online-music-licence accessed 6 November 2020.

[13] www.biem.org/index.php?lang=en accessed 6 November 2020.

a record deal, the terms of contract could include this type of work – but this can be negotiated. For instance, some contracts allow artists to undertake commissioned work for films or adverts which does not fall within the remit of the record label's attained copyright.

9.6 Extended collective licence

Extended collective licensing is a method of rights clearance originally developed in Scandinavian countries, and now also provided for by law in the UK. The scheme aims to enable the clearing rights for multiple copyright works to be established quickly and efficiently. It does this by allowing collecting societies to license the use of works by all relevant rightsholders within their class of rights, including copyright owners that are not members of the collecting society. However, rightsholders can choose to specifically opt out of the scheme. Fees collected on behalf of non-members are held for a certain period of time, but if unclaimed eventually end up funding social, cultural and educational activities for the benefit of non-member rightsholders.[14] That said, currently no UK collecting societies have successfully applied for the scheme.[15]

9.7 Blanket licence

Blanket licence is the term used to describe one of the ways in which collecting societies licence their repertoire. It simply allows the licence holder to use all the titles within the collecting society's copyright collection provided by their members, in accordance with certain terms and conditions.

9.8 Creative Commons

Creative Commons is a selection of six prescribed licences that all revolve around the idea of letting other people use your copyright work for free,

---

[14] UK Copyright and Rights in Performances (Extended Collective Licensing) Regulations 2014.
[15] In 2017 the collecting society for authors, the Copyright Licensing Agency (CLA), made an application; it later withdrew it, in 2018.

but with certain rules attached to them so that you can enforce conditions on the way that the work is used: for example, that it cannot be used for financial gain, or cannot be edited without your permission.[16] If you publish something under the Creative Commons scheme, you are able to enforce your chosen licence as if you had signed a contract with the user. For example, if you specify that third parties may use your work under a Creative Commons licence on the condition that you are credited as the creator and they do not make a financial gain from your work (this is called CC BY-NC)[17] but the third party does use it for commercial purposes, you are able to enforce your rights as a breach of contract.

Now that this chapter has explained assignment and licences, Chapter 10 takes a look at copyright on social media, including how the terms and conditions act as a licence that affects the ownership of the content.

---

[16] https://creativecommons.org/ accessed 6 November 2020.
[17] https://creativecommons.org/about/cclicenses/ accessed 6 November 2020.

10 Social media

Social media is growing in popularity, with an estimated 45 per cent of the world's population now using social media channels[1] and spending on average 136 minutes per day on social networks.[2] More than 95 million photos and videos are posted on Instagram every day.[3] More than 250 billion photos have been uploaded to Facebook – that equates to 350 million photos per day![4]

Social media has largely replaced the idea of fan clubs in the modern-day music industry. It is the best way to connect with your fans and the contemporary marketing arena. The content on social media is likely to be protected by copyright, so there are a few important things that you need to be aware of in order to know where you stand with regard to your own content as well as the use of other people's content. As such, this chapter covers who owns the content on social media, infringement of social media content and two platforms that are particularly relevant to the music industry: TikTok and YouTube.

Before we get stuck in, I would like to mention that I love social media – both from a personal perspective, as a user of literally all of them, and as a researcher. It can be transformative, a creative playground, and a way to build a connection with your fans or following. However, this chapter is here to let you know about the risks and ramifications of social media, because that is what lawyers do – and then you can make informed decisions about what you do and do not share.

---

[1] We Are Social and Hootsuite, 'Digital 2019: Essential Insights into How People Around The World Use The Internet, Mobile Devices, Social Media And E-Commerce' (2019) https://p.widencdn.net/kqy7ii/Digital2019-Report-en accessed 6 November 2020.

[2] 'Daily Time Spent on Social Networking by Internet Users Worldwide from 2012 to 2018' www.statista.com/statistics/433871/daily-social-media-usage-worldwide/ accessed 6 November 2020.

[3] www.omnicoreagency.com/instagram-statistics/ accessed 6 November 2020.

[4] www.brandwatch.com/blog/facebook-statistics/ accessed 6 November 2020.

Also, while this chapter focuses on social media, much of it applies to the internet more broadly. You should also be thinking about these topics in relation to your website or app should you decide to create one or have one created for you.

10.1   Copyright ownership on social media

This section looks at who owns the content uploaded or posted on social media. Usually the person who creates a photo or video would be the copyright owner of that work, except in circumstances that we have previously discussed, such as creating something in the course of employment – and also this one time when a monkey took a selfie and everyone lost their minds about whether the copyright holder of the photo was the monkey, the photographer who set up the camera, or maybe even the zoo where the monkey lived, or a charity that supports monkeys.[5]

So, you would think that the person uploading their own content to social media would be the owner of that material. However, the user of social media is bound by the terms of service of that platform, which impacts the rights. This is problematic because users do not tend to be in the business of reading long, complicated terms and conditions, and even if they did they would probably still just go ahead and use the social media platform anyway.

For example, Instagram reports that it does not take ownership of its users' content. Technically that is true. However, Instagram's terms of use state that users grant 'a non-exclusive, royalty-free, transferable, sub-licensable, worldwide license to host, use, distribute, modify, run, copy, publicly perform or display, translate, and create derivative works of your content (consistent with your privacy and application settings). You can end this license anytime by deleting your content or account.'[6] In addition, under platform policy it says: 'You grant us and our affiliates a non-exclusive, transferable, sub-licensable, royalty-free, worldwide license to use any data, content, and other information made available by you or on your behalf in connection with your use of our Platform. This

---

5   In the end the parties settled out of court … *Naruto et al v David Slater* No. 16-15469 (9th Cir. 2018).

6   Instagram, https://help.instagram.com/581066165581870 accessed 6 November 2020.

license survives even if you stop using the platform feature.'[7] So, while the user may remain the copyright holder, an extremely broad and generous licence is granted to Instagram to use the content in any which way they please without even telling you, let alone paying or crediting you.

There have been a few cases brought against social media platforms by consumer representative organisations, arguing that these terms were unreasonable. For example, in August 2018 the Paris Court of First Instance found that Twitter's Terms of Use were void and unenforceable because they were abusive towards users.[8] Additionally, in April 2019, the Paris Court declared that 430 clauses of the general conditions of use of Facebook were also abusive and unlawful, stating that the clauses relating to the transfer of copyright were significantly disproportionate, and that the terms on user-generated copyright content were unclear and confusing.[9]

The impact of these cases has been limited because they only applied in the country of that case, but I doubt very much that these will be the only cases we see on the issue. In the meantime, just remember that by uploading content to social media platforms you remain the copyright holder as the creator, but the platform can utilise the content for itself under the terms and conditions. This is the current situation, at least; however, it is important to note that the terms of social media platforms are continually updated and are therefore always subject to change!

10.2 Copyright infringement on social media

This section talks a little about copyright infringement on social media. Online enforcement is addressed in more detail in Chapter 20, which covers what to do if you think someone has infringed your copyright on social media or online.

---

[7] https://help.instagram.com/325135857663734/?helpref=hc_fnav&bc[0]=Instagram%20Help&bc[1]= Privacy%20and%20Safety%20Center accessed 6 November 2020.

[8] *Union Fédérale des Consommateurs v Société TWITTER Inc.* Décision du 07 août 2018, 1/4 social N° RG 14/07300.

[9] *UFC-Que Choisir v Facebook Inc.* TGI de Paris, jugement du 9 avril 2019.

Social media companies encourage their users to spend more time on their platforms and to share more content, in order to increase revenue.[10] This includes encouraging users to share both their own original content and others' content. The more time users spend on their platform sharing content, the higher the revenue they are able to receive through advertising. For example, Facebook earned $16.6 billion in advertising revenue for the second quarter of 2019, a 28 per cent increase year-over-year,[11] alongside an increase in registered users[12] and time spent on the platform by those users.[13] Social media companies financially benefit from encouraging users to share content and this is important to bear in mind when we consider how much responsibility the platforms should take in relation to informing and protecting their users.

In total contrast to this, the terms and conditions of the social media platforms state that users guarantee either that the content uploaded by them is their own original work or that they have permission from the copyright holder. We all know that this is not how social media works but agreeing to these terms helps protect the platform from being sued for copyright infringement – as do their notice and take down systems.

However, it does not protect the user. Posting copyright-protected material on social media without permission, a licence or the benefit of a copyright exception is copyright infringement. I have seen claims made and users pay for their sharing of other people's images on social media. It really does happen. It is becoming a more common occurrence due to technologies that enable copyright holders to upload their work and then scan social media channels for matches. This software searches online content,[14] locates copies and sends automated claims to social

---

[10] See Bosher H and Yeşiloğlu S, 'An Analysis of the Fundamental Tensions between Copyright and Social Media: The Legal Implications of Sharing Images on Instagram' (2019) 33(2) International Review of Law, Computers & Technology 164–86.

[11] 'Facebook Reports Second Quarter 2019 Results' https://s21.q4cdn.com/399680738/files/doc _financials/2019/Q2/FB-Q2-2019-Earnings-Release.pdf accessed 6 November 2020.

[12] https://about.fb.com/company-info/ accessed 6 November 2020.

[13] In 2005, 5 per cent of American adults used at least one social media platform; by 2011 that share had risen to half of all Americans, and today 72 per cent of the public uses some type of social media: Pew Research Center, 'Social Media Fact Sheet' www.pewresearch.org/internet/fact-sheet/social-media/ accessed 6 November 2020.

[14] Such as www.photoclaim.com, which operates on a no win no fee basis, taking 35 per cent of any claims, and claims to have gained 3819856.00 euros for copyright holders over 2,683 settled cases.

media account holders. There are no court cases about this because they tend to be settled out of court – this is because, legally speaking, it is an open-and-shut case, being technically copyright infringement.

There have been a number of high-profile disputes, particularly in the US. These disputes have also commonly settled out of court, as in the case of Khloe Kardashian,[15] after she posted a photo of herself on her Instagram profile – with the watermark removed – that was owned by Xposure Photos. The case settled after mediation in March 2018. American fashion model Gigi Hadid faced a similar claim in 2018, but decided to defend her case after being sued a second time for copyright infringement on her social media profile.[16] Hadid had also posted a picture of herself on her Instagram account, which she reportedly sourced from a fan account on Twitter.[17] The copyright holder claimed infringement and Hadid tried to argue several angles of defence including fair use, joint ownership and implied licence. Sadly, the case fell apart because the copyright holder did not register their copyright before bringing the claim – which is a requirement under US law![18]

The take-home message of this section is that while it is common practice to share others' content on social media, you should be aware that it is still technically copyright infringement, so the best thing to do is to share your own original content.

The final two sections of this chapter look at TikTok and YouTube. These social media platforms are particularly relevant to the music industry due to their heavy use of musical content.

10.3   Music and TikTok

The latest social media trend is, of course, TikTok. For those living under a rock, this is a social media platform where users create and share video content of 60 seconds' duration. Users can watch a video and save the

---

[15] *Xposure Photos UK Ltd. v Khloe Kardashian et al* 2:17-cv-03088.

[16] *X-clusive Lee, Inc. v Gigi Hadid* 1:19-cv-00520.

[17] G Hadid Instagram account, 2019.

[18] See Bosher H, 'Key Issues Around Copyright and Social Media: Ownership, Infringement and Liability' (2020) 15(2) Journal of Intellectual Property Law & Practice, 123–33.

audio clip in order to create their own version using the same clip. Users can upload original audio or choose a sound from the app. Much of the content involves fun challenges, dances or lip syncing to the tune of a catchy song – otherwise known as musical memes.

TikTok has had an incredible impact on the music industry: it has been instrumental in music discovery and pushing songs up the charts. TikTok is currently changing how hits are made. As a result, if you get a record deal, you might quickly see a TikTok campaign coming from the marketing department – especially after MMF signed a partnership deal with TikTok so that managers can work directly with them.[19] We've already seen everyone from Little Mix to The 1975, Dua Lipa and The Weeknd jumping on the proverbial bandwagon. In 2019 Lil Nas X's song *Old Town Road* first went viral on TikTok and now holds the title of longest-reigning Billboard Hot 100 No. 1 in the chart's history. Likewise, Megan Thee Stallion's 2020 hit *Savage* went viral after a choreographed TikTok dance that quickly became known as the 'Savage Challenge'.

At the same time, industry organisations were trying to negotiate and secure licensing deals with TikTok and threatening legal action against the social media platform for copyright infringement in the absence of such an agreement.[20] They believed that there should be royalty payments for the use of the sound clips used within the app.

In 2019, ICE (a joint venture representing the digital music rights of PRS in the UK, GEMA in Germany and STIM in Sweden) attempted to reach an agreement with TikTok. This ended up being referred to the UK's Copyright Tribunal. In December 2019 the dispute was withdrawn from the tribunal, as the parties announced that they would be entering into arbitration to agree the terms of a licensing deal that would include retrospective use of copyright material on TikTok. So far, the outcome of the arbitration has not been made public.

In July 2020 TikTok signed licensing deals with independent distributor Believe and its subsidiary TuneCore. Within days of that agreement, it was announced that TikTok had also agreed a licensing deal with the US

---

[19] www.musicweek.com/management/read/tiktok-teams-with-music-managers-forum/079854 accessed 6 November 2020.

[20] www.ft.com/content/1b3b78ea-32a3-4237-8b79-3595820eeb63 accessed 6 November 2020.

National Music Publishers Association (NMPA). This partnership deal gives NMPA members the ability to opt into a licensing framework that allows them to benefit from their works included on TikTok.[21]

The terms and conditions of TikTok state that by uploading content, users give permission for other users to re-use their content.[22] This is significantly different from other social media platforms, such as Instagram – as discussed above – which commonly state that users either upload their own original content or content that they have sought permission to use. From a social media perspective, these TikTok terms make practical sense because the whole point in the platform is sharing and re-using sound clips to re-create derivative videos. However, from a copyright perspective, this is a bit awkward because it undermines the whole idea of copyright on the platform.

The terms and conditions also state that while users remain the copyright holders of the content they upload, they grant TikTok an 'unconditional irrevocable, non-exclusive, royalty-free, fully transferable, perpetual worldwide licence to use, modify, adapt, reproduce, make derivative works of, publish and/or transmit, and/or distribute and to authorise other users of the Services and other third-parties to view, access, use, download, modify, adapt, reproduce, make derivative works of, publish and/or transmit your User Content in any format and on any platform, either now known or hereinafter invented'. Moreover, they explicitly say that by uploading a sound recording, users grant TikTok the right to reproduce it, publicly perform it and communicate it to the public on a royalty-free basis, including royalties to 'a sound recording copyright owner (e.g., a record label), a musical work copyright owner (e.g., a music publisher), a performing rights organization (e.g., ASCAP, BMI, SESAC, etc.) (a "PRO"), a sound recording PRO (e.g., SoundExchange), any unions or guilds, and engineers, producers or other royalty participants involved in the creation of User Content.'[23] Thereby completely undermining the entire music copyright system – no wonder the music industry

---

[21] www.billboard.com/articles/business/9422985/tiktok-nmpa-global-partnership-agreement-music -publishers accessed 6 November 2020.

[22] 'Users of the Services may also extract all or any portion of User Content created by another user to produce additional User Content.' TikTok Terms of Service as of October 2020 www.tiktok.com/ legal/terms-of-use?lang=en accessed 6 November 2020.

[23] www.tiktok.com/legal/terms-of-use?lang=en accessed 6 November 2020.

was *ticked* off! Essentially, as a TikTok user, if you upload your own song to TikTok you are surrendering your rights to receive royalty payments according to the terms of service. However, in general the music available from the TikTok music library is licensed and so artists do receive royalties for the use of their music on the social media platform. TikTok also operates a notice and takedown procedure for the removal of any infringing content.

In terms of the videos created on the platform, they are likely to be protected by copyright. The Chinese version of TikTok, called Douyin, successfully argued copyright infringement when a video that was originally uploaded to its platform was later uploaded to Huopai, a similar video-sharing platform. Huopai argued that there was no infringement because the video was unoriginal and therefore did not qualify as a copyright work, stating that there was limited room for creativity in a 13-second video. However, the court found that the video was an original work capable of copyright protection, stating: 'For the works created on the same theme by different authors, the expressions of which are creative and independently completed, the authors enjoy independent copyrights in relation to the corresponding works.'[24]

So, while TikTok offers opportunities for music discovery and is clearly pushing songs up the charts, it is also currently a copyright nightmare for the industry. However, *Music Week* recently reported that global head of music Ole Obermann was working hard to get the platform fully licensed and in November 2020 TikTok announced another new licensing agreement, this time with Sony Music Entertainment, so that TikTok artists can have legal access to sound clips from Sony Music artists.[25]

---

[24] *Beijing Weibo Shijie Technology Co., Ltd. v Baidu Online Network Technology (Beijing) Co., Ltd. and Baidu Wangxun Technology Co., Ltd.* [2018] Beijing 0491, First Instance Civil Judgment No. 1.

[25] Mark Sutherland, 'Ole Obermann: TikTok "Well Down the Road" to Being Fully Licensed' (*Music Week*, 2020) www.musicweek.com/digital/read/ole-obermann-tiktok-well-down-the-road-to-being -fully-licensed/081052 accessed 5 November 2020.

10.4 Music and YouTube

YouTube has been around for longer than TikTok, but there is still great controversy when it comes to its relationship with music copyright holders.

There is an important case ongoing in the EU at the time of writing, in which the EU court has been asked to consider if YouTube infringes the communication to the public of rights of copyright holders under EU law. The result of the case is not yet decided but the Advocate General has given his opinion[26] – which the court may or may not follow. The AG's opinion was that YouTube does not perform acts of communication to the public under EU law[27] and is protected by another law, which we call the hosting safe harbour.[28] The hosting safe harbour provides, in a nutshell, that platforms can avoid copyright infringement claims by putting in place certain processes, such as the notice and takedown system on YouTube. However, in the opinion the AG explicitly stated that his conclusion was decided under current EU law as existing prior to the adoption of the DSM Copyright Directive; therefore he was not applying Article 17, which created a new obligation that providers of online content-sharing services perform an 'act of communication to the public or an act of making available to the public' (that is, copyright infringement) when giving the public access to works protected by copyright or to other subject matter that has been uploaded by its users.[29]

YouTube uses a technology called Content ID, whereby rightsholders upload their material and the software scans the videos on YouTube for a match. If an infringement is detected, the rightsholder is offered options that they can take, including to mute, remove, monetise from advertising or leave the video as it is.[30] One of the criticisms of this system is that the technology cannot recognise the purpose of the use within the video and

---

[26] *Frank Peterson v Google LLC, YouTube LLC, YouTube Inc., Google Germany GmbH* (C-682/18), and *Elsevier Inc. v Cyando AG* (C-683/18) ECLI:EU:C:2020:586, opinion of AG Saugmandsgaard Øe.

[27] Information Society Directive, Article 3(1).

[28] Directive 2000/31/EC of the European Parliament and of the Council of 8 June 2000 on Certain Legal Aspects of Information Society Services, in Particular Electronic Commerce, in the Internal Market, Article 13.

[29] The reason the AG could not form his opinion based on this new law was that, while the DSM Copyright Directive is technically in force, it has not yet been transposed into national law.

[30] https://support.google.com/youtube/answer/2797370?hl=en-GB accessed 6 November 2020.

so it does not know if a copyright exception applies.[31] Therefore, copyright exceptions are only used by users who are knowledgeable enough to submit a counter-notification or dispute a Content ID copyright infringement claim. Even then, in the vast majority of cases, the parties do not have the same bargaining power and the procedure tends to favour the rightsholder. This is because the user has limited opportunity to speak to the rightsholder to try to persuade them, and ultimately the decision to block or transfer remuneration from advertising is in the hands of the copyright owners.

In September 2019, YouTube changed its policy on how copyright holders can respond to infringements of their music on the platform.[32] The changes affect the way that copyright is enforced on YouTube and are a recent example of social media self-regulation, meaning norm-setting and enforcement by private actors, without the intervention of the state. The change came after YouTube released a statement earlier in 2019 stating that it had noticed a trend of aggressive manual claiming of very short music clips used in monetised videos.[33] YouTube felt that this was unfair because this kind of claim on YouTube transfers all the revenue from the uploader to the copyright holder making the claim, regardless of the amount of music claimed. Therefore, YouTube changed its policy on this type of claim. Previously, with this type of claim, the rightsholder could choose to either block the video or prevent the uploader from monetising the video to receive the full revenue from a video that included any amount of their content.[34] Now, under the new policy, rightsholders can no longer use the manual claiming tool to monetise from creator videos that use very short or unintentional uses of music.[35] The result of this is that the options available to the rightsholder in these circumstances are to either leave the video or block the video.

---

[31] Jacques S, *The Parody Exception in Copyright Law* (OUP 2019) 208.

[32] https://youtube-creators.googleblog.com/2019/08/updates-to-manual-claiming-policies.html. See also Bosher H, 'YouTube Takes Copyright Law into Their own Hands with new Policy on Music Infringement', The IPKat 2019: https://ipkitten.blogspot.com/2019/09/youtube-takes-copyright-law-into-their.html accessed 6 November 2020.

[33] https://youtube-creators.googleblog.com/2019/08/updates-to-manual-claiming-policies.html accessed 6 November 2020.

[34] https://support.google.com/youtube/answer/9142671#manual_claiming accessed 6 November 2020.

[35] https://youtube-creators.googleblog.com/2019/08/updates-to-manual-claiming-policies.html accessed 6 November 2020.

There are some concerns about this new policy, which follows a trend of platforms self-regulating and enforcing copyright rules.[36] This policy is based on what YouTube feels is unfair, rather than what the law says. For example, what does YouTube think is 'very short' or 'unintentional' use of music in a video? One of the issues in these circumstances is that YouTube is only offering an all-or-nothing rule on the monetising of the video. Why not use a proportionate system that reflects the normal legal procedure, whereby a percentage of the revenue is shared with the copyright holder, for example by offering the rightsholder a percentage of the revenue?

There is also a new EU Directive in town. This is called the Digital Single Market Directive,[37] and is the one that people were protesting in the streets about in 2019. One of the new laws that this Directive brings into EU countries, under Article 17, was aimed at platforms such as YouTube. The new law says the opposite of what the AG said about the Information Society Directive above – that EU countries will make content-sharing service providers liable for communication to the public by giving the public access to copyright-protected works or other protected subject matter uploaded by its users. This law came as a result of some serious lobbying by the music industry representatives, organisations and communities. However, they were pretty disappointed overall, because the way the law is drafted could potentially give YouTube a get-out clause as it says that they are not liable if they 'made best efforts to obtain an authorisation'. It has been suggested that what YouTube already does with Content ID would be enough to overcome this hurdle,[38] although this totally depends on how the different EU countries transpose the Directive into their own national laws.[39] What happens with this law and the development of the YouTube case mentioned above is important for musicians, artists and music rightsholders, as it will directly impact the remuneration you receive from the use of your music on YouTube.

---

36 Hugenholtz PB, 'Codes of Conduct and Copyright Enforcement in Cyberspace' in IA Stamatoudi (ed) *Copyright Enforcement and the Internet* (Kluwer 2010) 304.

37 Directive (EU) 2019/790 of the European Parliament and of the Council Directive on copyright and related rights in the Digital Single Market and amending Directives 96/9/EC and 2001/29/EC.

38 Kivistö M, 'The DSM Directive: A Package (Too) Full of Policies' in T Pihlajarinne, J Vesala and O Honkkila (eds) *Online Distribution of Content in the EU* (Edward Elgar Publishing 2019) 19.

39 See https://ipkitten.blogspot.com/2019/05/dsm-directive-series-5-does-dsm.html accessed 6 November 2020.

Social media is fairly new terrain for copyright – the laws are just about beginning to adjust to the idea. As an alternative, rightsholders and their representatives are utilising licence agreements and self-regulation to try to ensure that use of copyright material on social media is remunerated.

This chapter concludes Part II on managing copyright. The next part looks at copyright infringement in the music industry.

PART III

Infringement

Part III covers infringement of copyright: what it is and how it works. It also covers what has been happening in the music industry, where artists have been suing each other for copying parts of their songs. It further includes a consideration of the somewhat contentious area of sampling. The first four chapters in the part are focused on copyright infringement of music and the last chapter looks at infringement of additional products related to music such as performances and merchandise.

Chapter 11 starts by explaining what copyright infringement is. This includes what constitutes primary or secondary infringement, the differences between civil and criminal infringement and other types of law that can apply to circumstances of copyright infringement.

Chapter 12 looks at cases of artists and rightsholders claiming copyright infringement for the copying of songs. It discusses the cases involving Robin Thicke and Pharrell Williams' *Blurred Lines*, Katy Perry's *Dark Horse*, Ed Sheeran's *Thinking Out Loud* and Led Zeppelin's *Stairway to Heaven*. In doing so it covers substantial similarity, the parts of songs that are protectable and not protectable, originality by selection and arrangement and the test for access to copyright works in the digital age.

Chapter 13 builds on the previous chapters, to bring some clarity to the difference between taking inspiration and copying. It considers the concept of creativity, before summarising what is and what is not copying for the purpose of copyright infringement. This includes an explanation of unconscious copying.

Chapter 14 discusses music sampling, how it is used and recent developments in the law that apply in these circumstances. It includes a brief con-
textual account of the history of sampling, before explaining the current
legal position regarding copyright infringement, copyright exceptions
and sample licences.

Chapter 15 looks at copyright infringement of products beyond the music
itself, such as counterfeit goods, unauthorised recordings of performances
and illegal merchandise.

11   What is copyright infringement?

In Part I we got to grips with what copyright is. Part II then covered who owns the copyright and how it is managed with contracts and licences. Part III now looks at when copyright is infringed. This chapter begins by explaining what the law says copyright infringement is, including primary and secondary infringement, criminal and civil liability, and online copyright infringement (elsewhere referred to as piracy). It also mentions other types of laws that can apply in situations of copyright infringement, such as fraud, breach of contract, passing-off, defamation and human rights law, including privacy and freedom of speech.

11.1   What is copyright infringement?

In Chapter 4 it was explained that the copyright holder has the exclusive right to perform the restricted acts, which are to copy the work; issue or distribute copies of the work to the public; rent or lend the work to the public; perform, show or play the work in public; communicate the work to the public; or make an adaptation of the work. So, doing these things without the rightsholder's permission, or without a copyright exception (explained in Chapter 5), would be an infringement of copyright.

11.2   Primary infringement

Primary copyright infringement occurs when a person does any of the restricted acts mentioned above without permission. But how do we know when the use of a work counts as an infringement? Essentially, infringement of a copyright work can be summarised as the taking of the whole, or a substantial part, of a copyright-protected work, without permission of the copyright owner or the benefit of a copyright exception.

If there has been a literal copy of the whole of the work this is pretty straightforward: if someone takes your song and distributes it without a licence, it would infringe your copyright. However, when it comes to copying a *substantial part* of a song, things get a little more interesting.

11.3 Taking a substantial part

It is a general principle of copyright law worldwide that the taking of a substantial part of a work constitutes infringement. What is meant by 'a substantial part' is mostly undefined in the statutory laws and is decided on a case-by-case basis. Each country has its own tests or factors which it will apply to determine if the part taken was substantial.

The first thing to know is that there is no numerical number or amount of a work that determines if it is substantial. There is no set number of notes that can be taken from a song, and no length of a sample, that we can say for sure would not constitute infringement. There is a common misconception that there is a minimum number of notes that people can take from a song, or a certain number of seconds from a video clip, in order to avoid infringement. This is incorrect.

Instead, it depends on the quality of what is taken – not the quantity. The quality of what is taken is determined by referring to the original aspects of the copied work. Remember that, as explained in Chapter 2, the work must be original to be protected by copyright. Originality means using your own skill and effort and making creative choices that reflect your own personal touch. Those are the parts of the work that not only enable copyright to subsist in it, but they are also the parts that cannot be copied. Substantial part is about the quality, importance and degree of originality of what has been taken. If the parts taken are commonplace, or just the idea is taken, this will not be copyright infringement, because copyright does not protect ideas.

In the UK, the meaning of substantial part is developed in the case law. The UK courts have said that it is to be a matter of quality, not quantity,[1] and that quality is to be determined by reference to the reason the work is

---

[1]   *Ladbroke (Football) v Hill (William) (Football)* [1964] 1 WLR 273.

protected by copyright: the originality.[2] This means that if the parts taken are the original elements of the work, it is more likely to be infringement. However, if the parts taken are the non-original or non-protectable parts, such as the general idea, then it is unlikely to be infringement.

One of the most prominent UK cases in which the judges defined substantial part related to a floral and striped fabric design, in which the defendant's design had both similarities and differences in the detail.[3] In the first instance the judge found that there had been copying, but on appeal it was held that the taking was not substantial. However, after a second appeal, the original judgment was restored by the House of Lords (as it was then – it is now called the Supreme Court), where it was clarified that while there had been no photographic or literal copying of the fabric design, there had been copying of certain ideas expressed in the design, which had involved the original skill and labour of the creator; this therefore constituted a substantial taking. In a more recent case the judge expanded on this definition, stating:

> In assessing the crucial question as to whether a substantial part has been taken, the court must have regard to all the facts of the case including the nature and extent of the copying; the quality and importance of what has been taken; the degree of originality of what has been taken or whether it is commonplace; and whether a substantial part of the skill and labour contributed by the author in creating the original has been appropriated.[4]

In the US, the basis of the question of substantial taking is the same – that it relates to the original elements of the work. The requirements for proving copyright infringement under US copyright law are, first, that the person bringing the claim owns a valid copyright; second, that the protected aspects of their work were copied, which includes two separate components: (a) copying and (b) unlawful appropriation. Therefore, the person bringing the claim must prove that their work was copied. If they do not have direct evidence of copying, they can attempt to prove it circumstantially by showing that (1) the defendant had access to their work and (2) the two works share similarities such that it is demonstrative of

[2] *Newspaper Licensing Agency Ltd (NLA) v Marks and Spencer Plc* [2001] 3 WLR 290, Lord Hoffmann 19.
[3] *Designers Guild Ltd v Russell Williams (Textiles) Ltd* [2000] 1 WLR 2416, Kitchin J, 85.
[4] *Paul Gregory Allen (Acting as trustee of Adrian Jacobs (Deceased)) v (1) Bloomsbury Publishing Plc, (2) Joanne Kathleen Murray (Professionally Known as JK Rowling)* [2010] EWHC 2560 (Ch).

copying. This type of probative similarity needs to show that the similarities between the two works are due to copying rather than coincidence, independent creation or prior common source. In making this assessment, the US has a two-part test (as recently clarified in the Led Zeppelin *Stairway to Heaven* case, which is discussed in Chapter 12): the intrinsic and extrinsic test. The extrinsic test has two steps in finding similarity: to identify first, the protectable elements, and second, whether those protected elements are objectively similar to the corresponding elements in the allegedly infringing work. The intrinsic test is a subjective test that asks whether the ordinary reasonable person would find the total concept and feel to be substantially similar, and is usually determined by a jury.

In Australia, one of the most high-profile cases of copyright infringement in music came after the pop song *Down Under*, recorded in 1979 and again in 1981 by Men at Work, included a flute riff which Larrikin Music Publishing claimed infringed their copyright in the children's musical round *Kookaburra Sits in the Old Gumtree*.[5] The court found that *Down Under* had reproduced a substantial part of *Kookaburra*, and as a result, EMI Records had misrepresented to collecting societies that it was entitled to 100% of the royalties.

This section has introduced the concept of substantial taking as the essence of non-literal copying. It is discussed in more detail in Chapters 12 and 13, with reference to specific case examples relating to similar songs.

11.4 Secondary infringement

Secondary copyright infringement relates to situations where a person has not themselves directly infringed, but contributed to the infringement. It is also sometimes referred to as indirect infringement, or associated infringement.

Secondary liability is an important aspect of copyright infringement that makes it illegal to deal in commercial counterfeit goods. It means that

---

[5] *Larrikin Music Publishing Pty Ltd v EMI Songs Australia Pty Limited* [2010] FCA 29; and [2011] FCAFC 47.

action can be taken even when it is not possible to know who made the infringing goods, as it can be taken against the person distributing or enabling the infringement. It is also used in cases against websites that provide access to illegal copies of copyright works, discussed below.

The main difference between primary and secondary copyright liability is that for secondary infringement, the person is not liable unless they knew or had reason to believe that they were handling infringing copies, or, in the case of a performance, that the performance would infringe copyright. An example of secondary liability would be permitting the use of premises for entertainment where musicians perform without a licence; to do this legally would require a licence from a performing rights society. (Organising a public entertainment event without a licence would likely be primary copyright infringement. For example, if a band is booked to perform in a club/pub, there is a clear responsibility for the venue to ensure that the appropriate licence is obtained.)

Some countries, such as the UK, include the rules on secondary liability within their copyright laws. Other countries use different laws, called tort law, to restrict the same activity. This is particularly so in civil law jurisdictions: for example, in the Netherlands, these activities have been found to be illegal under that country's laws of negligence. In Germany, promoting a concert and operating a restaurant or dance hall without a licence has also been found to be contrary to German law.

In the UK, the restricted acts which would amount to secondary infringement of a copyright work include doing things such as: importing infringing copies; possessing or dealing with infringing copies; providing means for making infringing copies; permitting use of premises for infringing performance; and supplying apparatus for infringing performance.[6] The UK law states that the defendant must have known, or had reason to believe, that they were dealing with unauthorised copies. This is a broad and objective test. The threshold for knowledge is generally considered to be low because of the words 'had reason to believe'.

---

[6] CDPA 1988, sections 22–26.

This issue of knowledge arose in a case in the UK courts relating to Eminem's first album *Infinite*, recorded in 1996[7] (kudos if you knew this was his first album!). The Bass brothers run a recording studio in Detroit known as FBT. They discovered Eminem in 1995 and signed a recording contract with him, releasing the *Infinite* album on their Web Entertainment label in 1996. In 1998 Eminem and the Bass brothers signed an agreement with Aftermath Entertainment, a division of Universal Music, following which Eminem released his second album, *The Slim Shady LP*, in 1999. A distribution agreement was signed between a company called Boogie Up and two distribution companies called Let Them Eat Vinyl Distribution and Plastic Head Music Distribution to create CD and vinyl copies of the album. We know from Chapter 9 on licensing that this is a mechanical licence that needs to be obtained from MCPS. When the Bass brothers approached MCPS, they were told that MCPS did not have the rights to this album and were therefore unable to grant the licence, but still approved the manufacture of a maximum of 2,931 vinyl copies, for which the 8.5 per cent royalty was charged. The copies were made and distributed by the distribution companies, who supplied them until 9 October 2016.

The Bass brothers claimed secondary copyright infringement against the two distribution companies. One of the issues was whether the distribution companies knew, or had reason to believe, that they were infringing after their response from MCPS. In the case, the judge pointed out that often where 'reason to believe' is an issue in a case, the decision of liability depends on what happened after the defendant received a notice of infringement. Some previous cases were referred to in the arguments, one of which said that a person who deliberately refrains from inquiry and shuts their eyes to that which is obvious cannot say that they lacked knowledge.[8] Another case explained 'reason to believe' as involving the concept of knowledge of facts from which a reasonable person would arrive at the relevant belief.[9]

The test the court applied was to ascertain whether, viewed objectively, a reasonable record distributor would have arrived at the belief that they

---

[7]   *FBT Productions, LLC v Let Them Eat Vinyl Distribution Ltd & Anor* [2019] EWHC 829 (IPEC) (2 April 2019).

[8]   *Columbia Pictures Industries Inc v Robinson* [1987] 1 Ch 38.

[9]   *L.A. Gear Inc v Hi-Tech Sports plc* [1992] FSR 121.

were infringing copyright. To do this, the court considered all the relevant facts known to the distribution companies regarding the copies of *Infinite* that they were distributing. In this situation the reasonable person is not a lawyer and belief does not include a realisation of the full details of why there was an infringement of copyright, such as the identity and nature of the copyright work in question, precisely who owns the copyright, or why there was no licence from the owner. It is enough, the court said, if the facts would have led a reasonable person to believe that dealing in the copies would be in breach of a right in the nature of copyright held by some other person. However, merely suspecting that this is the situation would not be enough.

In the end, the court said that the distribution companies acted to ensure that they obtained the correct rights by approaching MCPS and paying the licence fee; this fell in their favour as it demonstrated that they believed they were dealing in legal copies. Therefore, the distribution companies were not liable for secondary copyright infringement for the importing, offering for sale and selling of copies of the *Infinite* album, because they did not have knowledge, or reason to believe, that they were dealing in infringing copies. However, they were found to be infringing the copyright in the *Infinite* album by primary infringement for making the copies. (Why? Because there is no knowledge requirement for that type of infringement!)

At EU level, these rules are not harmonised because there are both common law and civil law countries in the EU, and therefore not all countries have a specific secondary liability law for copyright. The EU has been seen to make moves towards trying to harmonise these laws, for example by introducing a knowledge requirement within the scope of primary liability and thereby blurring the distinction between primary and secondary infringement.[10] This happened in the *Pirate Bay* case,[11] where the EU court relied on the notion of 'indispensable intervention' to find that online platform operators could be regarded as primarily liable for unauthorised acts of copyright infringement, by communication to the public, if they have full knowledge of the consequences of their actions.

---

[10] Rosati E, 'The CJEU Pirate Bay Judgment and Its Impact on the Liability of Online' (2017) European Intellectual Property Review 11.

[11] *Stichting Brein v Ziggo BV and XS4All Internet BV*, C-610/15 EU:C:2017:456.

The requirement of knowledge had previously only been applied in cases of secondary infringement.

In the US, secondary liability encompasses two aspects of infringement: (1) contributory infringement and (2) vicarious liability. Contributory infringement is similar to the UK secondary liability, which addresses situations where a person contributes to, causes or induces infringing conduct. This type of infringement also requires knowledge of the infringing activity. Vicarious infringement refers to situations where a person's right and ability to supervise the infringing activity combines with a direct financial gain in the exploitation of the copyright material. Vicarious infringement does not require knowledge of copyright infringement in order to find liability.

11.5 Criminal infringement

The acts restricted by copyright under primary infringement come under a sector of law called private law. This essentially means that it is a law that governs private action between people or companies, such as suing each other under contract or copyright law. The other sector of law is called public law and refers to the regulation of people or companies by the state, for example in criminal cases where the state will take an action against an alleged crime. An important distinction between private law and public law is the types of remedies that are available. In private law actions the courts will try to remedy the harm by the payment of damages, for example, whereas in public law cases defendants can be given a prison sentence (see Chapter 19 for copyright remedies).

Historically, copyright was a private commercial interest that was governed only by private law. However, the laws have been developed to criminalise copyright-infringing activities in certain circumstances. It was first criminalised in the UK in 1862. The first time that imprisonment was a remedy for copyright infringement came in 1906, for creating unlawful copies of musical works. (At that time, getting caught once meant a £5 fine and getting caught twice meant two months in prison!) Even though criminal proceedings for copyright infringement have technically been available to copyright owners in the UK since 1956, the law was less utilised then than it is now. One reason why this may be is that the laws have developed to broaden the scope of the criminalisation of copyright, as well as the remedies and sanctions available. Additionally, the previous law required actual knowledge on behalf of the infringer, but under the current UK law the knowledge threshold is lowered to 'knowing, or hav[ing] reason to believe'. This has therefore encouraged more rightsholders to pursue criminal remedies rather than, or as well as, civil remedies.[12]

The UK copyright law provides that it is a criminal offence to: make for sale or hire; import into the UK otherwise than for private and domestic use; possess in the course of a business with a view to committing any act infringing the copyright; in the course of a business, sell or let for hire, offer or expose for sale, hire, exhibit in public, or distribute an article which is known, or there is reason to believe, is an infringing copy of a copyright work.[13] It is also a criminal offence to specifically design something for making copies of a copyright work, or to have such an article in your possession, knowing, or having reason to believe, that it is to be used to make infringing copies for sale or hire or for use in the course of a business. On the question of 'reason to believe', a magistrates' court has held that broad knowledge of the items complained of and the nature of the infringement was sufficient.[14]

A rightsholder can choose whether to bring their claim under private or criminal law, even if that means that the defendant is unable to bring a defence which they would have been able to bring in different proceedings.[15] In fact, they are able to bring both types of action at the same time. The cases will be brought in different courts that handle those particular types of actions, and may well use different approaches to assessing a case; this means that a rightsholder may be successful in one court and unsuccessful in the other, when arguing about the same circumstances.

The criminalisation of copyright in the US was first adopted in 1897 and has gone through a similar expansion to include more activities, with

---

[12] Richardson A, 'Case Comment: Thames & Hudson Ltd v Design and Artists Copyright Society Ltd Times' (1994) 5(5) Entertainment Law Review 91–2.

[13] UK CDPA 1988, sections 107 (1)(a)–(e).

[14] Kinnier-Wilson J, 'Copyright: Criminal Copyright Infringement – Sections 107 and 110 CDPA 1988 – Copyright in a Photocopy' (1994) 16(11) EIPR 217–48, 295.

[15] *Thames & Hudson Ltd v Design and Artists Copyright Society Ltd Times*, 10 August 1994 (Ch D) (1994).

extended sentences and higher fines, particularly in response to the development of digital technology and content sharing. Section 11.6 briefly addresses the issue of online copyright infringement.

11.6   Online copyright infringement

My favourite music industry era is the one depicted in Cameron Crowe's film *Almost Famous*, set in the early 1970s. This was apparently when everyone in the industry was having the absolute time of their lives. By the late 1970s, the CD had been invented and this catapulted the industry into a time of unprecedented surge in profits. However, it was relatively shortlived, because not long after that the internet changed everything.

Previously, people relied on the radio to hear new music and went to record shops to buy music. The record store had an active influence on music discovery and trade, and this culture was pretty well sustained in the CD era. The way we thought about music consumption even remained similar from the CD era to that of downloading music on the internet, when digital music was first developed. It still felt like a commodity that people wanted to own. This perception is what caused the dispute between Bruce Willis and Apple, after the American actor realised that he could not leave his iTunes collection in his will.[16] This was the turning point at which people started to realise that under the iTunes terms and conditions, users only licensed their use of the music, and did not own it. ('Welcome to the party, pal.')

These days, of course, streaming is the norm and consumers are happy to simply have access to music – the desire to have ownership of it has fallen away. In addition to the legal developments, the music industry has adapted through new business models. Subscription services such as Apple Music, plus the advertising model of Spotify, have been the most effective remedy to users' need for access to all songs ever. Licensing agreements have also been made with social media platforms such as Facebook and YouTube to capture some of the income for artists when their music is used online.

---

[16]   www.theguardian.com/technology/shortcuts/2012/sep/03/bruce-willis-v-apple-owns-music-ipod

Initially, the internet – and, more specifically, online file sharing services – caused huge disruption for the music industry. However, while there are still challenges to overcome, the law and the industry's business models have come a long way in adapting to these new technological and behavioural developments. The law is now applied broadly in relation to this type of copyright infringement online. The restricted act of communication to the public has been key in this development since it was introduced in 2003, and is 'at the heart of modern copyright law'.[17] It provides for the restricted act of communication to the public by electronic transmission, including making a copyright work available in such a way that members of the public may access it from a place and at a time individually chosen by them.[18] The application of this section has been instrumental in the development of the law relating to online copyright infringement, in particular in UK cases such as *Newzbin*,[19] which found liability for communicating protected works to the public when indexing copyright protected content. After that, there was the case of the *Pirate Bay*[20] website, which was also found to be infringing copyright when acting as a search engine and providing links to copyright-protected content, along with its users.

However, despite the importance of this right, communication to the public has struggled to find a predictable interpretation.[21] The scope of the right has widened dramatically, particularly in light of new technological and behavioural developments, allowing copyright holders to essentially control any communication of their work.[22] It has been argued that there is a need for a clearer understanding of the scope of communication and public,[23] and cases are still being referred to the EU court for clarification on whether it applies to certain circumstances, such as on YouTube.[24]

---

[17] Keane B, 'Ill Communication? The Concept of a Communication to the Public under EU Copyright Law' (2013) 24(5) Entertainment Law Review 165–71, 165.

[18] CDPA 1988, section 20.

[19] *Twentieth Century Fox Film Corporation v Newzbin Ltd* [2010] EWHC 608 (Ch).

[20] *Dramatico Entertainment Ltd & Ors v British Sky Broadcasting Ltd & Ors* [2012] EWHC 268 (Ch) (20 February 2012).

[21] Ibid 167.

[22] Gillen M, 'File-Sharing and Individual Civil Liability in the United Kingdom: A Question of Substantial Abuse?' (2006) 17(1) Entertainment Law Review 7–14, 11 – arguing that the new right addresses the latest challenges to copyright: 'making available is the essence of file-sharing.'

[23] Mysoor P, 'Unpacking the Right of Communication to the Public: A Closer Look at International and EU Copyright Law' (2013) 2 Intellectual Property Quarterly 166–85, 167.

[24] *Frank Peterson v Google LLC, YouTube LLC, YouTube Inc., Google Germany GmbH* (C-682/18) and *Elsevier Inc. v Cyando AG* (C-683/18) ECLI:EU:C:2020:586.

Moreover, despite the rise in digital licences and collections of royalties for rightsholders, many research studies still argue that the portion of income for creators from digital revenue does not reflect the state of the market.[25] In other words, there is a mismatch between the volume of creative work being made available via online channels and the amount of royalties being returned to creators. This notion, coined the 'value gap', is highly controversial, and some argue that it is based on assumptions rather than independent empirical evidence,[26] or even that it is an almost entirely fabricated rhetorical device.[27] Regardless, it was the driving force for the development of the new law, the EU Digital Single Market Directive,[28] which included a rule particularly intended to address issues of the value gap on YouTube.[29]

In Parliament, before a law is changed or updated, there is a consultation process. When this was happening in 1951, the UK government heard from 29 organisations and 5 individuals. In 1981 this increased to several hundred, and by 1986 it had reached about 1,000[30] – showing a gradual increase in engagement with what copyright rules should look like. This peaked in 2019, when tens of thousands of people took to the streets across Europe to protest the Digital Single Market Directive, and a Change.org petition was signed by more than five million people. Anarchy! This might be my favourite copyright era, because who would have thought that there would be thousands of people marching in the street engaging in copyright policy? Irrespective of whether you agree with what the Digital Single Market Directive says or not, the point is that regulation of copyright online is something that affects the general public at a new level, and people are starting to pay more attention.

---

[25] CISAC's Global Collections Report 2018 www.cisac.org/CISAC-University/Library/Global-Collections-Reports/Global-Collections-Report-2018 accessed 6 November 2020.

[26] Giancarlo F, 'From Horizontal to Vertical: An Intermediary Liability Earthquake in Europe' (2017) 12(7) JIPLP 565–75, 568.

[27] Giancarlo F, 'To Filter, or Not to Filter? That Is the Question in EU Copyright Reform' (2018) 36(2) Cardozo Arts & Entertainment Law Journal 331–68.

[28] Directive (EU) 2019/790 of The European Parliament and of the Council Directive on copyright and related rights in the Digital Single Market and amending Directives 96/9/EC and 2001/29/EC.

[29] Rosati E, *Copyright and the Court of Justice of the European Union* (OUP 2019) 200.

[30] Bosher H, *Law, Technology and Cognition: The Human Element in Online Copyright Infringement* (Routledge 2020).

11.7 Other relevant laws

In this final section of this chapter, I just want to mention a few other laws to be aware of that can go hand in hand with copyright infringement. These are fraud, contract, passing-off or unfair competition, defamation and human rights.

In UK cases of copyright infringement, we sometimes also see claims brought under the laws of fraud, which provides that it is a criminal offence to: dishonestly make a false representation; be in possession of articles for use in fraud; and make or supply articles for use in frauds.[31] Copyright holders utilise these additional statutory measures as they believe that it might increase their likelihood of success or might offer alternative remedies, such as increasing the penalty or sanction against the infringer.

In cases where the rightsholder succeeds against the copyright infringer under both copyright and fraud laws the sanctions can be accumulated (as in, added together) or run concurrently (at the same time). For example, in the matter of *Wayne Evans*,[32] Mr Evans was operating a number of websites responsible for the illegal distribution of copyright-protected material, one of which had 168,000 users and facilitated 523,000 downloads of UK Top 40 singles. The court found Mr Evans guilty of two offences of distributing copyright-infringing articles,[33] and also of a further offence of possessing an article for use in fraud.[34] Mr Evans was sentenced to 12 months' imprisonment on the first count, 6 months' imprisonment on the second count and 10 months' imprisonment on the third. All sentences were stated to run concurrently and so the total sentence was 12 months' immediate imprisonment.

As explained in the chapters on contracts and licensing, another law that is relevant to the copyright holder is contract law. Where there is a legal agreement in place, enforcement of rights can be made through breach of contract. This also includes the use of non-disclosure agreements, as these

---

[31] UK Fraud Act 2006, sections 1, 6 and 7.
[32] *Regina v Wayne Evans* [2017] EWCA Crim 139.
[33] Under UK CDPA 1988, section 107(1)(e).
[34] Under UK Fraud Act 2006, section 6(1).

contracts enable the protection of ideas – which, as we know, copyright does not do – and can therefore extend the scope of protection.

As mentioned in relation to the *Rihanna v Topshop* case, in the UK there is a law called passing-off that can be utilised in circumstances of infringement of image or publicity rights that would apply in the US. Other countries have an equivalent to passing-off called unfair competition law, which is often used to stop someone riding off the reputation of your business by misleading the consumers into thinking that you are somehow associated.

Defamation and privacy laws are also used in relation to copyright matters. Defamation is a law that prevents people from having their reputation tarnished by lies (it is not defamation if it's true!). Human rights such as privacy and freedom of speech are also both drawn upon in situations relating to copyright infringement. Breach of privacy might be used in a case of an unpublished work, such as in the Meghan Markle case.[35] Freedom of speech becomes relevant when arguing for the use of a copyright exception.

In the next two chapters, we are going to look in more detail at the copying of music by other musicians. Chapter 12 looks at recent case law developments after some high-profile cases involving Robin Thicke, Led Zeppelin, Katy Perry and Ed Sheeran. In light of this, Chapter 13 considers where, in music production and songwriting, the line is between taking inspiration and copying.

---

[35] Bosher H, 'Meghan Markle Letter: What the Law Says about the Press, Privacy and the Public's Right to Know' (The Conversation, 2019) https://theconversation.com/meghan-markle-letter-what-the-law-says-about-the-press-privacy-and-the-publics-right-to-know-124619 accessed 19 July 2020.

12   Who copied my song?

As mentioned in the previous chapter, copyright infringement is taking the whole, or a substantial part of, someone else's copyright-protected work, without permission or an exception. This chapter tells the story of some recent cases where rightsholders have sued artists for copyright infringement, where they believe that the artist has taken a substantial part of their songs. These cases involve the songs *Blurred Lines* by Pharrell Williams and Robin Thicke, *Dark Horse* by Katy Perry, *Thinking Out Loud* by Ed Sheeran and *Stairway to Heaven* by Led Zeppelin.

12.1   Before *Blurred Lines*

Although these are recent developments, they are not the first cases of their kind.[1] The first case was over the 1927 hit song *Little Spanish Town* being copied by another song called *Why* in 1959; however, the claim was unsuccessful in both the UK[2] and the US.[3] The courts agreed that while there was a degree of similarity between the songs, there was no evidence that the writer of *Why*, Peter de Angelis, had ever heard *Little Spanish Town* and the level of similarity between the songs was not enough to infer copying; the songs were sufficiently different to support the possibility they had been created independently.

In the 1990s there was a dispute involving the Academy Award-winning song *Chariots of Fire*. This case came about after a UK shoe manufacturer (Clarks) wanted to use the song in an advert. After refusal from the rightsholders, Warner Music (since the song was already being used for a Ford car advert), Clarks sought out something similar from EMI Records. When its advert aired on TV featuring the song *City of Violets*,

---

[1]   See this online resource for record of copyright infringement cases: www.lostinmusic.org/Cases
[2]   *Francis Day and Hunter v Sydney Bron* [1963] 2 All ER 16.
[3]   *Leo Feist, Inc. v Debmar Publishing Company*, 232 F. Supp. 623 (E.D. Pa. 1964).

it all kicked off. EMI acquired the copyright in *City of Violets* in order to sue Warner and the writer of *Chariots of Fire* for copyright infringement. However, again, the claim failed, and in any event EMI had fluffed the purchase of the copyright.[4]

So, there were cases before *Blurred Lines*, but they were few and far between, and mostly unsuccessful. The next section will explain the *Blurred Lines* case and the aftermath as seen in the cases involving the songs *Dark Horse*, *Thinking Out Loud* and *Stairway to Heaven*.

12.2   *Blurred Lines* v *Got to Give It Up*

Blurred Lines was written and recorded in 2012 and released in March 2013 by Robin Thicke, Pharrell Williams and Clifford Harris (T.I.). The copyright in the song was divided between the writers; Pharrell Williams received 65 per cent of the royalties, Robin Thicke got 22 per cent, and Harris took 13 per cent, for his rap verse. The song hit number 1 in 25 countries. (This despite being criticised for both its lyrics and its music video, which resulted in the song being banned in more than 20 UK universities.)

The Marvin Gaye estate immediately took issue with the song, arguing that the introduction in particular had copied Marvin Gaye's *Got to Give It Up*. At the trial in 2015, the remit of the Marvin Gaye copyright was confined to the sheet music, so the decision about infringement was not based on the musical elements of the song (because, as we discussed before, the song was written in 1977 so the US copyright law of 1909 applies – which does not protect the sound of the music, only the sheet music as filed).

Nevertheless, the jury found that Robin Thicke and Pharrell Williams were guilty of copyright infringement and awarded the Marvin Gaye estate the largest amount of damages in music copyright history: $7.3 million! Thicke and Williams obviously appealed, but in March 2018 the US Court of Appeals upheld the verdict. It reduced the damages awards

---

4   *EMI Music Publishing v Papathanasiou, Spheric BV and Warner Bros* [1993] E.M.L.R. 306 (Ch).

to $5.3 million, plus a 50 per cent interest in any future royalties from the song.[5]

Some argued that while the *Blurred Lines* judgment might encourage potential litigants to come out of the woodwork, the case was heavily fact-specific and so would not have much of an impact.[6] Others totally freaked out and said that it would have a chilling effect on the music industry.

The aftermath indicates that the case did indeed have a bearing on the future of copyright infringement litigation. There was a wave of lawsuits on music infringement, including for Mark Ronson and Bruno Mars, who faced several copyright claims relating to their song *Uptown Funk*.[7] Drake was sued for a beat that featured in two of his songs, *In My Feelings* and *Nice for What*, from his 2018 album *Scorpion*.[8] In 2016 Ed Sheeran settled a dispute, alongside Johnny McDaid from Snow Patrol, that claimed their song *Photograph* had copied another song released by X Factor winner Matt Cardle, called *Amazing*. In 2017 Ed Sheeran was sued again, this time alongside Tim McGraw and Faith Hill, for their song *The Rest of Our Life*. This related to songwriters Sean Carey and Beau Golden and their track *When I Found You*, and was settled in 2018.[9]

Before *Blurred Lines* these kinds of cases were not seen to be successful. After the *Blurred Lines* verdict (and damage award), it seemed as though most people were keen to settle disputes outside of court. One case that did proceed to court – and seemed to confirm the concerns of those seeking to avoid a jury for fear of paying huge amounts of damages – involved Katy Perry's song *Dark Horse*. The case is explained in the

---

5   *Pharrell Williams v Frankie Christian Gaye* (No.15-56880) 21 March 2018.

6   Fiona McAllister, 'Will the Floodgates Open Now that There Are No More Blurred Lines?' Ent. LR (2019) 30(1) 1, 2.

7   Michelle Kaminsky, 'Bruno Mars and Mark Ronson's "Uptown Funk" Faces (Yet Another) Copyright Infringement Suit' (*Forbes*, 30 December 2017) www.forbes.com/sites/michellefabio/2017/12/30/bruno-mars-and-mark-ronsons-uptown-funk-faces-yet-another-copyright-infringement-suit accessed 6 November 2020.

8   Bosher H, 'Drake Sued for Copyright Infringement of a Beat' (*The IPKat*, 9 September 2019) https://ipkitten.blogspot.com/2019/09/drake-sued-for-copyright-infringement.html accessed 6 November 2020.

9   *Carey et al v Sheeran et al*, U.S. District Court, Southern District of New York, No. 18-00214.

following section – but there is also a plot twist after the Zeppelin case, so we will come back to that!

12.3 *Dark Horse* v *Joyful Noise*

In August 2018, Marcus Gray (also known as Flame) claimed that his song *Joyful Noise* had been copied by Katy Perry in her song *Dark Horse*. After a seven-day trial in the US Court of California in July 2019, a federal jury of nine decided that all of the songwriters, including Katy Perry; the producers; and all the corporations that released and distributed the song were liable for copyright infringement. Marcus Gray successfully convinced the jury that first, Katy Perry had heard his song, and second, the songs were so similar that she must have copied his. Here's how:

12.3.1 Access to the song

Since the principal right of copyright is to prevent someone copying the work, the first hurdle for a copyright infringement claim is to prove that the alleged copier has heard the song in the first place – because you can't copy something that you've never heard, right? As mentioned in the previous chapter, where there is no direct evidence of access to the first work, circumstantial evidence can be used to prove that the alleged infringer heard the song. This can be done in two ways. One way is to prove a particular chain of events that links the two parties and shows that access to that work occurred – for example, through dealings with the same publisher or record company. The second way, believe it or not, is to show that the song has been so widely disseminated that *of course* the infringer has heard it … In the Perry case, she testified that she had never heard of Gray's song. But the court accepted the second approach: that since *Joyful Noise* had accumulated 3.88 million views on YouTube, across six videos, and the album that the record is on was nominated for a Grammy, Perry and the co-authors must have heard the song.

I personally take issue with this reasoning. This is because 'across six videos' means that there was an average of 633,333 views per video, in more than a decade! (The song was released in 2008.) In the context of YouTube's daily usage (five billion videos are watched on YouTube every single day, YouTube gets more than 30 million visitors per day, and 10,113 YouTube videos have generated more than one billion views) this number of views is not that impressive. We will come back to this point later in the chapter, as I am not the only one who thinks that this access question is an issue in the digital age.

12.3.2 Infringement of the song

The crux of the alleged copying in the songs came down to a descending minor mode 8-figure ostinato. Gray's evidence argued that the similarities between the two ostinatos were substantial and significant, overlapping in rhythm, pitch content, melodic contour and timbre. Perry's evidence, on the other hand, highlighted key differences in the songs such as overall structures, chord progressions, harmonic rhythm, pitch sequences in the ostinatos, intervals between the pitches in the ostinatos, melodic rhythms in the ostinatos and the length of the ostinatos.

The jury agreed with Gray that the songs were substantially similar. As a result, they decided that Gray was owed 22.5 per cent of the profits from *Dark Horse*, which amounted to $2.78 million in damages, with Perry responsible for $500,000 and Capitol Records paying nearly $1.3 million. Producer Max Martin had to pay $253,000 and Dr Luke was ordered to pay $61,000, plus $189,000 from his company Kasz Money Inc.[10]

This case was controversial because it essentially said that quarter notes descending in a minor scale from a third degree was original enough to be protectable by copyright. My opinion at this stage of the case was that it went too far and did not uphold the copyright principle of only protecting the expression of ideas.[11]

The case was appealed. The outcome was reached after the *Stairway to Heaven* case was decided ... cliffhanger! At the same time, the case of the *Thinking Out Loud* and *Let's Get It On* songs was also ongoing. The next section will discuss what was happening in that case, before explaining what happened in *Stairway to Heaven*, and the impact of that on the other decisions.

---

[10]   *Marcus Gray et al v Katy Perry et al* (No.2:15-cv-05642).

[11]   Bosher H, 'Jury Awards Joyful Noise $2.8M in Copyright Infringement Damages for Katy Perry's Dark Horse' (*IPKat*, 2019) https://ipkitten.blogspot.com/2019/08/jury-awards-joyful-noise-28m-in .html accessed 6 November 2020.

12.4 *Thinking Out Loud* v *Let's Get It On*

This case is about another Marvin Gaye song, *Let's Get It On*, which was written by Ed Townsend, who owned two thirds of the royalties for the song when he died in 2003. The action for copyright infringement was brought in 2018 by Townsend's daughter, Kathryn Townsend Griffin, and Townsend's estate. In response, Sheeran denied copying and applied to get the case thrown out with an application for a summary judgment on grounds including that: (1) the scope of the copyright protection was limited to the sheet music; (2) the songs are not substantially similar; (3) any similarities are commonplace elements and therefore not protected by copyright anyway.

12.4.1 The scope of copyright protection

The parties argued over the scope of the copyright in *Let's Get It On*. Sheeran said it was limited to the sheet music. Both parties agreed that the deposit copy included the composition's key, meter, harmony (chord progression), rhythm, melody, lyrics and song structure, but Townsend argued that the composition was embodied on the Gaye recording. This would mean that Townsend could play the sound recording to the jury, which would include the vocals, bass and percussion. The court left this question to be decided at trial.

12.4.2 Are the songs substantially similar?

Both sides submitted musicologist reports and agreed to some similarities between the songs, such as the I–iii–IV–V harmonic progression, harmonic rhythm with anticipated second and fourth chords, melody, bass line and percussion. However, they disagreed on the similarity of the vocal melody, harmonic rhythm, harmony, bass line and percussion. There was no claim of similarities between the lyrics or song structures.

The judge was of the opinion that the key, tempo, meter and genre of the two compositions were similar, but those are unprotectable elements. Sheeran pointed to other elements – song structure, lyrics and tone – to highlight the difference in 'total concept and feel' between the works, submitting that *Thinking Out Loud* was characterised by sombre, melancholic tones, about long-lasting romantic love, whereas *Let's Get It On* was a 'sexual anthem that radiates positive emotions and encourages the listener to get it on'. Overall, the judge decided that the question whether *Thinking Out Loud* was substantially similar to *Let's Get It On* should be decided at trial.

12.4.3 Are the parts taken original or commonplace?

As explained, a copyright claim under US law needs to show that there was copying in that the songs are substantially similar. For this the court dissects the song into protectable and unprotectable elements. The copying of the unprotectable elements is not infringement; only copying of the protectable elements is.

Sheeran argued that the similar elements between the songs were not protected as they were commonplace elements. The parties disputed whether the basic I–iii–IV–V chord progression used in *Let's Get It On* was commonplace, or was commonplace before that song. Sheeran's expert identified at least 13 songs predating *Let's Get It On* that also used the same chord progression, and noted that it appears in at least two guitar method books. But only a dozen or so were identified which had contained this chord progression prior to the release of *Let's Get It On*.

The parties also disputed whether the harmonic rhythm of that four-chord progression – the second and fourth chords being anticipated or placed ahead of the beat – was protectable. Sheeran said it was a commonplace technique; Townsend claimed it was distinctive. Again, the judge said this was a question that needed to be decided at a trial. As such, the summary judgment was denied. However, before that could happen, the *Stairway to Heaven* case was re-opened and as a result the *Thinking Out Loud* trial was put on hold until the outcome of the Led Zeppelin case, which is now explained.

12.5 *Stairway to Heaven* v *Taurus*

The story of this case happens in two Acts. Act 1: In 2016, an action for copyright infringement was brought against British rock band Led Zeppelin. It was claimed that the band had copied an instrumental song called *Taurus* written by Randy Wolfe, the guitarist from the Southern California rock band Spirit. The copyright of the song was registered as an unpublished musical composition[12] in 1967 by filing a one-page deposit copy of the sheet music with the US Copyright Office. Michael Skidmore, on behalf of the Wolfe estate, brought the action against Led Zeppelin, claiming that guitarist Jimmy Page and vocalist Robert Plant copied *Taurus* in *Stairway to Heaven*. The jury found in favour of Zeppelin – that the two songs were not substantially similar.

But then, the decision was appealed, and in 2018 a three-judge panel decided that there should be a re-trial because jury instructions had been deficient, and as a result the case would go before all the judges of the Ninth Circuit Court of Appeal.[13]

Interval. Guitar solo from Stairway to Heaven *plays (5:34–6:44).*

Act 2: On 9 March 2020, the US Ninth Circuit Court of Appeal reversed the three-judge panel decision, meaning that it upheld the 2016 jury verdict that Led Zeppelin's *Stairway to Heaven* did not infringe the copyright of the song *Taurus*.[14] In the course of the judgment the court took the opportunity to clarify some of the key copyright issues relating to music infringement, which were then relied upon in the *Thinking Out Loud* case and the *Dark Horse* Appeal, discussed below.

12.5.1 Scope of the copyright in *Taurus* and *Let's Get It On*

The copyright for *Taurus* was registered in 1967, meaning that the one-page deposit copy defined the scope of the copyright since, under the US Copyright Act 1909,[15] copyright only extended to sheet music and not sound recordings.[16] Just like in the *Thinking Out Loud* case, Skidmore wanted to play the sound recording to the jury – arguing that the copyright extended beyond the sheet music, which he said was more of a reference point than a definitive filing. Obviously, this went against

---

[12] Published works could be protected with a copyright notice on each copy published, but musical compositions were only considered published if the sheet music was published; distributing sound recordings did not count as publication, so technically *Taurus* was an unpublished work.

[13] *Skidmore v Led Zeppelin*, 905 F.3d 1116 (9th Cir. 2018), reh'g en banc granted, 925 F.3d 999 (9th Cir. 2019).

[14] *Michael Skidmore v Led Zeppelin* (No.16-56057) 9 March 2020.

[15] Registration for an unpublished work can be obtained 'by the deposit, with claim of copyright, of one complete copy of such work' with the Copyright Office: US Copyright Act 1909, section 11.

[16] As explained, sound recordings were not protected under US copyright law until 1972.

both what the law said and the purpose of the deposit copy, which is to make a record of the claimed copyright. So, the court held that the original judgment, which was on appeal, had correctly declined Skidmore's request to play the sound recordings that contained further embellishments than the registered sheet music.[17]

This finding had a direct impact on the *Thinking Out Loud* case, which was continued immediately after the *Stairway to Heaven* judgment. On 24 March 2020 the court decided that as *Let's Get It On* was written in 1973, it also fell under the regulation of the Copyright Act 1909, and the scope of the copyright was restricted to the deposited sheet music.[18] This meant that Townsend would not be allowed to play the song to the jury at trial, which is significant to the case because the sound recording of *Let's Get It On* includes many elements – at least some of which appear in *Thinking Out Loud* – such as percussion, drums, bass guitar, guitars, Marvin Gaye's vocal performance, horns and flutes. These elements of the song are not protected by the copyright because they do not appear in the simple melody of the deposit copy, which is the sole definition of the copyright protected. The *Stairway to Heaven* judgment not only helped this case but will surely also deter any other historic claims predating the 1976 Act from surfacing.[19]

12.5.2 Protectable elements of *Taurus* and *Joyful Noise*

In the *Stairway to Heaven* case, Skidmore took issue with the instructions that were given to the jury. He objected to the list of unprotectable elements provided to the jury, which included descending chromatic scales, arpeggios or short sequences of three notes, as examples of common musical elements. However, the Appeal Court held that the instructions correctly listed the non-protectable musical building blocks of music that are in the public domain for everyone to use and which cannot be protected by copyright. The instructions did not exclude the particular use of

---

[17] *Michael Skidmore v Led Zeppelin* (No.16-56057) 9 March 2020 [22].

[18] *Kathryn Townsend Griffin, Helen MacDonald and the Townsend Estate v Edward Sheeran, Atlantic Records, Sony Music, Warner Music* (No.1:17-cv-05221) 24 March 2020; quoting *Skidmore v Led Zeppelin* (No. 16-56057) March 9, 2020 [20].

[19] You can't usually bring a claim this old to court; not bringing an action for a long time can be held against you, but in these types of cases the claims have been allowed where the copyright infringement is still ongoing.

those musical elements in an original expression that would be protected by copyright.

As mentioned, the infringement in the case of Katy Perry's song *Dark Horse* was based on a descending minor mode eight-figure ostinato. The appeal against the *Dark Horse* decision came just nine days after the *Stairway to Heaven* judgment, on 16 March 2020.[20] The question of substantial similarity was re-considered. As mentioned, there are two parts to the test when finding similarity: first, identify the protectable elements; second, establish whether those protected elements are objectively similar to the corresponding elements in the allegedly infringing work. So, the first question was whether the elements of the eight-note ostinato were protectable. The court said that while there is a generally low threshold for originality in copyright, as a result of the limited notes and chords available, many, if not most, of the elements in popular music are not individually protectable. It even said that music, perhaps more so than other types of copyright work, borrows, and must necessarily borrow that which is well-known and has been used before. It quoted the *Stairway to Heaven* judgment: 'these building blocks belong in the public domain and cannot be exclusively appropriated.'[21]

Gray had argued that there were five or six protectable elements in his ostinato, including the length (eight notes), rhythm, melodic content, melodic shape, timbre or quality and colour of the sound and the placement. On the other hand, Katy Perry's side argued that none of these elements were individually protectable, and the Appeal Court agreed. Therefore, the test for similarity failed on the basis that the individual elements of the ostinato were not protectable by copyright (called it!). The previous decision for infringement was overturned ... phew. Copyright order was restored.

12.5.3 Copyright protection in the selection and arrangement of unoriginal elements

In both the *Stairway to Heaven* and the *Dark Horse* cases, the claims attempted to rely on another back-up argument which was based on

---

[20]   *Marcus Gray et al v Katy Perry et al* (No.2:15-cv-05642) 16 March 2020.

[21]   *Marcus Gray et al v Katy Perry et al* (No.2:15-cv-05642) 16 March 2020 [10] quoting *Michael Skidmore v Led Zeppelin* (No.16-56057) 9 March 2020 [33].

a rule saying that originality can be acquired through selection and arrangement, meaning that the work comprises of a protectable combination of otherwise unprotected elements. In the *Stairway to Heaven* judgment, the court clarified that the word 'combination' does not mean any set of artistic building blocks and decided that Skidmore failed to properly present an argument for selection and arrangement.[22]

Subsequently, in relation to the *Dark Horse* case, the court stated that claims of selection and arrangement apply to works that consist of a mix of compositional elements presented throughout the compositional work as a whole, not within a single portion. The ostinato was not a particularly new or rare combination and was therefore not arranged in a sufficiently original manner to warrant copyright protection.[23] Just to make sure Gray got the message, the court added that even if the ostinato was protectable in theory, the evidence at trial did not prove that the two ostinatos were objectively, substantially similar anyway. The standard of similarity for selection and arrangement infringement is higher in that it would need to be *the same* selection and arrangement[24] – meaning that they would need to be virtually (but not absolutely) identical in order to be substantially similar.

12.6 Access through wide dissemination in the digital age

Lastly, I just want to circle back to the point about access. Remember the first hurdle of the infringement claim – you can't copy something you have never heard. So, the claim has to show that there was a reasonable possibility (not merely a bare possibility) that the alleged infringer had heard the protected work before. Where there is no direct evidence of access, circumstantial evidence can be used to prove access either by events that connect the parties' work or by showing that the work was widely disseminated.

---

[22]   *Michael Skidmore v Led Zeppelin* (No.16-56057) 9 March 2020 [46].

[23]   *Marcus Gray et al v Katy Perry et al* (No.2:15-cv-05642) 16 March 2020 [19].

[24]   *Michael Skidmore v Led Zeppelin* (No.16-56057) 9 March 2020 [46].

In *Stairway to Heaven*, the court noted that the idea of access has changed as a result of digital consumption behaviours and technologies. They acknowledged, in this context, that the test for access has become increasingly diluted. Recent cases have been able to easily overcome this hurdle with a trivial demonstration that the work is available on YouTube or some other platform. The judges therefore pointed towards raising the bar for establishing access beyond merely the fact that a song has a certain number of YouTube views or listens on Spotify.

As mentioned, I was particularly unimpressed with the access justification in the *Dark Horse* case – that *Joyful Noise* had 3.88 million views on YouTube across six videos. On appeal, the court acknowledged this point as raised in *Stairway to Heaven*, but still maintained that in the circumstances, access was shown due to factors such as the YouTube and Myspace views, plus a Grammy nomination and the billboard ranking.[25] A little disappointing, but *Stairway to Heaven* left the door ajar on this point, so I suspect we will be hearing more on this issue in future cases.

So, following the success of the *Blurred Lines* infringement claim, we did see an increase in similar cases. However, the *Stairway to Heaven* appeal provided an opportunity for the US courts to clarify and comment on the current state of the US law in music copyright infringement. The result turned over the *Dark Horse* case and supported the *Thinking Out Loud* claim. This clarification of the law could mean that we see fewer cases like this from now on.

---

[25] *Marcus Gray et al v Katy Perry et al* (No.2:15-cv-05642) 16 March 2020 [25].

13   Inspiration or infringement

This chapter builds on Chapters 11 and 12 to summarise and apply what copyright infringement is and what that actually means in relation to your own creative process. This chapter clarifies the difference between taking inspiration and copying, thereby enabling you to understand when it is okay to draw from other's work and when it would constitute copyright infringement. First, it sets the context of inspiration, by considering what creativity is. Then it summarises what is and what is not copying for the purpose of copyright infringement, including when someone copies unconsciously – that is, not on purpose.

13.1   Inspiration and creativity

Before attempting to clarify the spectrum from inspiration to copying, it is important to set this conversation within the context of creativity. Warning, this section gets a little bonkers – but I trust that's why you are here.

> *'But I don't want to go among mad people', Alice remarked.*
> *'Oh, you can't help that', said the Cat: 'We're all mad here. I'm mad. You're mad.'*
> *'How do you know I'm mad?' said Alice.*
> *'You must be,' said the Cat, 'or you wouldn't have come here.'*[1]

Taking inspiration from existing works is a quintessential part of the creative process. In some ways, all works draw on and contribute to the existing body of works. When we learn to play an instrument, we are all taught the same scales, and practice by playing other people's songs. When we interviewed the musicians on copyrightuser.org and asked 'do you use other people's work', some of them said no. While they may not

---

[1]   Carroll L, *Alice's Adventures in Wonderland* (Wordsworth Classics 2001) 87.

directly take from existing work, it is unlikely – if not impossible – that they do not draw inspiration from others.

Did you know the word inspiration has a historically theological meaning in English, meaning divine influence upon a person? From around the early fourteenth century, the word *enspiren* meant to fill the mind and heart with grace or influence from divine power. The root of the word comes from the Latin word for breath, *spirare*, meaning spirit. In the sixteenth century it also became a word meaning 'breathing life into'. You could say that inspiration is perhaps some kind of divine influence that enables a person to breathe life into their creativity. Even setting aside any religious or spiritual views, there is still something about creativity and inspiration that is mysteriously out-of-body. Often creators have explained their creative process as being meditative, or involving losing their sense of their worldly self.

Essentially, creativity is magic and cool, and I could talk about this for the rest of the book, but I shall not steer too far off-piste. This does come back to copyright, promise. I read a book once (/'this one time at band camp'), *Big Magic* by Elizabeth Gilbert, where Gilbert talks about her theory on how creativity works – something akin to a kind of collective consciousness. She tells a story in the book of an experience where she had an idea that she never got around to expressing, and she believed that as a result the idea was passed on to someone else, who later produced the same idea without discussion. I love this notion of creativity because it is humbling, and in that mindset there is a balance of understanding that you have copyright in the expression of the idea, but at the same time you are also a mere conduit for creativity, for the idea to be expressed through you.

Researchers study creativity and inspiration, but it is not something we can really pinpoint. There are a lot of misconceptions about creativity. (Like the struggling artists we talked about in Chapter 1.) Some argue that creativity is part of human nature, and we can all be creative. This depends on how broadly you think about the concept of creativity, which can include scientific discoveries[2] as much as poetry. There is also something of an archetypical creator who struggles with mental health – the

---

[2]   McLeish T, 'We Talk About Artistic Inspiration All The Time – But Scientific Inspiration Is a Thing Too' (*The Conversation*, 2019) https://theconversation.com/we-talk-about-artistic-inspiration-all-the-time-but-scientific-inspiration-is-a-thing-too-111439 accessed 6 November 2020.

idea that suffering is a required element of a great creator. This argument is often quickly supported by a retelling of how Vincent Van Gogh cut off his ear and then later shot himself. However, the story of Van Gogh can be told another way. He painted *despite* his mental health challenges, not as a result of them. In letters to his brother he wrote that painting helped him, and when things were bad, he only painted on good days. Research indicates that a positive mood enhances creativity,[3] and that creativity can enhance happiness.[4] As Mozart famously said:

> When I am, as it were, completely myself, entirely alone, and of good cheer – say traveling in a carriage, or walking after a good meal, or during the night when I cannot sleep – it is on such occasions that my ideas flow best, and most abundantly. Whence and how they come, I know not, nor can I force them.

Having said that, there is also staggering research that clearly shows musicians are suffering with their mental health. In 2019, Record Union found that 73 per cent of independent musicians have battled stress, anxiety and depression.[5] After the tragic loss of many artists to suicide in recent years, there has been an increase in services, resources and openness about mental health in the music industry.[6]

In summary to this part: we don't exactly know what creativity or inspiration is, but it can be found somewhere between magic, mystery and the last door on the left. It apparently makes us happy even though lots of us are sad. Drawing inspiration from existing works is part of the creative process.

Copyright does not regulate inspiration. It regulates copying.

---

[3]   Davis M, 'Understanding the Relationship Between Mood and Creativity: A Meta-Analysis' (2009) 108(1) Organizational Behavior and Human Decision Processes 25–38.

[4]   Haller CS and Courvoisier DS, 'Personality and Thinking Style in Different Creative Domains' (2010) 4(3) Psychology of Aesthetics, Creativity, and the Arts 149–60.

[5]   www.the73percent.com/ accessed 6 November 2020.

[6]   Help Musicians www.helpmusicians.org.uk/; Music Industry Therapists & Coaches http://musicindustrytherapists.com/; Music Support www.musicsupport.org/; Tour Support www.lighthopelife.org/tour-support; Backline https://backline.care/; AFEM Mental Health Guide for the Electronic Music Industry www.associationforelectronicmusic.org/afem-mental-health-guide-for-the-electronic-music-industry/; Musicares www.grammy.com/musicares/about accessed 6 November 2020.

13.2   What is copying

Let's recap what copying is. From the perspective of copyright law, copying means taking the whole of a copyright-protected work, or a substantial part of it, without permission from the rightsholder, unless it is being used within the rules of a copyright exception.

Taking the whole of a copyright-protected work and copying it is copyright infringement. This means reproducing it and includes sharing it or selling it.

Taking a substantial part of a copyright-protected work is also copyright infringement. This means taking the original and protectable aspects of a copyright work. It relates to the quality of what is taken, not the quantity. The original and protectable aspects of a copyright work are the parts where the creator has expressed their own individual creativity and made their own personal choices.

Once a claim proves reasonable access and substantial similarity, it turns to the alleged infringer to try to demonstrate that they created their work independently, without the influence of the existing work. This is where keeping a record of your creative process can come in handy.

13.3   What is not copying

Not copying, then, according to copyright laws, is creating an original work, by using your own skill, labour, judgement and effort, or creating your own intellectual creation by making free and personal choices.

It is not copyright infringement to draw inspiration from other people's work.

Moreover, it is not copying to take unprotectable elements from existing works. For example, the twelve-bar blues – one of the most prominent chord progressions in popular music – has a distinctive form in phrase, chord structure and duration. This common chord progression would not be protectable by copyright; there are no free creative choices in using it as it appears.

It is not copyright infringement to copy an idea, because copyright does not protect ideas, only the individual expression of an idea. The idea of a romantic song or a song to celebrate birthdays is freely available and you can create your own expression of these ideas without infringing any copyright.

13.4   Unconscious copying

Unconscious copying, from a psychology perspective, is where a person's implicit memory influences their behaviour even though the individual is not aware of its influence. In other words, it is the influence of previous experience on task performance without conscious referral to stored information; essentially, learning without awareness.[7]

From a copyright law perspective, primary infringement does not require knowledge of the infringement. While, as we discussed, it does need to be shown that the alleged infringer heard the song, it does not need to be shown that they copied on purpose, or even that they knew that they were copying. For this type of infringement, the evidence provided to convince a court of infringement is likely to be much more significant.

In the UK, the argument for unconscious copying was presented in the case about the song *Little Spanish Town* (discussed in Chapter 12), but the court made no comment.[8] In the US, unconscious copying was argued in a case involving George Harrison from The Beatles.[9] A claim was brought against Harrison that his song *My Sweet Lord* copied the Chiffons' 1962 hit song *He's So Fine*. The songs had similarities that were considered to be unique, and Harrison acknowledged that he had heard the song *He's So Fine* before writing *My Sweet Lord* – although Harrison argued that he had created it independently. The court decided that the two songs were musically identical except for one phrase, and while Harrison did not deliberately copy, he was still liable for copyright infringement. The

---

[7]   Cohen NJ et al, 'Different Memory Systems Underlying Acquisition of Procedural and Declarative Knowledge' in David S Olton, Elkan Gamzu and Suzanne Corkin (eds) *Memory Dysfunctions: An Integration of Animal and Human Research from Preclinical and Clinical Perspectives* (Annals of the New York Academy of Sciences 1985).

[8]   *Francis Day & Hunter Ltd v Bron* [1963] Ch. 587.

[9]   *Bright Tunes Music Corp. v Harrisongs Music, Ltd* 420 F.Supp. 177 (1976).

court said that while Harrison was playing around with multiple possibilities for combinations of notes, a particular combination pleased him because he unconsciously already knew it had worked in a song which his conscious mind did not remember at that moment. Therefore, it was an infringement of copyright, even though unconsciously accomplished.

Some researchers argue that as a result of the sheer number of songs, compared with the finite number of notes and arrangements of music, originality in music is on its way out.[10] All the Music is a project that uses software to generate all mathematically possible combinations of melodies to challenge the idea of originality in musical melodies.[11] One researcher, Castanaro, argued that courts should allow unconscious copying to function as a defence to copyright infringement, but require defendants to overcome a rebuttable presumption that any copying was conscious.[12]

13.5   How many notes can be taken from someone's song?

This chapter concludes by answering the commonly asked question: how many notes can be taken from a song without infringing the copyright?

Applying the rule of substantial taking, there is no number of notes that can be used from someone else's song which we can say would or would not be copyright infringement. This is a misguided question: it should not be asking *how many*, but rather *which ones* can be used. Again, this is about taking a substantial or insubstantial amount; the quality of what is taken, not the quantity. It is decided on a case-by-case basis, looking at the importance of the parts taken and their degree of originality.

---

[10]   Castanaro VM, '"It's the Same Old Song": The Failure of the Originality Requirement in Musical Copyright' (2008) 18 (5) Fordham Intellectual Property Media & Entertainment Law Journal 1271, 1274.

[11]   http://allthemusic.info/faqs/ accessed 6 November 2020.

[12]   Jaeger CB, '"Does That Sound Familiar?" Creators' Liability for Unconscious Copyright Infringement' (2008) 61(6) Vanderbilt Law Review 1903–34.

14   Sampling

The previous chapters in this part of the book discussed copyright infringement. This chapter focuses on a particular type of potential copyright infringement: sampling. It gives a brief overview of what sampling is and its historical development, then considers whether sampling is copyright infringement or if it can benefit from copyright exceptions, such as fair use in the US or quotation throughout the EU. It then explains sampling licences, including the layers required for permission to use the sound recording and the musical work.

14.1   Started from the sample, now we're here

Sampling, at its most basic description, is taking a fragment of a song and using it to create a new track. Sampling is a fundamental pillar of hip hop culture[1] which evolved from around 1965 in the South Bronx, New York with live hip hop DJ sets, where the DJ would mix together record breaks, cuts and scratches.[2] The concept of sampling is much more than simply extracting parts of another song; rather, it is the transforming, re-contextualising and essentially converting of an aspect of culture from one context into another. From a copyright perspective, a work made out of another previous work is called a derivative work. A derivative work is capable of having its own copyright protection as long as it still meets the criteria of an original expression of an idea, within the types of works that copyright protects, as explained in Chapter 2.

---

[1]   Hip hop culture has four principal elements: MCing, DJing, break dancing and graffiti, all of which involve aspects of sampling, borrowing and transforming others' work as part of their creative expression.

[2]   For a detailed history of the development of hip hop culture and sampling see Said A, *The Art of Sampling: The Sampling Tradition of Hip Hop/Rap Music & Copyright Law* (Superchamp Books 2015); or watch the documentary series *Hip-Hop Evolution* directed by Darby Wheeler and Rodrigo Bascunan.

Since the development of sampling in hip hop and rap music, it has become an art form used in all genres of music. The most sampled song ever is the 1969 song *Amen, Brother* by the American funk and soul group The Winstons. The song was a B-side that went relatively unnoticed at the time and The Winstons didn't really take off beyond that record. The copyright in the song is owned by The Winstons' lead, Richard Spencer. The song itself also contains samples of two other songs by The Impressions; it uses the hook from their version of the song *Amen* (originally written by them for the film *Lilies of the Field*), plus multiple elements from *We're a Winner*. Incidentally, *We're a Winner* was also used to create *Move on Up* by Curtis Mayfield, which was in turn sampled in other tracks such as *Touch the Sky* by Kanye West … following sample threads is a merciless game that never ends!

The four-bar drum break in *Amen, Brother*, which was performed by Gregory Coleman, is now synonymous of two entire music genres: drum and bass and Jungle. The drum loop was used by Salt-N-Pepa in their 1986 song *I Desire*, and it became particularly mainstream after it was used in *Straight Outta Compton* by N.W.A, as well as in other tracks, including *Keep It Going Now* by Rob Base and DJ EZ Rock. In 1997, Oasis used it in their song *D'You Know What I Mean*; later, Skrillex used it in *I Know Who You Are*, and Chase & Status have sampled it in many of their tracks, including *Love's Theme, In Love* and *Time*. Talking about the Amen Break, a member of Chase & Status said: 'I don't know if the music would exist without it', and British drum and bass DJ and producer Fabio said 'anyone that's into drum and bass … will have to say, love it or hate it, it is the greatest break of all time'.[3]

There are nearly 5,000 other examples of the Amen Break being sampled.[4] In 1986, the sample was included on a compilation of old funk and soul tracks with clean drum breaks for DJs to use, called *Ultimate Breaks and Beats*. It also features on similar compilation albums, the copyright holders of which have then licensed it to be used by others in music and advertising.

---

[3] Radio 1 and 1Xtra's Stories: Chase & Status on the Amen Break www.bbc.co.uk/sounds/play/p00hb4q6 accessed 6 November 2020.

[4] By the time you search this it will probably be even more. For the most used samples see www.whosampled.com/most-sampled-tracks/ accessed 6 November 2020.

Neither Richard Spencer nor Gregory Coleman received any royalties for the use of their song and, tragically, Gregory Coleman is said to have died homeless. Richard Spencer was interviewed on BBC Radio 1 in 2011 and said that he felt that he had been left out where others had made millions from his work. He asked that people do the right thing and pay him for legal use of his copyright-protected song.[5] After that, in 2015, two British DJs, Martyn Webster and Steve Theobald, set up a GoFundMe campaign which remains open indefinitely, for the sole benefit of Richard Spencer.[6]

The fact that the artists were never compensated for the use of their track is, in my humble opinion, an injustice that goes against everything good that copyright stands for. I read somewhere that one of the reasons why a claim could not be brought was the rule that puts a time limit on when you can bring a claim. This limitation is a defence that someone can use if they have been infringing your copyright for a long period of time and you have never previously said anything about it. But in these circumstances it is nonsense, because the defence does not stand where the infringement is ongoing. In the *Stairway to Heaven* case, the claim was brought 43 years after the release of the Led Zeppelin song! The court said that the claim was able to overcome this defence because the infringement was ongoing.[7] If a claim for copyright infringement was brought, would it succeed? This is discussed in the next section on whether sampling without permission is copyright infringement.

14.2 Is sampling copyright infringement?

We know by now that copyright infringement means taking the whole, or substantial part, of a protected song without permission or a copyright exception. So, the question of whether sampling is copyright infringement comes down to the question of whether the sample is a substantial part.

---

[5] You can listen to the interview here: www.bbc.co.uk/sounds/play/p00hb618 accessed 6 November 2020.

[6] www.gofundme.com/f/amenbrother and www.gofundme.com/f/amenbrother2 accessed 6 November 2020.

[7] *Skidmore v Led Zeppelin*, 106 F. Supp. 3d 581, 589–90 (E.D. Pa. 2015) referring to *Petrella v Metro-Goldwyn-Mayer*, Inc., 572 U.S. 663, 668 (2014).

We also know that a song has more than one copyright; there is copyright in the musical work and in the sound recording. So, using the sample of the sound recording would require the permission of the copyright holder in the sound recording, as well as the permission of the copyright holder in the musical work.

As mentioned, in traditional hip hop culture sampling was the bedrock, and part of that movement meant that borrowing was fair game. There was, however, a kind of ethical understanding that the sample would be used to recreate something new and original, in your own style, so it did not validate simply copying someone else's work.

Regardless, the sharing mentality did not last for long. First came the Sugar Hill Gang's song *Rapper's Delight*, which sampled the bass riff from Chic's track *Good Times* without permission ('say whaat?'). Sugar Hill Gang had recreated the bass riff themselves rather than using a copy of the master, so they only infringed the musical work and not the sound recording, but they settled out of court for royalties and credit on the song.

Subsequently, a string of similar disputes ensued and likewise settled, including the Beastie Boys' track *Hold it Now Hit It*, which settled with The Jimmy Caster Bunch for using their song *The Return of Leroy Pt.1*. De La Soul settled with The Turtles after The Turtles' song *You Showed Me* was sampled in De La Soul's skit *Transmitting Love from Mars*. Vanilla Ice settled with David Bowie after the bassline from Queen and Bowie's *Under Pressure* was used in *Ice Ice Baby*.

The first case of this kind to actually be heard in court occurred after rapper Biz Markie sampled Gilbert O'Sullivan's song *Alone Again (Naturally)* in his song *Alone Again*.[8] (Didn't even bother to come up with his own title – I mean, come on. Although his next album after this happened was called *All Samples Cleared*. Lesson learned.) The court confirmed that the sampling was copyright infringement and granted an injunction, although the analysis was limited in this early case.

The legal status of sampling in the US matured in 2005, when a case was brought against hip hop group N.W.A. after their song *100 Miles and*

---

[8]   *Grand Upright Music, Ltd v Warner Bros. Records Inc.*, 780 F. Supp. 182 (S.D.N.Y. 1991).

Runnin' sampled a two-second guitar chord from Funkadelic's track *Get Off Your Ass and Jam*. In the first instance it was decided that there was no copyright infringement, but on appeal this was reversed. The appeal judge eloquently set the record straight by saying: 'Get a license or do not sample.'[9] Roger that.

14.3   Sampling as an exception to copyright

Despite the clear legal position, some people argue that since sampling is the art of making something new out of something old, it should therefore be allowed under copyright exceptions, such as under fair use in the US or quotation under EU and UK law.

In the EU, this argument was put forward in a court case in Germany in 1999, which only in 2020 came to the conclusion that sampling does not fall under the copyright exception for quotation. The case involved a two-second rhythm sequence sampled from Kraftwerk's *Metall auf Metall* in the song *Nur Mir* by Pelham and Haas (yes, you heard me correctly – 21 years of litigation for a two-second sample!).[10]

The case confirmed that recognisable sampling will usually infringe copyright under German law. In particular, it found that a sample that is recognisable to an average music listener will infringe copyright regardless of how short the sample is. The court also stated that copyright exceptions and limitations for quotation, parody and caricature and incidental inclusions do not permit reproduction by sampling. It is likely that other EU national cases on copyright and music sampling would come to a similar conclusion.

As such, music sampling is likely to be copyright infringement and does not fall within the copyright exceptions. Even if you could argue for an exception in your particular circumstances, remember that these exceptions are defences. This means that you would have to argue your case for

---

9   *Bridgeport Music, Inc. v Dimension Films*, 410 F.3d 792 (6th Cir. 2005).

10   *Hutter v Pelham (Metall auf Metall)* (C-476/17) ECLI:EU:C:2019:624; first heard in the Regional Court of Hamburg in 1999 (308 O 90/99) and concluded in German Federal Court of Justice, I ZR 115/16 – *Metal on Metal IV (Pelham v Hütter)*, 30 April 2020.

the exception in response to a copyright infringement claim; essentially, this is a risky and expensive game. In any event, if you are looking to sign a record deal or a publishing contract, the companies that you sign with will not take this risk. Therefore, you will need a licence to use a sample.

14.4   Sampling licences

To use a sample of another song, a licence is required. If you want to use part of a sound recording, you will actually need two licences, giving the permission of both the copyright holder in the sound recording and the copyright holder of the musical work. If you create your own version of the sample, you will not need the sound recording permission, but you will still need a licence for the musical work.

Licensing for samples is now common practice and you will see in any recording or publishing contract that there is a clause specifically requiring that all the rights have been cleared for any sample used. It is also common practice for copyright holders to want to hear your use of the sample before they calculate how much to charge you for it. So, you could invest time and money in creating a song with a sample which you haven't yet received permission to use – eek!

The cost of the sample, or the percentage of royalties that the copyright holders will want, depends on several factors, such as who you are and your use of the work, as well as the popularity of the song you are sampling, how much and in what way you used the sample and whether it features heavily in the new song.

However, negotiating the cost of a sample after you've used it rather than before publication becomes much more expensive in lieu of copyright infringement proceedings. For example, the pre-chorus in Ed Sheeran's song *Shape of You* was apparently 'loosely inspired'[11] by the pre-chorus from TLC's 1990s hit *No Scrubs*. The writers of *Shape of You* maintained that they had not taken a substantial part. However, negotiations clearly took place between the parties because the writers of *No Scrubs* now

---

[11]   Bosher H, 'Oh Why, Oh I, Wonder If It Is a Substantial Part...' (IPKat, 2018) http://ipkitten.blogspot .com/2018/08/oh-why-oh-i-wonder-if-it-is-substantial.html accessed 6 November 2020.

appear on the copyright registration in the US and the UK, receiving 15 per cent of the royalties for the musical work.

As it happens, this came up in a case that has been ongoing for several years in the UK courts, in which a copyright infringement claim is being made against the writers of *Shape of You* for allegedly copying another song, called *Oh Why*, by Sam Chokri. The reason why *No Scrubs* became relevant is because Chokri and his music publisher wanted to rely on similar fact evidence to support their argument that Ed Sheeran and the other *Shape of You* songwriters were, consciously or subconsciously, in the habit of copying other music in their songwriting sessions. Another example included the song *Strip That Down*, which the same writers created, was later recorded by Liam Payne, and also became the subject of a copyright dispute. As a result, the credits for *Strip That Down* now include the creators of the song *It Wasn't Me*, who receive 25 per cent of the PRS royalties.[12] Indeed, it is much better to negotiate a sample licence *before* publication.

Arguably, one of the most iconic samples in hip hop is the use of *The Edge*, by David MacCallum, in *The Next Episode* by Dr Dre featuring Snoop Dogg, Nate Dogg and Kurupt. The sample was more recently used by John Legend in his song *Actions*, but he used the evolved version which included Snoop Dogg's 'la-da-da-da-daa' vocals ('Snoop doooooogg'). In this scenario John Legend recorded his own versions of both these samples; playing the hook on the piano and singing the vocals himself, so presumably he took a licence for the musical work of *The Edge* and potentially also sought permission for the musical work of *The Next Episode* for using Snoop Dogg's melody.

Things can get very complicated when sampling a track that was already in itself created using samples. (Sample inception.) For ex-sample, in Busta Rhymes' song *Turn It Up (Remix)/Fire It Up*, he sampled three tracks; the *Knight Rider Theme*, Rick James's *Fire It Up* and Shelly Thunder's *Kuff*. So, he's looking at minimum three, maximum six sample licences (depending on if he used the master or recreated his own version). Subsequently, Panjabi MC created a song called *Mundian to Bach Ke* which samples *Turn It Up (Remix)/Fire It Up*. Since sample licences do not come with

---

12 Bosher H, Sheeran v Chokri Part 2: Admission of Similar Fact Evidence (IPKat, 2020) http://ipkitten .blogspot.com/2020/01/sheeran-v-chokri-part-2-admission-of.html accessed 6 November 2020.

sub-licence clauses, Panjabi MC would have needed anything from two to eight licences! (Am I just being a massive nerd, or should someone make a board game out of this?)

In summary, sampling requires a licence; just how many and for how much depend on what you sample and how you use it. Obtaining the right sampling licences can be a challenge, but there are sample-clearing companies and experts that are able to help with this.

The final chapter in Part III of the book, about copyright infringement, covers infringement of additional materials such as merchandise and counterfeit goods. Part IV moves on to talk about enforcing your rights where there has been an infringement.

15   Counterfeit goods

Part III of this book has explained what copyright infringement is, and when the invisible line between inspiration and copying is crossed over into substantial taking. To conclude this part, this chapter serves as an FYI regarding other types of copyright infringement that are relevant, beyond the musical work and sound recording. It covers counterfeit goods and includes infringement of performances, artwork and merchandise.

15.1   Counterfeit goods

Counterfeit goods are products that are made illegally without the permission of the rightsholder. They typically infringe several intellectual property rights as well as copyright, including trade marks. The law says that copyright counterfeit goods are any goods which are copies made without the consent of the rightsholder, or person authorised by the rightsholder, in the country of production, which are made directly or indirectly from an article where the making of that copy would have constituted an infringement of copyright under the law of the country of importation. Basically, the law says it is illegal to make and import a good that uses a copyright work without permission – things like knock-off merchandise or unlicensed CDs.

An EU study looked at the impact of counterfeit goods on the music industry; it covered both physical infringing goods when the product involves the use of media such as CDs, and digital copyright infringement online. The main finding of the research was that in 2014 the recorded music industry lost approximately €170 million of sales revenue in the EU as a consequence of the consumption of recorded music from illegal sources. This total corresponds to 5.2 per cent of the sector's revenues from physical and digital sales. These lost sales were estimated to result in direct employment losses of 829 jobs. When they took into consideration both direct and indirect effects of infringement of intellectual property in this sector, the researchers estimated that it caused approximately €336 million of lost sales to the EU economy, which in turn led to employment losses of 2,155 jobs and a loss of €63 million in government revenue (not including revenues from music distributors and retailers).[1]

In another report, *Mapping the Real Routes of Trade in Fake Goods*,[2] it was recognised that trade in counterfeit goods is a worldwide phenomenon that continues to grow in scope and magnitude. The research suggested that most counterfeit products are transported by sea, but use of courier services and postal mail is also increasing in the movement of smaller goods. And a further study, *Situation Report into Counterfeiting in Europe*,[3] identified that there had been a shift towards online trade in counterfeit goods.

The UK Intellectual Property Office (IPO) published a report on the impact of social media on intellectual property infringement.[4] The main objective of the research was to assess the role of social media in the sale of counterfeited products. In order to do this, the IPO undertook research, gathered statistics and conducted interviews with stakeholders such as representatives from Google, Facebook and Twitter. In the second phase, the researchers designed and developed monitoring tools to locate, track and trace the possible infringement of 12 products on Facebook, Twitter and Google. In addition, an online survey of 3,000 respondents was conducted, focusing on purchasing goods through social media. The third phase assessed the potential harm of purchasing counterfeit goods through social media by undertaking industry surveys.

[1] European Union Intellectual Property Office (2016) 'The Economic Cost of IPR Infringement in the Recorded Music Industry' https://euipo.europa.eu/tunnel-web/secure/webdav/guest/document_library/observatory/resources/research-and-studies/ip_infringement/study7/Music_industry_en.pdf accessed 6 November 2020.

[2] OECD/EUIPO, *Mapping the Real Routes of Trade in Fake Goods* (OECD Publishing 2017) http://dx.doi.org/10.1787/9789264278349-en accessed 6 November 2020.

[3] Europol and EUIPO, 'Situation Report on Counterfeiting and Piracy in the European Union' (Europol and EUIPO 2017) www.europol.europa.eu/publications-documents/2017-situation-report-counterfeiting-and-piracy-in-european-union accessed 6 November 2020.

[4] UK Intellectual Property Office (2017) 'Share and Share Alike, The Challenges from Social Media for Intellectual Property Rights' www.gov.uk/government/publications/share-and-share-alike accessed 6 November 2020.

The research found that according to industry groups, government and private enforcement agencies, counterfeiting online encompasses a range of activities, such as impersonation, fan pages, social media pages transacting business, promotion and the proliferation of websites selling counterfeits and offering fake special offers. As such, social media plays a significant and growing role in the sale and distribution of counterfeited goods. The consumer data supports these claims that platforms enable infringement. The researchers described social media as a haven for counterfeiters, who disseminate through open and closed group pages, as well as utilising likes and retweets and fan pages. Evidence from Trading Standards indicates that social media sites were the second most common location for investigations into counterfeiting.

So counterfeit goods continue to be an issue for the music industry, although there is much more focus on digital copyright infringement, and in particular the marketing of counterfeit goods through social media. Section 15.1.1 will look at counterfeits made within your national country, followed by what happens when someone tries to import counterfeit goods.

15.1.1 National counterfeit goods

At national level, countries have departments or officers who deal with the marketing and distributing of counterfeit goods. In the UK there is Trading Standards, which aims to protect consumers by helping them to purchase goods and services from reputable businesses. Trading Standards operates locally to assist in protection again counterfeit goods. Here is an example of the kind of thing that it does: West Yorkshire Trading Standards received an anonymous tip-off alleging a large-scale illegal counterfeit operation that was selling music CDs from a website. It undertook a two-year operation, collating 50,000 pages of evidence and seizing counterfeit music merchandising worth £473,000. As a result, the infringer – a Mr Hawken – pleaded guilty to four counts of making copyright articles for sale without a licence and was jailed for 18 months.[5]

---

5   UK Intellectual Property Office, 'Trading Standards Successes IP Crime and Enforcement Report 2018/19' www.gov.uk/government/publications/annual-ip-crime-and-enforcement-report-2018-to -2019 45 accessed 6 November 2020.

In 2013, a specific police department was set up in the UK to deal with intellectual property infringements. Called the Police Intellectual Property Crime Unit (PIPCU), its agenda is to investigate and deter serious and organised intellectual property crime. PRS for Music forms part of a partnership with PIPCU called Operation Creative; this is a multi-agency initiative designed to disrupt and prevent websites from providing unauthorised access to copyrighted content. It is a unique partnership between the City of London Police and the creative and advertising industries. Partners include FACT (Federation Against Copyright Theft), the BPI (British Phonographic Industry), IFPI (International Federation of the Phonographic Industry), PRS for Music, The Publishers Association, UKIE (The UK Interactive Entertainment Association), MPA (Music Publishers Association), MPA (Motion Picture Association) and the Gambling Commission.

In the US the equivalent trading standards organisation is the Federal Trade Commission. In Australia there are Offices of Fair Trading in each state and in New Zealand there is the Ministry of Consumer Affairs.

15.1.2 Importing counterfeit goods

At international level it is agreed that all countries that are members of the World Trade Organization are required to provide procedures authorising national customs authorities to suspend the importation of counterfeit goods, upon the rightsholder's request.[6] The TRIPS agreement also allows countries to apply these procedures to parallel imports.[7] The law allows for the option to apply these procedures to exportation of goods as well as importation. Countries can also decide if they want to add a limitation to this rule that allows for small quantities of goods brought into the country by a traveller for non-commercial purposes, in their personal luggage.

---

[6] TRIPS Agreement, Article 51.

[7] Parallel imports are goods which are placed legally onto a market in another country with the rightsholder's permission, but then imported into the home market without their permission, thereby competing with the goods sold in the home market under a territorial licence.

In the EU there is a specific Regulation[8] on how all EU countries must deal with the importation of counterfeit goods. (A Regulation is different to a Directive; EU Regulations automatically become the law in each Member State country, whereas a Directive is implemented through local law.) The EU Regulation applies the rules set by the TRIPS agreement, as mentioned above, but also goes further to apply in general to goods that infringe intellectual property rights. It does exclude parallel imports (because that would contradict the whole idea of the EU as a single market)[9] and goods of a non-commercial nature from travellers' personal luggage.

The EU regulation sets out the actions that customs authorities can take where goods imported are suspected to be infringing intellectual property rights. They are required to conduct adequate customs control and to take proportionate identification measures in order to prevent infringing goods entering the EU territory. The customs authorities can detain goods, and even destroy or release them, unless they are held while a copyright infringement case goes ahead.

In the US, there are two relevant laws. First, there is a rule that restricts the importation of counterfeit goods made without the permission of the rightsholder, in line with the TRIPS agreement. Second, it is also illegal to import goods that have been made lawfully in another country, but where the importation of these goods would violate the terms of a territorial licence agreement with the copyright owner. These laws authorise US Customs and Border Protection to therefore block the importation of counterfeit goods and goods that would infringe exclusive territorial licences.

In the UK, HM Revenue and Customs border control can confiscate property on behalf of the rightsholder upon entry into the country.[10] One benefit of this action is that the costs of the resources fall on the state rather than the rightsholder.

---

[8] Regulation (EU) No 608/2013 of the European Parliament and of the Council of 12 June 2013 Concerning Customs Enforcement of Intellectual Property Rights and Repealing Council Regulation (EC) No 1383/2003.

[9] For that reason, a licence to produce CDs, records or merchandise usually considers the EU as one territory.

[10] Under the UK Proceeds of Crime Act 2002 (Commencement No.5, Transitional Provisions, Savings and Amendment) Order 2003 (SI 2003/333).

The final sections of this chapter cover other types of illegal goods, including the recording of performances, visuals and artwork and merchandise.

15.2   Bootlegging – illegal recorded performances

Bootlegging[11] is the illegal recording of live performances, without permission from the performers, which are then illegally manufactured, marketed, distributed and/or sold. At its peak this was a $250 million industry.[12]

In 1993, British artist Phil Collins brought an action against a distributor in Germany.[13] Without his consent, a recording was made of Phil Collins performing in the US, which was then marketed and distributed on CD in Germany. The case was joined together with another dispute of similar circumstances relating to unauthorised recordings of Cliff Richard performing in the UK, then being distributed in Germany by another company. The courts in Germany referred to the EU court to ask whether the rights of copyright holders in other countries applied in these circumstances, and if so, whether EU law prevents the legislation of a Member State from denying to rightsholders from other Member States the right to prohibit the marketing, in its national territory, of a phonogram manufactured without their consent, where the performance was given outside its national territory. This case happened before the 2013 EU Regulation was implemented, but the court answered to the same effect. Therefore, Collins and Richard were able to bring their claim and enforce their rights against the distribution companies selling bootlegs of their performances in Germany.

In a more recent UK case, a police raid in 2005 found that Robert Langley was in possession of £11,500 worth of Led Zeppelin bootlegs, £1,790 of Rolling Stones bootlegs and £885 of Beatles bootlegs. When the case went to court in Glasgow, Scotland, Jimmy Page of Led Zeppelin testified,

---

[11]   The term comes from the 1890s, when alcohol was smuggled in bottles hidden in boots!

[12]   See Heylin C., *Bootleg! The Rise and Fall of the Secret Recording Industry* (Omnibus Press 2004).

[13]   *Phil Collins v Imtrat Handelsgesellschaft mbH and Patricia Im- und Export Verwaltungsgesellschaft mbH and Leif Emanuel Kraul v EMI Electrola GmbH* (joined cases C-92/92 and C-326/92) 20 October 1993.

saying that Langley was 'breaking the rules legally and morally'. Langley pleaded guilty and was sentenced to 20 months in prison in 2007.[14]

Likewise, US law provides that anyone who, without the consent of the performer or performers involved, fixes (records) or transmits a live performance, or distributes a fixation of a live musical performance shall be infringing copyright.[15]

15.3 Merchandise

Counterfeit goods are not only illegal copies of CDs or unauthorised recordings of performances, but also include knock-off merchandise. Counterfeit merchandise will infringe a range of intellectual property rights. It is a criminal offence to create it and, as explained in Chapter 11, secondary copyright infringement to handle the infringing goods.

An example of a case of this nature in the UK involved an industrial-scale screen printing operation that illegally printed clothing and distributed it globally via eBay and Amazon. The clothing infringed the intellectual property rights of Arctic Monkeys, The 1975, Motörhead, Ramones, Beyoncé, 5 Seconds of Summer, Ed Sheeran, Nirvana and a number of others. The infringers generated global counterfeit sales of £472,898 over a five-year period. During searches of the infringers' properties in 2016, it was found that the defendants were making clothing to order, and large numbers of heat transfers for music industry brands were seized. Investigators also relied on analysis of a significant number of eBay, PayPal and Amazon records to evidence the extent of the offending in this case. When sentencing the infringers at Bradford Crown Court, the judge described the crimes as 'well organised fraud'. The infringers were sentenced to two years' imprisonment suspended for two years, ordered to complete 300 hours of unpaid work and banned from acting as directors of limited companies for three years. For his part in the conspiracy, a supplier of the counterfeit branded heat transfers was sentenced to eight

---

[14] *R v Robert Langley*, Glasgow Sheriff Court, 2007, unreported.
[15] 17 U.S. Code § 1101 – Unauthorized fixation and trafficking in sound recordings and music videos.

months' imprisonment, suspended for 18 months, together with 180 hours of unpaid work.[16]

15.4 Artwork and visuals

Lastly, it is also worth noting that copyright applies to artwork, photographs and visual designs. This means that the artwork accompanying your music is also protected by copyright, including album covers and merchandise. As with all the types of infringement discussed throughout Part III, it is an infringement of your copyright in your visuals, artwork or photographs for someone to use the whole, or a substantial part of it, without your permission or the benefit of a copyright exception. Likewise, their production of goods with your artwork appearing on them would also infringe your rights.

This concludes Part III of the book, on infringement. Part IV covers what to do if you think your copyright has been infringed.

---

[16] UK Intellectual Property Office, Trading Standards Successes IP Crime and Enforcement Report 2018/19 www.gov.uk/government/publications/annual-ip-crime-and-enforcement-report-2018-to -2019 45 accessed 6 November 2020.

PART IV

Enforcement

Part IV focuses on enforcement; it takes the reader through the journey of enforcing copyright in music. While the previous chapters discussed what copyright is and when there is an infringement, Part IV considers the practicalities of moving forward with a claim. Its five chapters cover the topics of how a claim is initiated, where it can be brought, in which court and in which country; it looks at the kind of evidence used in a copyright infringement claim, in particular focusing on musicology reports; and goes on to cover remedies and online enforcement.

Chapter 16 starts at the beginning, explaining who can bring a claim for copyright infringement and what happens at the start of an action, including preliminary action and a mention of settlement deals.

Chapter 17 turns to where the claim can be brought, both in terms of country and court. It explains the rules on deciding which country the claim should be made in, as well as the UK court options, including the Intellectual Property Enterprise Court, the High Court and the Copyright Tribunal. It also refers to costs and alternative dispute resolution.

Chapter 18 considers the evidence that can be brought to support a case for copyright infringement. It mentions collating evidence and then focuses on expert evidence that can be provided by a musicologist.

Chapter 19 discusses the remedies available after a copyright infringement claim is successful, including injunctions, damages and, in criminal cases, prison sentences.

Chapter 20 looks at online copyright infringement and the kind of enforcement options available against online infringement, using notice and takedown procedures and blocking injunctions.

16 Starting a copyright infringement claim

Part I described what copyright is; Part II explained how to manage music copyright; Part III was all about what copyright infringement is; and now Part IV explains how copyright is enforced when a rightsholder believes that there has been an infringement. The chapters in this part explain the processes and some of the rules around bringing an action, but I feel the need to reiterate at this point that this does not count as legal advice and will not equip you to bring your own claim. What it does do is help you to understand what a claim would look like and what some of the rules are; it also clarifies some of the key aspects of that process. If you plan to bring a claim in court, you should hire a lawyer.

Likewise, it is worth mentioning that this chapter is written from the perspective of bringing a claim. If someone is bringing a claim against you, the same principles and processes apply.

This first chapter of Part IV covers who is eligible to bring the action in the first place and what happens at the beginning of a copyright infringement action. This is called preliminary action, or pre-action.

16.1   Who brings a case?

This section explains who can initiate a claim for copyright infringement. All actions for copyright infringement are brought under the specific rules of the country in which the claim is made. There are no rules at international level that harmonise the way in which an action needs to be brought, or the remedies that are available if the claim is successful. The international agreements do require that signatory countries provide enforcement procedures that enable effective action to be taken.[1] At EU level, an Enforcement Directive[2] was adopted in 2004 which sets minimum standards with regard to the remedies available to rightsholders, discussed further in Chapter 19.

One circumstance can give rise to both criminal and civil action. This means that a claim can be brought against a potential infringer in both the criminal and the civil courts at the same time – although they do not tend to proceed at the same pace and the outcome may be different, as the judges will be applying a different set of rules.

16.1.1 Criminal case

Criminal proceedings are brought by the state, or the government. If you suspected criminal activity of copyright infringement, the process would be to simply report the matter to the relevant authority – for example, the police, or specifically the UK Police Intellectual Property Crime Unit, or the relevant trading office or customs authority for your region or country – as explained in Chapter 15.

In the US this is usually commenced through the US Attorney's office, in coordination with a law enforcement agency such as the Federal Trade Commission. Then you let them handle the case, although you might be invited to be involved as the rightsholder at some stage, for example in giving evidence. The remedies and sanctions available from criminal action are discussed in Chapter 19.

16.1.2 Civil case

A civil copyright infringement case refers to a private action where the rightsholder brings a claim against another individual or company for copyright infringement – for example if someone has copied a substantial part of an existing song, or used a sample without permission.

---

[1]   TRIPS Agreement, Part III.

[2]   Directive 2004/48/EC of the European Parliament and of the Council of 29 April 2004 on the Enforcement of Intellectual Property Rights.

An infringement of copyright is actionable first and foremost by the copyright owner.[3] As discussed in Chapter 6, the owner of the copyright is usually the creator of the work in the first instance; this is unless it was created in the course of employment, in which case it is usually owned by the employer. The copyright owner may also be an inheritor of the right if the work has been transferred through a testamentary disposition or will.[4] If the claim is being brought in the US, the rightsholder must register the copyright with the US Copyright Office *before* bringing the action.[5] It is also difficult to bring a copyright infringement claim in China without first registering the right there.

Second, an exclusive licensee can also bring an action for copyright infringement. The exclusive licensee has the same rights and remedies available to them after the granting of the exclusive licence as if the licence had been an assignment, meaning as if they were the copyright owner. Likewise, the person against whom the claim is brought will have the same defences available to them as if the case were brought by the copyright holder.[6] In the circumstances of an action for infringement relating to a copyright work in which the copyright owner and the exclusive licensee have concurrent rights (wholly or partly), the parties must be joined together as the parties bringing the claim or added as a defendant against the claim.[7]

Third, in the EU, since the implementation of the 2001 Information Society Directive,[8] a non-exclusive licensee can also bring an action for infringement of copyright in certain circumstances.[9] If the infringing act was directly connected to a prior licensed act of the licensee, then the licensee may bring an action, provided that the licence (1) is in writing, (2) is signed by or on behalf of the copyright owner, and (3) expressly grants the non-exclusive licensee a right of action. If these criteria are met, the non-exclusive licensee has the same rights and remedies as if they were the copyright owner.

---

[3]   For example, in the UK under CDPA 1988, section 96(1).

[4]   UK CDPA 1988, section 90(1).

[5]   US Copyright Code, Title 17, section 104.

[6]   CDPA 1988, section 101(3).

[7]   CDPA 1988, section 102(1).

[8]   Directive 2001/29/EC of the European Parliament and of the Council on the Harmonisation of Certain Aspects of Copyright and Related Rights in the Information Society.

[9]   UK CDPA 1988, section 101A.

So, in summary, the people who can bring an action for copyright infringement are:

(1) The copyright owner, who may be:
    (a) the creator, or
    (b) an employer of the creator, or
    (c) the inheritor of the copyright.
    (d) This includes an individual or company to whom the copyright has been assigned by the rightsholder and is therefore the copyright owner.
(2) A person or company that is the holder of an exclusive licence from rightsholder.
(3) In some circumstances, a non-exclusive licence holder.

16.2   When a claim can be brought

Most countries have a law that limits the timeframe within which a claim for copyright infringement can be brought – this issue was mentioned in relation to the *Amen Break* sample in Chapter 14. This is referred to as the limitation period. Some countries have a set time; others set the time from the point when the infringing activity stops. So, don't waste any time: not taking action can be seen as being okay with the infringement and can come back to bite you if you change your mind in the future.

As mentioned, if you are bringing a claim in the US, you need to do this after you have registered the copyright, if you haven't already done so.

16.3   Preliminary action

In the event that a rightsholder believes their copyright has been infringed, there are a number of preliminary actions available before court action. This section sets out these options that may be utilised by a copyright holder before, or instead of, litigating the issue in court.

In the UK, pre-action is expected. According to the Practice Direction on Pre-Action Conduct, parties are expected to cooperate in exchanging information about prospective claims prior to issuing proceedings, with a view to narrowing down or settling the issues.[10]

However, pre-action protocol is not mandatory,[11] and there are no provisions that allow for protection against groundless threats of copyright infringement. This was demonstrated in the *Golden Eye* case,[12] where the judge said that sending letters claiming £700 for infringement were excessive and that threatening to make an application to the recipient's ISP to slow down or terminate their internet connection was unjustifiable, but the letters were not exactly illegal.

The Intellectual Property (Unjustified Threats) Act 2017 now provides for protection against groundless threats of infringement proceedings by the holder of other types of intellectual property rights, including patent, trade mark, unregistered or registered design right, but not copyright. The decision to omit copyright from this regulation followed a consultation[13] which included justifications such as the fact that there are not yet any existing provisions for unjustified threats in copyright law. In addition, as copyright is not a registered right, it would not be possible for a recipient of a Letter Before Claim, for example, to check a register to confirm the infringement.[14] Nevertheless, there remains a lack of protection for recipients of unjustified threats relating to copyright infringement.

In civil law countries, such as Germany, it is actually more common to file legal proceedings before corresponding with the other side. Nevertheless, more often than not cease and desist letters tend to be effective. It is common for a letter to be enough to either inform an unknowing infringer or concern a knowing infringer sufficiently to either stop or settle as per the arrangements offered in the letter.

However, it is also important to know that you do not have to send a letter, and in certain circumstances sending one could actually undermine your case. For example, if there is a situation of serious copyright infringement,

[10] Practice Direction on Pre-Action Conduct, paras 3, 6 and 12.

[11] Fox A, *Intellectual Property Enterprise Court: Practice and Procedure* (Sweet & Maxwell 2016) 67.

[12] *Golden Eye (International) Ltd & Ors v Telefonica UK Ltd* [2012] EWHC 723 (Ch).

[13] Law Commission, *Patents, Trade Marks and Design Rights: Groundless Threats* – Consultation Paper No. 212 (The Stationery Office 2013).

[14] Unregistered design rights are included to prevent the abuse of allowing threats to be made in respect of unregistered designs, when the true issue is registered designs.

writing a letter could give notice to the infringer, who might then destroy evidence, or move their operation. In these circumstances it is better to act quickly and hire a lawyer who will apply to the court for a claim, or if appropriate an interim injunction.[15]

If you receive a letter making a claim against you, now is the time to be pleased about keeping that record of your creative process, as this could help you quickly conclude the issue if there is no infringement. I would strongly recommend hiring a lawyer to look over the letter and prepare a response, particularly if you are in the UK, as the lawyer will be able to correctly follow the pre-action protocol. This is important if the claim ends up making it to court; as discussed in more detail in Chapter 19 on remedies, additional amounts of damages can be added for failing to comply with these rules.

16.4   Formal preliminary action

Beyond writing a letter, there are formal preliminary actions available that can be granted by a court. This includes a range of options that can be applied for, such as interim injunctions, search orders, freezing orders, orders for delivery up and disclosure orders. These types of remedy are discussed more in Chapter 19.

If the copyright infringement is taking place online, you can also make a notice and takedown request. This is discussed in Chapter 20, which covers online enforcement.

Guidance on preliminary action is also available through the Chartered Trading Standards Institute,[16] Business Companion,[17] the Citizens Advice Bureau, the British Library IP Centre, the Federation Against Copyright Theft (FACT), the IP Pro Bono Initiative and Anti-Copying in Design (ACID).

---

[15]   Injunctions are explained in Chapter 19 on remedies.

[16]   www.tradingstandards.uk accessed 6 November 2020.

[17]   www.businesscompanion.info accessed 6 November 2020.

16.5   Settlement

You might think it is a little ambitious to talk about settlement when we have only just started off on the journey of bringing the copyright infringement claim, but honestly, sometimes this can be the best option for everyone. In my personal opinion, settling a dispute out of court can be great, for the following reasons:

1. The parties can decide between themselves the terms of the settlement: this offers much more flexibility than anything a court could offer. The remedies that courts can provide are restricted by laws that regulate limitations on the types of remedy that can be provided, as well as the amount. One significant aspect of this is that in court the judgment only applies in that particular country, so if it was a worldwide issue you would have to take action in other countries too, in accordance with their legal rules and remedies. However, a settlement agreement can be effective across jurisdictions and even globally.
2. It's less risky. Going to court is always a risk. As we have discussed throughout the book so far, the law can be illusive; it changes all the time, cases can be won and then lost on appeal, and then the appeal can be appealed, and things can change again. When you are arguing over lofty concepts such as whether something is a substantial part, whether it is an idea, whether the amount taken is fair, you can never be 100 per cent sure of the outcome.
3. IT SAVES SO MUCH TIME AND MONEY. And time. And money. Court cases are long and expensive – and for some people, extremely stressful. When I was a law student, for a while I worked at a firm that provided family law. I will never forget the couple who went through the time, expense, stress and emotional toll of divorce proceedings, only to get married again on the day their divorce was legally finalised! When they talked about it afterwards, they said that 'things just got out of hand' and they were 'just angry'. (Usually when I am talking about a situation getting out of hand it refers to drinking unnecessary espresso martinis after midnight, not *literally* years of arguments hosted in courtrooms facilitated by expensive lawyers!) The moral of the story is not to let things get out of hand, and that if there is a *fair* settlement offer on the table, you should not refuse it just because you are angry.
4. Settlement agreements are confidential. Court judgments are pub-

lished for everyone to see, and often get press coverage – sometimes this is helpful for you; sometimes it's humiliating. Settlement agreements are almost always confidential, and there is a non-disclosure clause included within the agreement, so it stays between the parties.

In common law countries it is usual that settlement discussions between parties are not disclosed to the court, should an agreement not be reached. This is referred to as 'without prejudice', which means that any discussions that happen in view of attempting to reach a settlement cannot be used against the parties later on in court. If a settlement agreement is reached but a party does not keep to their side of the bargain, legal action can be taken in court to enforce the agreement – this then becomes an issue of breach of contract.

I am not saying that settlement agreements are always appropriate. Sometimes a matter has to go to court in the interests of justice. Where cross-examination is necessary or disclosure becomes an issue, the courts could be a more suitable option. And if you cannot agree a fair settlement, I will march you to the judicial gate myself.

The next chapter considers where to take a claim, if you have decided to bring one.

17 Where to make a claim

If you decide to take a claim forward, the next thing to consider is where to go with it. This can mean two things: in what country's jurisdiction, and then within that country in what forum, meaning which court, tribunal or alternative dispute resolution option. This chapter first discusses the rules about which country a copyright infringement claim can be made in, including in circumstances where the parties and the infringement are in different countries, and when there is a breach of licence agreement or contract. It then goes into more detail on the court systems relating to criminal and civil actions, in particular the court options that rightsholders have in the UK. Lastly, it mentions alternative dispute resolution options where claims can also be resolved.

17.1   Which country: jurisdiction

As explained, copyright laws are territorial, meaning that the laws of one country do not apply in another. Each country has their own copyright laws and rules on the procedure of bringing a claim. The international agreements specify that if you bring a case in a country other than the one you are resident in, then your copyright is treated as if it was that of a national of that country, so that's reassuring. However, usually you want to bring the claim in the country you are in, since this is where your lawyers are and where the law that you know about is.

Having said that, sometimes people want to bring a case in another jurisdiction because those laws are more favourable to their case. This is called forum shopping. But it is not quite as simple as it sounds – you can't just 'add to basket' and declare to the other side that you are suing them in Yemen.

A court must have jurisdiction to decide the case. This means that it is legally entitled to hear the case in its country or state. A straightforward example would be if both the copyright holder and the alleged infringer live in the same country, where the infringement is also taking place; that country would therefore be the appropriate place to take court action. There becomes a choice when the parties are resident in different countries, or if the infringing activity takes place in another country.

In the US, the law gives jurisdiction to federal courts in cases where there is a foreign element in the story, as long as an act of infringement takes place inside the US. Sometimes, however, the courts also take a case where the infringing activity is outside the US, such as in a dispute between a UK copyright holder and a New York licensor where the infringement took place in six Latin American countries.[1]

The rules on jurisdiction in the EU are governed by conventions that are also signed by, and therefore apply in, EFTA states (Switzerland, Norway, Iceland and Liechtenstein). The agreement provides a general rule that a claim is made against a person in the country they are living in, regardless of their nationality.[2] The exceptions to this rule are: (1) when there is a contract, a person can be sued in the country where the obligations of the contract are performed; (2) when the dispute is about a tort – meaning a wrongful act such as copyright infringement – the person can be sued in the place where the harm occurred. For instance, in a case where French publishers sued Google for scanning and digitalising French books, they were able to successfully sue in France because that is where the harm occurred. Incidentally, they won the case for copyright infringement in France,[3] but Google Books was found to be permitted by fair use in the US[4] – showing how the laws in different countries can have diverse outcomes with the same circumstances.

Common law countries have a rule where they can decide to dismiss a case from their jurisdiction if it is not the most appropriate forum.

---

[1] *London Film Productions Ltd v Intercontinental Communications Inc* (1984) 580 F Supp 47 S.D.N.Y.

[2] Regulation (EU) No 1215/2012 of the European Parliament and of the Council of 12 December 2012 on Jurisdiction and the Recognition and Enforcement of Judgments in Civil and Commercial Matters (recast) from Council Regulation (EC) No 44/2001.

[3] As a result Google paid €300,000 in damages and had to remove the infringing digital books from their search engine, and as the icing on the cake, they had to publish a copy of the judgment to let everyone know they had messed up! *La Martinière and French Publishers Association v Google* (2009) Paris Court of Appeal.

[4] *The Authors Guild, et al. v Google Inc.*, 2016 US Supp. 15-849.

Usually this comes after one of the parties argues for a different jurisdiction. This was argued in the case of *PRS v Qatar Airways*, mentioned in Chapter 7. After being unable to obtain a licence for use of music, PRS filed a copyright infringement case against Qatar Airways in the UK. Qatar Airways accepted that it had been served in the UK and therefore the UK High Court had jurisdiction to hear the case, but argued that the court should not do so on the basis that the appropriate forum for these proceedings was Qatar. The rules for deciding can be summarised as:[5]

(1)   Is there another available forum which is clearly and distinctly the natural forum, that is to say, the forum with which the action has the most real and substantial connection?

(2)   If there is, is England nevertheless the appropriate forum, in particular because the court is not satisfied that substantial justice will be done in the alternative available forum?

In answering the first question, there are four factors to consider: (1) the personal connections the parties have to the countries in question; (2) factual connections which the events relevant to the claim have with the countries; (3) applicable law; and (4) factors affecting convenience or expense, such as the location of witnesses or documents. These are explained below.

1. Personal connections

PRS is primarily based in the UK, as is its employees and representatives. Qatar Airways is of course based in Qatar, but has 128 offices in 73 different countries and approximately 46,000 staff worldwide, including Vice President Legal Mr Rehan Akram, who is a graduate of the University of Cambridge in England and qualified as an English solicitor. As such, PRS and Qatar Airways both have close and genuine links to their home state, but Qatar Airways had stronger links to the UK than PRS had to Qatar. The degree of that difference was considered by the court to be small, however.

2. Factual connections

The events relevant to the claim are the playing of music in Qatar Airways' aircrafts. Where that occurs depends on where the aircrafts are.

---

[5]   Following the leading UK case, *Spiliada Maritime Corp v Cansulex Ltd* (The Spiliada) [1987] AC 460.

About 98 per cent of Qatar Airways' flights either start or finish in Qatar; by contrast, 5 per cent of their flights either start or finish in the UK, and in fact UK destinations represent only 3.4 per cent of the destinations served by the airline. As such, the aircrafts spend more time in Qatar than in the UK. However, the court also agreed that relevant acts do take place in the UK, and a great deal of the activity in issue takes place in other countries – neither Qatar nor the UK.

3. Applicable law

If you thought you were spoilt for choice when searching for flights, just wait until you hear about the myriad of jurisdiction-shopping options there are for aircrafts. When an aircraft is in a destination country or its airspace, the law of that country applies. As such, when the aircraft is in Qatar, Qatari law applies, and when in the UK, it is subject to UK law. When in international airspace, Qatari law will apply; this includes when the aircraft is in the airspace of a non-destination country. Since the aircraft spends more time in Qatar than in the UK, Qatari law applies for more of the time than UK law. Nevertheless, UK law is still the applicable law in relation to those acts carried out in the UK. Likewise, the law of other states of destination countries will also be engaged. As such, the judge noted that a large number of states' laws are relevant to this dispute; while it may not be necessary to examine every single one of those laws distinctly, whichever court handles the case will be required to examine laws other than its own.

The parties took divergent views of Qatari law and procedure and of how a Qatari court would go about dealing with foreign law. However, the judge was not satisfied that the courts of Qatar were not capable of dealing with and applying foreign law appropriately in a case which required it.

4. Factors affecting convenience or expense

The dispute about how the on-flight entertainment system of the Qatar Airways app operates will require witnesses based in Qatar, and the production of some documents which are in Qatar. However, the judge stated that this is not a complicated issue; it is merely a simple question of when and how users access the system. Equally, there may be evidence from witnesses based in the UK. If infringement is established, both Qatar Airways and PRS are likely to want to call evidence about contracts and licensing. Therefore, for whichever court hears the matter, there will be a need to translate into or out of English or Arabic – so the costs will be high regardless of where the case is held.

A major part of Qatar Airways' argument at stage 1 was that a factor strongly favouring Qatar as the natural forum was that Qatari law will apply to the vast majority of the acts complained of, and many more than those to which UK law will apply. It was accepted that in terms of amount of time, or the number of plays of a work, Qatari law will apply to many more of those instances than will UK law. However, the case is not a Qatari copyright dispute in which the events in and law of the UK and other countries are a kind of ancillary aspect. Every non-domestic flight engages the copyright laws of at least two states. The judge said: 'The case is really a global copyright dispute between a UK holder of those global rights and a Qatari user of the protected content who is using it all over the world. The dispute has a connection to every state to and from which Qatar Airways flies planes.'[6]

Overall, the judge decided that the dispute had more of a real connection with the UK and Qatar than it does with any other state. As between the two, the fact that a higher share of any damages may be due for acts to which Qatari law is applicable than those for which UK law is applicable does not make Qatar clearly and distinctly the forum with which the dispute has the most real and substantial connection. As such, the application by Qatar Airways to move the case from the UK to Qatar was dismissed, so the case will now proceed in the UK. This case demonstrates some of the key issues with copyright infringement jurisdiction: usually the challenge is the internet rather than an aircraft, but the same principles would apply.

17.1.1 Jurisdiction for breach of contract

Any licence or contract worth the paper it is written on will include a clause towards the end called jurisdiction, in which it will specify in which country any legal action arising from a breach of the terms in the contract must be taken. In fact, a good contract will specify not only choice of forum but also governing law.

---

[6] *Performing Right Society Ltd v Qatar Airways Group QCS* [2020] EWHC 1872 (Ch) (17 July 2020) 69.

Civil law countries generally honour the forum selection decided in the agreement. Common law countries also honour the forum selection of the contract, but are slightly more open to the idea of overriding it if any of the above-mentioned criteria convince them that there is a more appropriate option.

In the US, the courts have said that the contractual agreement will be followed unless there are reasons that would make it unreasonable and unjust to do so.[7]

17.2 Criminal or civil action

As mentioned in the previous chapters, depending on the type of copyright infringement, you will need to decide if you are going to pursue criminal or civil action, or both if appropriate.

Criminal and civil action takes place in different courts with different systems. Within those two categories there are also different courts available. The following sections will explain the different court options available in the UK, followed by costs and alternative dispute resolution.

17.2.1 UK High Court

In England and Wales, the Business and Property Courts is an umbrella term[8] that covers the specialist IP courts, including the Intellectual Property Enterprise Court (IPEC) and the High Court (Chancery Division and Patent Court). Eligible parties, such as rightsholders, owners or exclusive licensees of copyright and other intellectual property rights, can bring certain types of IP cases to the IPEC or the High Court in England and Wales, the Court of Session in Scotland, the High Court in Northern Ireland or Her Majesty's High Court of Justice of the Isle of Man.[9] In some cases, it is also possible for the eligible parties to bring a case in the County Court in England and Wales, in the Sheriff Court in Scotland and in the

---

[7] *Bremen v Zapata Off-Shore Co.* (1972) 407 US 1.

[8] www.gov.uk/courts-tribunals/the-business-and-property-courts accessed 6 November 2020.

[9] UK CDPA 1988, sections 115(3), 205(3) and 215(3).

County Court in Northern Ireland.[10] In relation to appealing a case from these courts, rightsholders can bring their cases in the Court of Appeal in England and Wales, in the Court of Session in Scotland or in the Court of Appeal in Northern Ireland.

The IPEC is a specialist intellectual property court. It technically forms part of the High Court of England, but offers two routes for action: multi-track and small claims track. The IPEC multi-track has a limit on the maximum amount of damages that can be awarded, of up to £500,000. Costs orders are made in proportion to the nature of the dispute and are subject to a cap of no more than £50,000.

The small claims track is for suitable claims in the IPEC with a value of up to £10,000. These options make it much easier for rightsholders to bring smaller claims. The action tends to be faster than in the High Court, and there is less risk due to the caps on damages and costs.

Between 2013 and 2016, a project led by Kretschmer and Burrow[11] presented empirical data on the use of the small claims track as part of the then newly established IPEC. The study revealed data on the number of cases issued, the number of claimants, the number of first-time litigants, the number of industries and the types and values of claims.[12] Another benefit of the IPEC is that the judges are specialised in intellectual property matters and often have a technical background,[13] which also makes it an attractive forum for bringing your copyright case. An independent review of the IPEC commissioned by the UK IPO found that there was a substantial increase in the number of intellectual property cases at the IPEC after it introduced a cap on the amount of costs in October 2010; as a result, this greatly improved the ability of small and medium-sized enterprises and individuals to gain access to justice.[14] The IPEC is considered to be something of a success, as it provides an efficient and cost-effective forum for the resolution of intellectual property disputes in the UK.[15]

---

[10] UK CDPA 1988, sections 115, 205 and 215.

[11] Kretschmer M and Burrow S, *Assessing the Small Claims Track* (CREATe 2013–16).

[12] Burrow S, *Assessing the Small Claims Track* (EPIP 2015).

[13] Taylor Wessing, *5th Global Intellectual Property Index* (Taylor Wessing 2016) 37.

[14] www.judiciary.uk/publications/evaluation-of-the-reforms-of-the-intellectual-property-enterprise -court/

[15] Fox J, *Intellectual Property Enterprise Court* (Sweet & Maxwell 2016).

17.2.2 UK Magistrates' Court

Criminal copyright infringement cases are initially heard in the Magistrates' Court, where all criminal proceedings start in the UK. Magistrates have limited sentencing powers such as community sentences, fines of up to £5,000 and short custodial sentences of up to six months in prison (or up to 12 months in total for more than one offence).[16] If the court considers there is a need for a longer sentence the case will be passed to the Crown Court, which has a wider range of sentencing powers.

As mentioned, usually these cases are brought by the state. However, rightsholders can rely on criminal prosecution to protect their copyright where criminal offences occur, and any person can initiate criminal proceedings instead of the Crown Prosecutors.[17] In other words, it is possible for rightsholders to start a criminal prosecution privately. In the field of intellectual property criminal enforcement, it is common practice that trade bodies, such as Trading Standards, industry bodies and collecting societies, perform criminal prosecutions against intellectual property crime. Often these proceedings are initiated after the rightsholder raises a complaint with the aforementioned official bodies, but the decision to take forward the case is entirely at the bodies' discretion.[18] Where the scale of the crime is more serious, the Crown Prosecution Service may take the cases investigated by the police or trade body and carry out a public criminal prosecution.[19]

17.2.3 UK Copyright Tribunal

The UK Copyright Tribunal is a non-departmental public body, sponsored by the government Department for Business, Energy and Industrial Strategy. The primary purpose of the Copyright Tribunal is to resolve commercial licensing disputes between copyright owners or collecting societies, and between the licensor and the business using the copyrighted material, the licensee.

---

[16] www.gov.uk/courts/magistrates-courts accessed 6 November 2020.

[17] Prosecution of Offences Act 1985, section 6(1).

[18] Crozier R, Criminal Prosecutions – An Underused Remedy (*IP Magazine*, 2012) www.clarkewillmott .com/wp-content/uploads/2015/08/criminal-prosecutions-an-underused-remedy.pdf accessed 6 November 2020.

[19] UK Prosecution of Offences Act 1985, section 3.

After the increased success of PRS, there were some conflicts between PRS and some of its licensees. As a result the Copyright Tribunal was set up in 1956,[20] to settle any disputes between PRS and user organisations – in particular, at the time, the BBC.

17.3   Costs

The cost of private legal action is no joke. It is a factor that needs to be taken into consideration. It costs money to hire a lawyer, make an application to court, collate evidence and make it through trial, and then there could be appeals.

Each country has its own costs and fees for such things, but they all pretty much range between expensive and extortionate – although in most countries you can get your costs paid back to you by the losing side if you win the court case overall. This is a general rule, and is subject to many factors, including the procedure rules of the court and whether the party followed the correct preliminary procedures. In the UK the courts have been seen to hold this against parties, including if they were unreasonably unwilling to participate in alternative dispute resolution[21] – discussed below. A refusal to do so does not necessarily automatically mean that you won't get your costs back, however; it depends on the circumstances.[22] Some courts, such as the IPEC discussed above, will make case management decisions to help parties keep the costs down.

Some organisations, such as those listed in Chapter 7 – including collecting societies and trade associations – provide organisational support for obtaining evidence and tracking down potential infringers. As we have seen in the examples given, these organisations will also represent their members in civil action, as well as conducting their own private criminal cases.

---

[20]   UK Copyright Act 1956.
[21]   *Halsey v Milton Keynes General NHS Trust* [2004] EWCA Civ 576; [2004] 1 WLR 3002.
[22]   *PGF II SA v OMFS Company 1 Limited* [2013] EWCA Civ 1288.

17.4   Alternative dispute resolution

Although the IPEC has improved accessibility to proceedings for copyright holders, alternative dispute resolution continues to be encouraged, with the aim of leaving court action as the last resort – although, of course, for alternative dispute resolution to proceed, both parties need to agree to engage with the process.

Alternative dispute resolution is a formal negotiation and settlement between the parties that involves an independent third party. It can be in the form of mediation or arbitration, depending on the circumstances of the dispute.

Mediation can be utilised by the copyright holder to resolve disputes relating to infringement or licensing issues. It is generally cheaper and quicker than litigation. Parties agree a resolution between themselves in the presence of a mediator and therefore this tends to produce results that benefit both parties, rather than a more winning-and-losing-party approach. The UK IPO provides a mediation service which can be utilised either in person or on the telephone.[23]

Use of alternative dispute resolution can reduce the costs and, as mentioned, is encouraged by the UK government.[24] The courts are increasingly willing to view refusal to engage in alternative dispute resolution, and the preliminary actions discussed in the previous chapter, as a factor to be taken into account when assessing costs. In particular, mediation provides a strong mechanism for IP rightsholders to pursue their disputes without resorting to litigation.

Chapter 18 discusses the evidence that can be brought in a copyright infringement case.

---

[23]   www.gov.uk/guidance/intellectual-property-mediation accessed 6 November 2020.
[24]   Weatherall K et al, *IP Enforcement in the UK and Beyond: A Literature Review* (SABIP 2009) 36.

18 Evidence and musicology reports

The previous two chapters have discussed what happens when starting a copyright infringement claim and where the claim can be made. This chapter looks at the evidence that can be brought to support the case. It first considers gathering of evidence for a claim, and then focuses on the use of expert witnesses who produce musicology reports.

The overall structure of this book, and of Part IV, is loosely arranged in the format of the rightsholder journey: from knowing what the rights are, to managing those rights, understanding when an infringement might occur and actualising a claim against an infringement. However, in reality this is not meant to be a chronological to-do list, written in order of what action to take. You don't actually start collecting evidence for a claim that you made in court *after* starting proceedings. In fact, there is some evidence that you should collate and keep from the day you started creating, as explained in Part I.

18.1 Gathering evidence

As mentioned in Chapter 2, one of the things you should do from the very beginning is keep a dated record of your creative process. This can help to show how and when your work was created by you. If a claim is made against you for copyright infringement, and you can show that your work was created before the other work, then that immediately puts an end to the dispute. In certain countries, such as the US, you should also consider registering the copyright. The registration can be used for the same purposes but is also a requirement for being able to bring a copyright claim in the first place. As part of gathering the evidence to bring a copyright infringement action, this documentation is needed to show that first and foremost the thing that has been copied is rightfully yours.

One way to prove the existence of a digital file, particularly if you are in a country where registration is not necessary, is by using the World Intellectual Property Organization (WIPO) global online service called WIPO PROOF. The service was set up in May 2020 and produces tamper-proof evidence which you can use to prove that your digital file existed at a specific point in time. The benefit of this system is that it provides verifiable confirmation that the work existed at the point of registration.

Thereafter, evidence would be required to show that the infringement has taken place, and there would be a need for details of the parties involved and the extent of the infringement. The specific type of evidence needed would depend on the type of copyright infringement taking place, including whether it is criminal infringement – for example, a company illegally distributing copies of your music – or a civil infringement, such as someone copying your song in their own. There are national laws that govern how evidence can be collected, preserved and made admissible to a case.

In terms of collating evidence of the activities of the alleged infringer, if necessary, it is possible to get a search order granted by a court to allow for the search of relevant property, including to take photographs and seize any infringing articles. As this is quite extreme, this kind of order is only granted in situations where the case is strong, there is actual or potential serious damage to the rightsholder and there is clear evidence of the existence of incriminating documents or possessions that the infringer may destroy.

Another type of court order that can be made in the process of gathering evidence is a discovery order, which requires a person to reveal information relevant to the claim. This information might include things such as relevant names and addresses, dates and quantities of imported goods and sources of imported goods.

Cases go through different types of hearings – this is where there are proceedings before a court. A trial is like a type of hearing, but it is specifically about examining the evidence of the case in order to decide the case. Typically, you might have one or two hearings before the trial and another after, depending on the issues that need to be decided. Sometimes these hearings can happen in person but they can also be on paper – or even online or via telephone, should you find yourself at court in the midst of a global pandemic.

As part of your case, you(r lawyers) may bring witnesses to take the stand in court and give their version of events, in order for the court to decide the facts of a case. Expert witnesses can also be brought as part of a case; these are people who are not directly involved with the case, but who have the expertise to explain and analyse a particular aspect of a case for the judge. In music infringement cases these are called musicologists, and they are the focus of the remainder of this chapter.

18.2   Musicology reports

Musicology is the study of musical works. A forensic musicologist is someone who has experience in musicology, usually with degrees in music, and who provides information to the court, such as musical analysis and comparison of songs.

When there is a copyright infringement claim that argues that a substantial part of a song has been copied, it is now common to see musicology experts appearing for both parties on each side of the case. The normal practice is that musicologists are hired by a party to analyse the similarities and differences between the songs and produce a report of their findings for the court. Often, the musicologist is also brought to appear as a witness before the court, should the case make its way to trial.

This is a fairly recent development in the assessment of music copyright cases. Before the 1950s the question of substantial similarities was determined by the impression left on the untrained ears of everyday listeners. In the US this might have been the jury; in the UK we do not have a jury for civil cases, so it would have been decided by the judge. Subsequently, experts were introduced who could translate music into legal evidence with scientific analysis.[1]

---

[1]   Mopas M and Curran A, 'Translating the Sound of Music: Forensic Musicology and Visual Evidence in Music Copyright Infringement Cases' (2016) 31(1) Canadian Journal of Law and Society – Revue Canadienne Droit et Société 25.

The case involving Vangelis' *Chariots of Fire*,[2] mentioned in Chapter 12, was one of the first times that we saw musicologists becoming seriously involved in copyright infringement cases, and it came about in somewhat of a serendipitous manner. The circumstances of the case were that a UK shoe manufacturer (Clarks) wanted to use the song in an advert, but after refusal from the rightsholders, Warner Music, Clarks went looking for something similar from EMI Records. When Clarks' advert aired on TV featuring the song *City of Violets*, the case commenced. Geoffrey Bush was the expert witness – not so much as a musicologist, but rather based on his reputation for developing strategies against copyright infringement claims, having already provided evidence in a number of other cases on the degree of musical similarity between songs.[3] He was a copyright expert in that sense.

However, Vangelis' legal team was joined by a young apprentice who reportedly stumbled upon the case by mistake and wanted to get involved (is it a fairy tale?). His name was Guy Protheroe and he was a composer and conductor who became an expert witness for the case. This was the first time someone with no knowledge of copyright litigation had been used as an expert witness in this type of case, and it paved the way for the forensic musicologists that are now common practice. Protheroe eventually became one of the main forensic experts in British music copyright in the late twentieth century. During the 1990s, he provided advice to an average of 30 clients per year.[4]

Protheroe provided the musicology expert evidence in the *Spandau Ballet* case,[5] discussed in Chapter 6. The judge deciding the case put a huge amount of emphasis on Protheroe's evidence, relying on it heavily in the judgment. For example, when dismissing the claim, the judge said: 'Mr Protheroe said that in general the saxophone[s] … were not in themselves particularly memorable, tuneful or original … Mr Protheroe did not consider that they were in themselves elements in the musical work.' This shows the importance that courts give to this kind of evidence and

2   *EMI Music Publishing Ltd v Papathanasiou* [1993] E.M.L.R. 306.
3   *Francis Day and Hunter Ltd v Bron* [1963] 2 All ER 16; *Ledrut v Meek* [1968] 57 R.I.D.A. 180; *Roberton v Lewis* [1976] RPC 169.
4   Bellido J, 'Forensic Technologies in Music Copyright' (2016) 25 Soc & Legal Stud 441.
5   *Hadley v Kemp* [1999] E.M.L.R. 589.

shows why it has become increasingly popular. (And they lived happily ever after.)

Another musicologist frequently providing this type of expert evidence is Peter Oxendale,[6] who reported working on 450 cases a year in 2017, after the *Blurred Lines* case.[7] In fact, nowadays, musicologists are even being hired *before* a song is published in order to ensure there hasn't been any subconscious copying.[8]

The law provides specific rules relating to how expert evidence can be used. In the UK, the courts must provide permission and, when doing so, will consider the objective of dealing with cases justly and at proportionate cost. The rules also state that even though the expert witness might be hired by the party in the case, the expert has an overriding duty to the court, and they must show that they have conformed with certain standards of objectivity.[9]

In the US, expert evidence is only admissible if it assists the court in understanding unfamiliar or complex issues in determining the facts. Nevertheless, when the musicologist's evidence is brought, it is also often heavily relied upon by the court. This is what happened in the copyright infringement case brought by Seth Swirsky and Warryn Campbell against Mariah Carey,[10] which claimed that her song *Thank God I Found You* infringed their song *One of Those Love Songs* (performed by Xscape). The musicologist for Swirsky and Campbell was Dr Robert Walser, chair of the Musicology Department at the University of California. Dr Walser's method of comparing the two songs looked at the pitch sequences, basslines, melodies, measure structures, choruses and rhythms. The courts found this methodology selective and noted that the analysis was not wholly objective, but it was still enough to throw out Carey's motion for summary judgment (a summary judgment is where you are so confident that the claim is nonsense you ask the court to decide at a summary hearing that it needn't go any further).

---

[6]   www.oxendale-music.co.uk/ accessed 6 November 2020.

[7]   www.bbc.co.uk/sounds/play/b08md9xf accessed 6 November 2020.

[8]   www.theguardian.com/money/2015/jan/20/how-become-forensic-musicologist accessed 6 November 2020.

[9]   UK Civil Procedure Rules 1998/3132, Part 35.

[10]   *Swirsky v Carey*, 376 F.3d 841, 843 (9th Cir. 2004).

Musicologists are able to use their knowledge of music to translate the language of music, and the fingerprint of a song, into a format that judges can understand, aiming to give the court a way to objectively analyse a song. It has been said that 'those who can speak the language of music and translate it into a textual format have tremendous currency in copyright infringement cases'.[11] Musicologists have played a significant role in development of the copyright infringement cases, particularly those discussed in Chapter 12, such as the *Blurred Lines, Stairway to Heaven* and the *Dark Horse* cases.

In the *Blurred Lines* case, the musicologist for the Marvin Gaye side was Judith Finell. She stated in her report of October 2013 that the songs *Got to Give It Up* and *Blurred Lines* both contained substantially similar constellations of defining features, and many of the same deliberate creative choices were made by their respective composers. Finell stated that consequently, rather than merely resembling one another stylistically, the two works sounded substantially similar in many of their most distinctive features. In particular, the main vocal and instrumental themes of *Blurred Lines* are rooted in *Got to Give It Up*, such as the signature phrase, vocal hook, backup vocal hook, their variations and the keyboard and bass lines. In addition, she noted that both songs departed from convention in the same way, such as the unusual cowbell instrumentation, omission of guitar and use of male falsetto. As a result, Finell believed that the ordinary observer would recognise the substantial similarities between these songs. And we all know how that case turned out.

In the Katy Perry case about her song *Dark Horse*, the crux of the alleged copying came down to a descending minor mode eight-figure ostinato. Both sides hired musicologists that reported opposing evidence – as is the norm in these situations! Perry's musicologist highlighted key differences in the songs, such as overall structures, chord progressions, harmonic rhythm, pitch sequences in the ostinatos, intervals between the pitches in the ostinatos, melodic rhythms in the ostinatos and the length of the ostinatos. The expert also concluded that the ostinato in question contributed only a negligible amount to the *Dark Horse* song. On the other hand, Gray's evidence claimed that the similarities between the two ostinatos

---

[11] Mopas M and Curran A, 'Translating the Sound of Music: Forensic Musicology and Visual Evidence in Music Copyright Infringement Cases' (2016) 31(1) Canadian Journal of Law and Society – Revue Canadienne Droit et Société 25.

were substantial and significant, overlapping in rhythm, pitch content, melodic contour and timbre.

One issue that continues to be raised around musicology evidence is that musicologists are music experts and not copyright experts. So, their use of the words 'substantially similar' may not be the same as the legal definition. As we know, two songs sounding similar does not necessarily mean copyright infringement. This was illustrated during disposition when Gray's musicologist answered 'no' to the question 'so you don't know whether when you're using the term "substantially similar" it tracks with the legal definition or not; you don't know one way or the other?'

Sometimes the use of a musicologist does not always help the case. An example is the Led Zeppelin case, where they were being sued by Skidmore for allegedly copying the song *Taurus* in their record *Stairway to Heaven*. Skidmore's own expert musicologist, Dr Stewart, agreed that musical concepts like the minor chromatic line and the associated chords have been used as building blocks in music for quite a long time. This really supported the Led Zeppelin argument, which was described by their expert Dr Ferrara: that the chromatic scale, descending or ascending, is as a musical building block that no one can possibly own. Knowing the important influence of these experts, Skidmore even attempted to stop Zeppelin's musicologist from testifying at trial on the basis of conflict of interest, but it was denied by the court.

However, overall, it is clear that musicology reports are now common practice in cases that turn on the question of whether two songs are substantially similar. We have seen that the courts are keen to rely on this type of evidence when deciding the facts of a case.

Chapter 19 discusses the different remedies available at the conclusion of a copyright infringement case.

19 Remedies

When taking a case of copyright infringement to court, a number of remedies are available for the copyright holder should the claim be successful. The types of remedy available are different for civil and for criminal action. In civil proceedings the rightsholder may be able to obtain an injunction and damages, as well as any destruction or surrendering of infringing materials. In criminal matters, there is also the possibility that a person found guilty of copyright infringement could receive a prison sentence.

This chapter will first cover the pre-action and temporary remedies that can be extremely beneficial for copyright holders, including interim injunctions and measures to preserve evidence. It then covers other types of injunctions, damages, and lastly prison sentences.

There are only a few minimum standards set at international level for copyright infringement remedies. This means that the types of remedy available depend on the country of the action, as well as the amount of damages or length of prison sentence that may be imposed. The international agreements do set out that countries will enable rightsholders to have effective action against infringement, including the availability of remedies that not only compensate the rightsholder but also act as a preventative deterrent to future infringements. Courts can grant preliminary remedies, meaning that they take action in a matter before it has been decided at trial, and permanent remedies, which come after the outcome of the case is decided. The preliminary remedies are discussed below, followed by the permanent remedies. In addition, specific remedies available for dealing with online copyright infringement are discussed in Chapter 20.

19.1 Pre-Action Remedies

Remedies that can be granted by a court before the matter goes through to trial can be extremely helpful for the copyright holder. This is because sometimes action needs to be taken to prevent more damage later, or even to preserve evidence that would be needed for the proceedings. At international level, it is agreed that all nations will provide provisional measures that can help to prevent infringement from taking place, including stopping infringing goods entering the country via customs. These provisional measures are only available as part of legal proceedings that need to be issued within a certain timeframe – usually a month, but it depends on the country.

These measures allow authorities to seize infringing goods, whether that be to prevent them from entering the market or as preservation of evidence, to stop them being destroyed by the alleged infringer. Preservation of evidence can be done with an order to allow for the confiscation of infringing materials and includes the ability to require the alleged infringer to open their premises for inspection. (There's a *The Office* joke in there somewhere.)

An injunction means to stop someone doing something. A preliminary injunction is an injunction that is granted to stop someone doing something before they do it, until the outcome of the case has been decided. It is also called an interlocutory injunction and could be used, for example, to stop a song being published before infringement proceedings are decided. In the UK and Canada this is common practice in copyright cases. To decide if a preliminary injunction can be granted, the courts look at the merits of the case and its probability of success.

In the US, the equivalent is a temporary restraining order or a temporary injunction that can be used to preserve the position of the parties in lieu of proceedings. In deciding whether to grant these injunctions, the US court considers four factors: likelihood of success on the merits of the case; irreparable injury to the parties; balance of hardships; and public interest.

Sometimes these injunctions are granted without the alleged infringers being able to defend their case before the judge; this is called a without notice injunction, or sometimes we lawyers like to go fancy in Latin and call it an *ex parte* injunction. It enables the rightsholder to take swift action to protect their copyright without giving the infringer the chance to destroy evidence or delay action.

It is also useful to know that once a copyright infringement claim is made against an artist for taking the substantial part of another song, collecting societies may also suspend the royalty distribution for that song. For example, PRS for Music operates a system whereby it suspends royalties until the outcome of the dispute is resolved. For this to take effect, at least one of the parties bringing the proceedings needs to be a member of PRS or an affiliated society, and must then make a written communication to PRS to formally notify them of the dispute, in accordance with their rules governing infringing claims.

19.2   Injunctions

As mentioned, injunctions can be preliminary, meaning before the dispute is resolved, or permanent, which are effective after the court case is decided. A permanent injunction aims to prevent the continuation of any infringement, by stopping the infringer from continuing to use the copyright material. An injunction is made in the form of a court order which sets out exactly what the infringer must do or stop doing. If the order is breached, and the infringer goes against what is set out in the injunction, they could face a fine and even imprisonment.

Injunctions can be granted against the infringer and any other third parties involved. This includes intermediaries such as internet service providers. These are called online blocking injunctions and are discussed further in Chapter 20 on online enforcement. The injunctions usually involve the delivering up or destruction of any remaining infringing goods.

19.3   Damages

Damages is monetary relief that is awarded in copyright infringement cases, where money is paid to the copyright holder. There are different types of damages: compensation, account of profits, hypothetical royalties, punitive and additional damages, and costs.

If a copyright infringement claim is successful, a court can order the infringer to pay the copyright holder damages to compensate them for the loss or injury caused by the infringement. This is agreed at international level in the TRIPS Agreement.[1] In most countries, aside from the US, these types of damages are only awarded where the infringer knew or had reason to believe that there was an infringement.

It is also agreed at international level that courts can grant damages in the form of any profits made by the infringer, whether they were aware of the infringement or not. This is called account of profits. Another common type of damages awarded in copyright infringement cases is the hypothetical royalty. This is where the amount of damages is calculated based on the amount that would have been paid if there had been a licence for the work in place.

In some cases, the courts can also take into account other non-economic factors, such as the moral prejudice caused by the infringement. On top of this, the courts can award further damages as a punitive measure, with a view to deterring future infringement.

In the US, the law provides that copyright holders can reclaim the actual damages suffered by them as a result of the infringement, as well as any profits made by the infringer. As an alternative to recovering the actual damage and account of profits, in the US rightsholders can sue for statutory damages. Statutory damages can be notoriously high, covering all infringements within the circumstances. The amount can range from $750 to $30,000 per infringement as determined by a jury, and where the infringement is determined to have been wilful, this can extend to $150,000 per infringement! For example, in a case where the infringer had downloaded 24 sound recordings at home using peer-to-peer sharing software Kazaa, the jury awarded $9,250 per song in the first instance, awarding $222,000 in damages. At retrial the jury went up to $80,000 per song, awarding $1,920,000 in damages. After several other appeals, the court reinstated the original $222,000 award.[2]

---

[1] TRIPS Agreement, Article 45(1).

[2] *Capitol Records v Thomas-Rasset* 799 F Supp 2d 999 (2011) and 692 F 3d 899 (2012).

US law also provides that a successful copyright holder can be awarded the costs of their attorney fees. In the EU, successful parties can be awarded reasonable and proportionate legal costs and expenses.[3]

In the UK, there are two basic models of how damages are decided: (1) damages are awarded in order to restore the claimant to the position they would have been in if the infringement had never occurred; (2) account of profits from the infringer's illegal gains.

On top of this, additional damages can be granted, which may be awarded at the discretion of the court.[4] Additional damages can be helpful where the costs of the hypothetical licence would not deter the infringer from committing the same offence again, if all that the infringer stood to lose was the original cost of the licence. Therefore, the additional damages are added in order to be dissuasive.[5] Additional damages have been applied in the UK, Australia and New Zealand. It is at the court's discretion to grant additional damages where the infringer has acted in a flagrant manner. When deciding if additional damages can apply, the court can take into consideration whether it would be dissuasive. In this context, dissuasive can mean in relation to both the infringer in the case and any actual or potential other infringers.[6]

19.4　Prison sentences

As mentioned, in cases of criminal copyright infringement, infringers can be sentenced to imprisonment. The maximum sentence available as a sanction against copyright infringement recently increased to up to ten years' imprisonment for online infringement. This matches the maximum sentence for offline infringement. The UK law now provides that a person found guilty of an offence of criminal copyright infringement is liable to either six months' imprisonment and a fine, or both; or on indictment to a fine or imprisonment for a term not exceeding ten years, or both.[7]

---

[3]　EC Enforcement Directive, Article 14.

[4]　CDPA 1988, s 97(2).

[5]　*Absolute Lofts South West London Ltd v Artisan Home Improvements Ltd* [2015] EWHC 2608 (IPEC).

[6]　*PPL v Hagan* [2016] EWHC 3076 (IPEC).

[7]　CDPA 1988, s 107(4).

In the *Wayne Evans* case,[8] the defendant was sentenced to 12 months' imprisonment for copyright infringement. However, it was pointed out in this case that there were no definitive guidelines setting out how a court would decide the length of sentencing in this type of case. Therefore, the court offered guidance on the length of a sentence in these circumstances, stating that in offences of this kind the sentencing court must retain flexibility and take into account the circumstances of the particular offence or offences, as well as the circumstances of the particular offender. In addition, the court offered the following (non-exhaustive) considerations that are likely to be relevant in sentencing cases involving the unlawful distribution of infringing copyright articles:

(1) First, illegal downloading and distribution is very often difficult to investigate and detect. It can give rise to serious problems and losses (none the less real for not being readily quantifiable) to the music and entertainment industry. Deterrent sentencing in such a context is appropriate.

(2) Second, the length of time (and including also any continuation after service of cease and desist notices) of the unlawful activity will always be highly relevant.

(3) Third, the profit accruing to the defendant as a result of the unlawful activity will always be relevant.

(4) Fourth, and whether or not a significant profit is made by the defendant, the loss accruing to the copyright owners so far as it can accurately be calculated will also be relevant: as will be the wider impact upon the music industry even if difficult to quantify in precise financial terms: because wider impact there always is.

(5) Fifth, even though this particular type of offending is not the subject of any Definitive Guideline there may be cases where it will be helpful to a judge to have regard to the Definitive Guidelines on fraud, bribery and money laundering offences. In some cases, such as the present, that will positively be required because one or more of the counts on the indictment, as here, will be a count which comes within the ambit of the guideline itself. But even where that is not the position there may be some cases where a judge, at least if only as a check, may wish to refer to the Definitive Guideline to get a feel, as it were, for the appropriate sentence. However, there will be other cases where the Definitive Guideline may be of marginal, and perhaps no, assistance at all. That will be a matter for the assessment of the judge in the individual case. Where the Definitive Guideline is required to be taken into account because one of the counts on the indictment is within the ambit of the guideline, that of itself will no

---

8   *Regina v Wayne Evans* [2017] EWCA Crim 139, 14 February 2017.

doubt lend assistance in deciding what the appropriate overall sentence will be.

(6) Sixth, personal mitigation, assistance to the authorities and bases and pleas of guilt are to be taken into account in the usual way.

(7) Seventh, unless the unlawful activity of this kind is very amateur, minor or short-lived, or in the absence of particularly compelling mitigation or other exceptional circumstances, an immediate custodial sentence is likely to be appropriate in cases of illegal distribution of copyright infringing articles.

Applying the above-mentioned list to the *Wayne Evans* case, it would seem that since the offender did not make a financial gain (point 3), had mental health issues (point 4) and pleaded guilty (point 6), the considerations of more influence might be deterrence in favour of the copyright owner (point 1) and length of time, particularly after receiving cease and desist notices (point 2).

In this case, the judge stated that there was both a loss to the copyright owners in a quantified manner and also a wider detrimental impact on the music industry and its profitability. Therefore, deterrence sentencing was justified in this context.[9] However, research as to the effectiveness of deterrence is inconclusive. In particular, deterrence theory requires that there must be knowledge of the sanction in order to be deterred.

In 2018, according to the Ministry of Justice, 25 people were found guilty of offences under UK copyright law, and the number of people cautioned was four.[10] For example, in *R v Mather*, the case involved a company that illegally produced and distributed music products for the karaoke industry. The defendant pleaded guilty to four offences and was sentenced to eight months' imprisonment.

In summary of this chapter, when bringing a copyright infringement claim, a copyright holder may apply for preliminary remedies such as a temporary injunction or measures for the preservation of evidence. If the copyright infringement claim is successful, the rightsholder will be entitled to a permanent injunction and damages. There are different types of damages that are calculated in different ways, and this also depends on

---

[9] *Regina v Wayne Evans* [2017] EWCA Crim 139, 14 February 2017, 19.

[10] https://assets.publishing.service.gov.uk/government/uploads/system/uploads/attachment_data/file/842351/IP-Crime-Report-2019.pdf accessed 6 November 2020.

the country in which the claim is brought. If the copyright infringement proceedings are brought in the criminal courts, an infringer can face a fine and/or a prison sentence.

20   Online enforcement

To conclude Part IV, which has covered enforcing your rights, this chapter focuses on copyright enforcement online. First it will discuss the issue of online copyright infringement, then it will cover notice and takedown procedures and blocking injunctions.

20.1   Online infringement

Online copyright infringement remains an issue for rightsholders. In 2017, the UK IPO's *Online Copyright Infringement Tracker*[1] reported that an estimated 15 per cent of UK internet users aged 12+ had consumed at least one item of online content illegally in the past three months. This equates to a quarter of all consumers of any of the six key content types. Levels of infringement varied by the type of content: TV programmes recorded the highest levels of infringement (8 per cent) among internet users, followed by music (7 per cent) and films (6 per cent). The report suggests that the main reason for infringement was convenience: this was the most commonly cited reason (45 per cent), overtaking 'because it is free' as a result of a drop in the proportion claiming this as a motive to do so (from 49 per cent in 2016 to 44 per cent in 2017). The report also showed that the most common reason that would deter infringement was 'If everything I wanted was available legally', with 22 per cent of infringers claiming this to be the case. In addition, 17 per cent claimed they would be deterred 'if everything I wanted was available legally online as soon as it was released elsewhere' and 21 per cent claimed that 'if legal services were cheaper' it would discourage them. Finally, 22 per cent stated that they would be deterred 'if it was clearer what is legal and what isn't'.

---

[1]   UK IPO, *Online Copyright Infringement Tracker: Latest Wave of Research* (UK IPO 2017).

In 2018, the Eighth Wave of the *Online Copyright Infringement Tracker*[2] reported that the percentage of UK internet users who had consumed at least one item of online content illegally in the preceding three months was the same as in 2016 and 2017. This demonstrates no change or improvement in the level of content illegally consumed online. In terms of content type, however, it was seen that illegal consumption of computer software had declined significantly, from 26 per cent in 2017 to 20 per cent. The reasons for infringing also remained largely the same in 2018 as in 2017: convenience (41 per cent) and 'because it is free' (44 per cent). This suggests that not enough is being done to address consumers' need for convenience. On the other hand, reasons for infringement that relate to the user being able to 'try something before I buy it' declined to 15 per cent, from 16 per cent in 2017. A more significant decline was seen in the reason 'because I can', which reduced to 13 per cent in 2018, down from 18 per cent in 2017. This is an encouraging statistic that suggests, perhaps, the success of technical protection measures and blocking injunctions which make it more difficult for users to access illegal content.

The latest version of the annual study, published in early 2020,[3] found that 87 per cent of its survey participants used at least one legal source to download music and 70 per cent used only legal sources (those aged 45–54 were most likely to have used only legal sources). In terms of illegal downloading of music, 30 per cent had used at least one illegal source to download music and 13 per cent had used only illegal sources to download music, with those aged 16–24 most likely to have used an illegal source. Interestingly, those who demonstrated a high level of passion for music were more likely to access music illegally – 36 per cent, compared with 18 per cent of those with a low level of passion for music. The study also showed that 17 per cent had used a mix of legal and illegal sources; this behaviour was highest among those aged 16–24 (23 per cent) and 25–34 (22 per cent). Again, those with a high level of passion for music had used a mix of legal and illegal sources (25 per cent) more often than those with a medium level of passion (10 per cent).

We also know that online platforms and social media sites contribute to increasing distribution of counterfeit goods. Products sold via the internet are usually distributed in small parcels via postal services, often directly

2   UK IPO, *Online Copyright Infringement Tracker: Latest Wave of Research* (UK IPO 2018).
3   UK IPO, *Online Copyright Infringement Tracker: Latest Wave of Research* (UK IPO 2020).

to customers. This can be a challenge for copyright enforcement due to a number of constraints, such as the need to coordinate cross-border investigations and tackle new technologies used by infringers to hide their locations and activities.[4]

The UK IPO also published a report on the impact of social media on intellectual property infringement to assess the role of social media in the sale of counterfeited products.[5] The research found that according to industry groups, together with government and private enforcement agencies, counterfeiting online encompasses a range of activities, such as impersonation, fan pages, social media pages transacting business, promotion and the proliferation of websites selling counterfeits and offering fake special offers. As such, the researchers argued that social media plays a significant and growing role in the sale and distribution of counterfeited and pirated goods. The researchers described social media as a haven for counterfeiters, who disseminate through open and closed group pages, as well as utilising likes and retweets and fan pages. The survey evidence from Trading Standards put forward in the study indicated that social media sites were the second most common location for investigations into counterfeiting. However, there has been subsequent coordinated action, in particular an agreement between Trading Standards and Facebook that allows Trading Standards to refer to Facebook potentially infringing content which it feels should be removed, subject to meeting criteria.

The IP Crime Group Enforcement Report 2018–2019[6] noted that there has been overall growth in the trade in counterfeit goods, despite Anti-Counterfeiting Group (ACG) members combined with Trading Standards and police generating more than 50 law enforcement investigations and more than 70 raid actions across the UK in 2018. The Report highlighted that effective action against IP crime can only be taken if agendas are coordinated at all levels, from the local to the global.

---

[4] Europol and EUIPO, *Situation Report on Counterfeiting and Piracy in the European Union* (Europol and EUIPO 2017).

[5] UKIPO, *Share and Share Alike: The Challenges from Social Media for Intellectual Property Rights* (UKIPO 2017).

[6] IP Crime Group, *IP Crime and Enforcement Report 2018–19* (IP Crime Group 2019).

20.2 Online blocking injunctions

An online blocking injunction is another type of injunction that can be used to block websites. It is an order that can be granted by a court to make an internet service provider prevent or disable access to a specific website for its users. These cases are also more often brought by trade associations or rightsholder companies rather than by individuals. However, when a case is brought, it tends to be successful. In the UK more than 30 successful blocking orders have been made, covering hundreds of websites.

The case against The Pirate Bay,[7] a well-known illegal content-sharing website, was a success for rightsholders after the judge found that the website operators and the users were all guilty of copyright infringement. This case was technically the second order of this kind made in the UK, but it was really the start of the development of the law of online blocking injunctions, providing rightsholders with a clear list of things that they needed to acquire in order to be successful in this type of claim, including the type and extent of evidence the UK courts would accept for the order to be granted. Blocking injunctions are now pretty standard in the UK. They have advanced to become quite the sophisticated enforcement tool, and now include live blocking injunctions, which enable websites to be blocked during certain times, for example during a match, game or even a sports season.

These types of blocking injunctions have been made in 25 different countries and are considered an effective measure against online copyright infringement, as the data shows they are able to reduce access to content by 90 per cent.[8]

---

[7] *1967 Ltd, Dramatico Entertainment Ltd, Infectious Music Ltd, Liberation Music PTY Ltd, Simco Ltd, Sony Music Entertainment UK Ltd, Universal Music Operations Ltd v British Sky Broadcasting Ltd, British Telecommunications plc, EE Ltd, Talktalk Telecom Ltd, Virgin Media Ltd* [2014] EWHC 3444 (Ch).

[8] Allgrove B and Groom J, 'Enforcement in a Digital Content Under EU Copyright: Positive and Normative Perspectives' in Aplin T, *Research Handbook on Intellectual Property and Digital Technologies* (Edward Elgar 2020).

EU law does prevent rightsholders from obliging service providers to generally monitor content.[9] However, there is another type of online injunction – though far more rarely used – that can be granted by a court to oblige the provider of a file-hosting service to search third party websites for links leading to the provider's service, which was what happened in a German court in the case against the popular cyberlocker Rapidshare.[10]

20.3 Notice and takedown

Notice and takedown refers to the procedure of removing illegal copyright content from online platforms. It is an important tool for copyright holders to use to enforce their rights online. It enables the removal of unlicensed content and the sale of counterfeit goods.

Some of these notice and takedown procedures are in place as a result of legal rules,[11] and others are set up following private agreements between rightsholders and internet service providers. For example, in 2011, the European Commission set up a voluntary scheme to which rightsholders and the major internet platforms signed up, committing to taking down adverts upon notification that the advertised item was a counterfeit and to taking steps against service users who are generally engaged in counterfeiting.[12]

Notice and takedown procedures have been shown to be useful for rightsholders and tend to be used more by trade associations than by individual rightsholders. For example, in a study looking at notice and takedowns in relation to the US law, it was found that 58.6 per cent of the notices came from three particular trade associations, led by the UK recording industry association the British Phonographic Industry, together with the International Federation of the Phonographic Industry and the Recording Industry Association of America.

---

[9]   Although this is subject to change as a result of the DSM Copyright Directive.

[10] *Atari v Rapidshare*, BGH, 12 July 2012, I ZR 18/11.

[11] US Digital Millennium Copyright Act 1998.

[12] See European Commission, Memorandum of Understanding on the Online Sale of Counterfeit Goods (2016) at http://ec.europa.eu/DocsRoom/documents/18023/attachments/1/translations accessed 6 November 2020.

Notice and takedown procedures are used across online platforms, search engines and social media sites. YouTube's Content ID technology is an example of one of these systems, as mentioned in Chapter 10. This allows rightsholders to manage their content online. Utilising the system, rightsholders are able to identify user-uploaded videos that contain their copyright work and then decide how they want to proceed. For example, a rightsholder can request that the video be blocked, access data around the video or monetise the video with advertising (more than 90 per cent choose this option). In Google's most recent report, it stated that the Content ID technology scans videos uploaded to YouTube against more than 600 years of audio and visual reference content, with more than 98 per cent of copyright issues resolved via this system. In relation to music in particular, 99.5 per cent of reported claims were generated and resolved automatically with the copyright holders' preferred action. This meant that the copyright holder only had to intervene in 0.5 per cent of cases.[13]

A common approach taken by copyright holders has been to manage the use of their work rather than use notice and takedown to have it removed, in order to benefit from its use. As noted, this is particularly common on YouTube: it has paid out more than $2 billion to rightsholders who have monetised their content, and more than 90 per cent of all Content ID claims across the platform result in monetisation, where rightsholders have opted to leave the content up and monetise through advertising rather than make an infringement claim or remove the content.[14]

This chapter has provided some insight into online infringement and online enforcement measures that can be used to tackle it, such as blocking injunction and notice and takedown procedures. This concludes Part IV of the book, on enforcement. The final part of the book turns to look at the future of the music industry, from the perspective of copyright, artificial intelligence and blockchain.

---

[13] Google, *How Google Fights Piracy Report* (Google 2017) 26.
[14] Ibid 6.

PART V

Looking to the future

This final section of the book looks to the future of the music industry and copyright, considering how new technologies such as artificial intelligence and blockchain might influence the future of music, for example in relation to copyright, creativity, registration and licensing.

Chapter 21 looks at artificial intelligence and music. It considers copyright authorship in the creation of music using AI and, in those circumstances, who becomes the copyright owner. It also discusses copyright infringement in relation to the material input into the AI system, as well as the content generated by AI.

Chapter 22 considers blockchain in the music industry, considering the impact of this technology on copyright registration, licensing and payments, as well as copyright enforcement.

21 Artificial intelligence and music

The use of artificial intelligence (AI) technologies is evidentially growing steadily across all sectors and industries. This includes in the creation and development of music, which raises some interesting copyright questions about authorship, ownership and infringement. This chapter will look at the impact of AI on these principles of copyright in the context of music creativity.

21.1 Artificial intelligence in music creativity

There is no agreed definition of exactly what artificial intelligence is, or what a technology needs to be able to do to be considered AI. One definition is that it is the ability of a non-natural entity to make choices by an evaluative process.[1] It can be distinguished by two classifications: narrow and general. Narrow AI is where a system is able to achieve certain specified goals, such as translation or navigation, whereas general AI has the ability to achieve an unlimited number of goals and even independently set new goals.

In the arena of creativity, AI is expected to become an integrated part of the industry in the somewhat near future. New AI technologies present exciting opportunities but, of course, there are social, economic and ethical implications that need to be addressed alongside these developments. This includes the adjustment of copyright and policy. As discussed at the beginning of this book, copyright regulation has always adapted to the development of new technologies and AI is one of the next major challenges for copyright in seeking to keep up to date. In particular, AI

---

[1] Turner J, *Robot Rules Regulating Artificial Intelligence* (Palgrave 2019).

raises questions about the way that copyright principles of authorship, ownership and infringement will apply in this context.

In light of this, the World Intellectual Property Organization (WIPO) launched a public consultation to consider measures for encouraging technological innovation.[2] The study began in 2019 with the *WIPO Technology Trends Report*, offering evidence-based projections to inform global policymakers on the future of AI. In September 2019 WIPO held a 'Conversation on IP and AI', bringing together Member States and other stakeholders to discuss the impact of AI on IP policy, with a view to collectively formulating the questions that policymakers need to ask. In December 2019, WIPO published an issues paper with a call for comments from the widest possible global audience. Responses were provided from the music industry, including from UK Music, the BPI and the Music Publishers Association. We will look at the industry's thoughts on the impact of AI in the music industry throughout this chapter.

In the BPI's response to the WIPO consultation it highlighted the ways in which AI is currently being used in the music industry, including the following examples:

- Streaming music services use AI to analyse data and personalise the user's experience of their service by creating playlists or recommendations.
- Artists use AI tools in their creative processes – for example, tools that can master or remix a recording automatically using algorithms derived from data on previous recordings, or that find suitable samples for use in a piece of music.
- Record labels use AI to analyse streaming and social data, or recordings themselves, to identify potentially successful artists (A&R) or to plan marketing campaigns or tours.
- Music production companies use AI to generate music that can be used as background music online, or in advertisements.

---

[2] WIPO Begins Public Consultation Process on Artificial Intelligence and Intellectual Property Policy, PR/2019/843 (13 December 2019) www.wipo.int/pressroom/en/articles/2019/article_0017 .html accessed 6 February 2020.

The use of AI in the creation of music has been employed by companies such as Google's Magenta[3] and Sony's Flow Machines,[4] both of which use AI technology to write and produce songs. Another example is AIVA,[5] an AI tool that is used to compose classical music and was recognised as the author of an album titled *Genesis*.[6]

However, the BPI argues that the application of AI in the music industry is currently still in its infancy, having only a marginal impact on the supply and demand of music. The nature, extent and future impact of the uses of AI in the music industry remain unclear, and therefore any new laws and policies need to wait until these developments are better understood.

This is certainly a wise move: often when laws are made too quickly, without first seeing the impact of the new technology, the rules can be stifling to creativity and not actually relevant or specific enough to address the issues. That said, it is time to start thinking about how copyright rules will apply to AI, because without clarity on matters such as who is the creator, who is the owner and whether a licence is needed, the dissemination of creativity can also be affected.

What follows considers who is the author, for the purposes of copyright, when AI assists in creativity or even creates independently. Following that, what this means for copyright ownership is addressed.

21.2   AI and copyright authorship

You may have heard that AI has created works, such as a song or a painting. However, the method of creativity with AI is not quite that straightforward and the whole process needs to be taken into account when we are thinking about how copyright will apply. For example, an AI portrait of Edmond de Belamy (which sold for $432,500!) was signed as authored by an algorithm. The algorithm was created by Obvious, a collective consisting of Hugo Caselles-Dupré, Pierre Fautrel and Gauthier

---

[3]   https://research.google/teams/brain/magenta/ accessed 6 November 2020.

[4]   www.flow-machines.com accessed 6 November 2020.

[5]   www.aiva.ai accessed 6 November 2020.

[6]   https://soundcloud.com/user-95265362/sets/genesis accessed 6 November 2020.

Vernier, using what they call GAN: Generative Adversarial Network. The algorithm consists of two parts: the Generator and the Discriminator. Caselles-Dupré, Fautrel and Vernier input a dataset of 15,000 portraits, and the Generator uses this data to make a new image. The Discriminator tries to spot the difference between a human-made image and one created by the Generator.[7]

Another example of AI-generated work is Sunspring, which claims to be the first ever screenplay written entirely by artificial intelligence. But of course, it also required a human to develop the software, and to collate and input the hundreds of screenplays used as the dataset.[8]

A recent European Commission report on AI and IP[9] stated that we could be moving towards AI autonomy, at least to a level at which the human contribution is 'trivial to the creative or inventive process', and therefore we could be entering into an era where machines will 'not only assist humans in the creative process but create or invent all by themselves'. However, we are not presently at that stage and AI technology is not currently truly autonomous. In fact, in a typical machine-learning system there is human involvement and human intervention at a number of points, such as in choosing how to set the system up, which involves the writing and choosing of the algorithm (including which learning models to use); choosing and collating data, which often includes the undertaking of data cleansing or other actions on the data, such as looking at how it is structured; providing feedback; reviewing output; and revising the model. In addition, the data itself is from human-created sources. Therefore, it would be a mistake to consider that AI is completely autonomous, when in fact AI systems are highly dependent on programmers, developers and data input through human intervention to train intelligent algorithms. The UK Music response to the WIPO consultation noted that in the music industry, an AI-generated work of music or lyrics entirely depends on human input. This human input usually involves first, the creation of the existing copyright works that are then used as data by the AI application, and second, the use and training of the AI application to do this.

---

7   www.christies.com/features/A-collaboration-between-two-artists-one-human-one-a-machine-9332 -1.aspx accessed 13 February 2020.

8   www.thereforefilms.com/sunspring.html accessed 13 February 2020.

9   Iglesias M, Shamuilia S and Anderberg A, *Artificial Intelligence and Intellectual Property – A Literature Review*, EUR 30017 EN (Publications Office of the European Union 2019).

When it comes to the authorship of copyright works, it seems that the AI system would be at the most a co-author – certainly not the sole author of a work that it created. AI-generated works often arise as a result of collaboration between several humans and the machine. In that sense the AI system is more of a tool, or, in the case of music, like an instrument.

However, the degree of contribution by the AI will of course differ depending on what it is doing. For example, something like auto-tuning is clearly a human work, assisted by technology. But if the AI software generates its own song, this might be considered joint authorship.

If we think back to the discussions on originality and creativity throughout this book, particularly in Chapter 13, and put them in the context of AI we are faced with new questions. Does the AI use of data to create something new from that data equate to originality? Or is it copying? Did it take a substantial part? As we know, copyright arises when a creator uses their own intellectual creation, expressing their creative abilities in the production of a work by making free and creative choices that allow them to stamp the work with their own personal touch.[10] In the context of AI, is it possible for a machine to have a personal touch?

These are important discussions that need to be considered by policymakers before new laws are made. Should we recognise AI-generated content as original for the purpose of copyright protection? Or should we create a new category of work for AI-produced content, which could acknowledge it as an unoriginal work – in the same way that sound recordings do not need to be original for copyright protection?

In its response to the WIPO consultation, UK Music argued that a work created using AI technology should either be fully protected by copyright or not at all, and either way, copyright should not be applied in the AI context in a way which devalues the role or rights of human creators. In particular, UK Music is concerned that any policy-driven enablement of AI innovation should, from a copyright perspective, still put the human creator first.

The Music Publishers Association's response to the WIPO consultation noted that the impact of AI technologies on the administration of musical

---

[10]   *Painer* (C-145/10) ECLI:EU:C:2011:798, 88–92.

works is different to that of using AI to assist in the creative process. It said that AI-assisted works still protect the human endeavour of the composer using applications, and that AI-generated works are ultimately based on works created by humans, mainly ingested in the machine-learning process. As a result, it believes the existing copyright framework that rewards human endeavours and the creation of musical works is already adequate to cover AI-assisted works.

The BPI's response to the WIPO consultation also highlighted that AI's ability to produce outputs of any value comes only as a result of being trained with quality input materials, therefore depending entirely on human intervention and previous human creativity. The BPI also emphasised that ensuring human creativity is not undermined is essential to create the conditions from which AI innovation can flourish. It too believes that the current copyright framework can be applied to AI and that it is not necessary at this stage to look for solutions to a series of theoretical difficulties. It would prefer that, instead of making new laws, we consider how the existing framework would address AI-generated and AI-assisted works. In particular, it suggests that the question to be answered is: what degree of human involvement would be required for copyright protection to be obtained?

The next question is: if a work that was created using AI was to be given copyright protection, who would be the owner of that copyright? This is discussed in section 21.3.

21.3 AI and copyright ownership

In some countries there are already laws in place for computer-generated works that can be applied to material created using AI – for example in the UK, South Africa, Hong Kong, India, Ireland and New Zealand. In these countries, the owner of the copyright is the person who made the necessary arrangements for the creation of the work.

In the UK, the law says that 'in the case of a literary, dramatic, musical or artistic work which is computer-generated, the author shall be taken to be the person by whom the arrangements necessary for the creation of the work are undertaken'.[11] A computer-generated work is defined as a work that is generated by a computer where there is no human author of the work. For this type of work, copyright protection lasts for 50 years after it was made.[12] This law follows the economic justification of copyright, discussed in Chapter 1, which rewards the person who invested their resources into the development of the AI.

Use of the input material will be further discussed in the next section, but it is important to note at this stage that the data used by the AI system in order to create could be copyright protected. For example, scientists at SONY CSL Research Lab published a song credited to AI, where the input material was songs by The Beatles, in order to produce a new song in the style of The Beatles called *Daddy's Car*.[13] It could be argued that the copyright holders of The Beatles' songs would have a stake in the ownership of *Daddy's Car*. Luckily, in this instance Sony are already the owners of The Beatles' catalogue!

Nevertheless, there have already been reports of AI-generated works being recognised as being created by the AI, such as the examples given above of the painting, screenplay and songs. However, it is likely that this is mostly for commercial effect – they might be signing works as authored by AI, but the names on the copyright register belong to people.

For example, in 2019, Warner Music signed a record deal with Endel,[14] an algorithm developed by a start-up based in Berlin. They agreed a 50/50 distribution deal, covering a total of 20 albums. Endel creates tailor-made custom sound frequencies based on personal user inputs such as weather, time of day, location and biometric details such as heart rate.[15] In this case, the co-founders and software engineers were listed as the songwriters in order to register the copyright of the music.

---

[11] UK CDPA 1988, section 9(3).

[12] UK CDPA 1988, section 12(7).

[13]   https://soundcloud.com/user-547260463 accessed 6 November 2020.

[14] https://endel.io/ accessed 6 November 2020.

[15] Bosher H, 'Warner Music Signs Distribution Deal with AI Generated Music App Endel' (IPKat, 2019) https://ipkitten.blogspot.com/2019/03/warner-music-signs-distribution-deal.html accessed 13 February 2020.

This was not the first time that AI music had formed part of a distribution deal. Aiva Music[16] is a composition algorithm that famously became the first AI to register with a collecting society (SACEM) and recently partnered with Believe Distribution (owned by Song Records) to release its latest album. Sony's Flow Machines[17] project, which involves an algorithmic composition tool, is credited as the songwriter, producer, instrumentalist and vocalist in all of the tracks on its debut album *Hello World*. Still, the creators also include a list of human contributors who provided songwriting, instrumentation, mixing and mastering support.

The Endel–Warner deal is, however, a step forward in that there are no human collaborators in the generation of the output sounds. Of course, there was in the development of the AI and the input data – some of the inputs, or instrumental stems, were created by Endel's co-founder and sound designer Dmitry Evgrafov. Each sound was then allocated metadata according to certain parameters which the app can read and use to generate a soundscape. So, while it may seem as if the sounds are created with a click of a button, in fact 1.5 years of work went into developing the algorithm and creating and tagging the stems. This highlights the level of human effort that goes into AI-generated music.

In the final section of this chapter, we turn to consider the input materials in more detail, to think about whether this would qualify as copyright infringement, if a licence would be needed or if a copyright exception might apply.

21.4 AI and copyright infringement

The fact that AI systems are highly dependent on input material has been emphasised. This is important not only with regard to the human intervention but also in respect of the copyright status of the material used to train and feed the AI. This material, which we often refer to as data in this context because it is being used as such, can be copyright protected, which means that in principle the developers should obtain permission to access and use it for that purpose.

---

[16] www.aiva.ai/ accessed 6 November 2020.
[17] www.flow-machines.com accessed 6 November 2020.

UK Music's response to the WIPO consultation stated that using existing copyright-protected works for the purpose of machine learning could constitute a copyright infringement, depending on the context of what is being used, how extensively it is used and what will be produced as a result. This argument was also put forward in the Music Publishers Association's response, which argued that using works in this way requires a copyright licence from the respective rightsholder. Likewise, the BPI stated that the value of the work generated using AI depends on the material input to the system.

Therefore, it is suggested that using copyright-protected material for the purposes of AI learning, development and creation could be copyright infringement, if done without permission. As such, licensing solutions need to be considered to enable this type of permission to use works for AI purposes, unless a copyright exception applies.

In relation to copyright exceptions, some people argue that current copyright exceptions might apply in these circumstances. Fair use, in the US, is an example. Georgia Tech researcher Mark Riedl posted an AI-generated lyric video featuring the instrumental to Michael Jackson's song *Beat It*, using his machine-learning model Weird A.I. Yankovic, which generates new rhyming lyrics for existing songs. The video was removed after a notice and takedown procedure was issued by the International Federation of the Phonographic Industry. Riedl argued that his use of the work fell under the copyright exception for fair use as it was a type of parody.[18]

One contentious issue within the EU copyright system would be whether the material input into the AI is treated as copyright material or as data. This is because there is an exception that applies to text and data mining, and therefore the way we deal with the input material would have an impact on whether the exception would apply. When policymakers are deciding whether AI infringes copyright, they will need to be specific about the use of the input material for AI learning and AI generation of new content. Whether the AI output material is substantially similar to the input material and therefore constitutes copyright infringement is

---

[18] www.vice.com/en_ca/article/m7jpp3/the-record-industry-is-going-after-parody-songs-written-by-an-algorithm accessed 6 November 2020.

another question altogether. Consequently, the law also needs to consider who would be liable for the infringement.

The music industry appears to be in consensus that the current copyright framework is equipped to apply to the developments in AI technology, and that the focus of copyright should remain on the human creator. However, clarification is needed on how exactly the current laws will apply in these circumstances.

The final chapter of this book takes a look at another type of technology that we could see having an impact on copyright and the music industry in the future: blockchain.

22 Blockchain in the music industry

Following on from Chapter 21, which considered the impact of artificial intelligence technology on copyright and the music industry, this chapter considers another type of technological development: blockchain.

Blockchain is, simply put, a technology that can provide a secure, transparent record of information that can be used to log and monitor transactions. For copyright and music, this could mean being able to track and trace uses of copyright material, as well as potentially to facilitate transactions such as licences and registration.

There are already several blockchain initiatives operating in the music industry. For example, Mycelia[1] is a research and development hub for music makers, founded by Imogen Heap, that provides an open-source, public, blockchain-based distributed computing platform featuring smart contract functionality. Imogen Heap used her own music as a test case for Mycelia to issue music on the blockchain by releasing her album *Tiny Human* on Ethereum's public blockchain in 2015. Although the experiment was not a commercial success, it was a part of a bigger movement towards developing and adopting blockchain technologies. This chapter will discuss the use of blockchain technology in copyright registrations, licence and payments and copyright enforcement.

22.1 Blockchain and copyright registration

As mentioned previously in this book, copyright does not need to be registered in order to subsist in a work. However, in certain countries, such

---

[1] http://myceliaformusic.org/ accessed 6 November 2020.

as the US, you do need to register your copyright in order to fully benefit from the right and enforce it.

We may see blockchain facilitating the registration process in the future. A blockchain registration system could allow an author to provide robust evidence of ownership and would also give the user a unique identifying address. A sophisticated blockchain registration service could also act in conjunction with other management elements, such as allowing payments.

While a decentralised and immutable record of ownership may sound appealing, there are also a number of issues that currently remain a challenge to this ambition. One of the major challenges to blockchain is that currently the record is immutable, raising the risk that incorrect authors could be forever recorded in the blockchain. The technology needs to be flexible to changes and amendments – for example, if, as a result of an infringement claim, other authors needed to be added to the registered right – without creating security issues. Other challenges include the security of the technology; privacy issues; the regulation of that technology, including for disputes arising in relation to the technology and the data; and where the liability for any illegality would fall.

Although this might seem farfetched, blockchain is already being assessed as a tool to maintain other registration of rights. For example, in Denmark, blockchain is facilitating the registration and transfer of ownership of vehicles by the Danish Customs and Tax Administrators.[2] Copyright scholars have argued that a blockchain copyright registry could record copyright transfers, reduce transaction costs and facilitate licensing.[3]

22.2 Blockchain licences and micropayments

It has been suggested that blockchain technology could be used to track the dissemination of a copyright work, as well as to record information

---

[2] www.nets.eu/perspectives/Pages/Blockchain-technology-could-add-transparency-to-buying-and-selling-a-car.aspx accessed 6 November 2020.

[3] Mostert F, 'Digital Tools of Intellectual Property Enforcement: Their Intended and Unintended Norm Setting Consequences' in Aplin T (ed) *Research Handbook on Intellectual Property and Digital Technologies* (Edward Elgar 2020).

about its use. It could then, potentially, initiate a licence and facilitate a payment between the user and rightsholder. However, despite the early hype, blockchain may not be a suitable solution for the music industry's data challenges. In particular, as it is an immutable ledger, blockchain is more appropriate for dealing with data that doesn't change; however, music data is very much a changing dataset.

Licensing of content through blockchain technology would need to operate on partnership agreements between rightsholders and users, as well as app developers and platforms. It could provide rightsowners with remuneration for use of their material, while also allowing users to legally create content using copyright-protected material. Blockchain technology could be used to facilitate the agreements between the user and the copyright holder. Although this initiative has not yet gained momentum in the industry, it may be the start of new ways to facilitate easier licensing.

Nevertheless, some initiatives are working towards this goal. Three of the largest member-owned collection societies in the world – the American Society for Composers, Authors and Publishers (ASCAP); the Society of Authors, Composers and Publishers of Music (SACEM); and PRS for Music – have partnered with IBM to work on a new shared system of managing music copyright information using blockchain technology. It aims to improve the processes of royalty matching, which in turn will speed up licensing, reduce errors and reduce costs.[4]

If it works, blockchain licensing could increase both licensing efficiency and the autonomy of creators, resolving issues of orphan works, where the copyright holder or author is unknown. It could also assist in fair remuneration for and allocation of copyright. However, as mentioned, there remain challenges to this emerging technology. In addition to those mentioned above, when it comes to the actual licence this would be a type of smart contract, which comes with its own limitations.

A smart contract is a computer protocol which digitally facilitates, verifies or enforces the performance of a contract, without the need for human intervention. In this context the contract could, for example, agree the licence and make the royalty payment. These transactions are trackable,

---

[4] www.prsformusic.com/press/2017/prs-for-music-ascap-and-sacem-initiate-joint-blockchain-project accessed 6 November 2020.

which is great; but they are irreversible, which could cause problems if something goes wrong.

Blockchain could also facilitate a micropayment marketplace for copyright works. Blockchain could enable an efficient record of the use of copyright works in a public ledger, and that use could be charged to the user's electronic wallet. This could allow creators to obtain monetary reward through cryptocurrencies. Spotify has purchased music blockchain startup Mediachain,[5] which is one of many companies working on applications for blockchain technology to track transactions, content rights ownership and attribution.[6]

While micropayments may seem like another fabulous use of blockchain technology, there are also a number of challenges that would need to be overcome before this would be effective. For example, cryptocurrencies have been stunted in their growth and utility as a method of payment due to lack of scalability, slow transaction rates and potential high transaction costs. In the end, the main problem may be one of business models and commercial realities. Subscription systems such as Spotify, Netflix, Apple Music and Amazon Prime have proven extremely successful, and this could be because consumers prefer to make a monthly payment that covers all access rather than making pay-per-listen micropayments.

22.3   Blockchain copyright enforcement

Another proposed use of blockchain technology in copyright is as an enforcement mechanism. This could happen by having a copyright-protected work represented as a unique address on a blockchain, which would also be attached to a registration system; it would then be able to inform the rightsholder when a work is used. Under this system, browsers and media players could be built to play only authentic works registered on the blockchain. Already we have seen companies, such as Sony, developing this type of technology. However, at this stage

---

[5]   https://copyrightandtechnology.com/2017/04/27/spotify-acquires-blockchain-startup-mediachain/ accessed 6 November 2020.

[6]   See Music 2025, *The Music Data Dilemma: Issues Facing the Music Industry in Improving Data Management* (UK IPO 2019) 113–17.

the technology is still emerging, and organisations are still exploring its potential.

Some people argue that blockchain can be used to address illegal use of content online. However, from a copyright perspective, one major limitation of this approach would be that it does not allow for copyright exceptions. This would severely limit the public domain, which would be detrimental to the entire copyright system, human rights and society as a whole.

In other industries blockchain is being used to track authentic goods and could therefore be used as a tool against counterfeit goods. It has the potential to transform, or at least to assist in, copyright management in the music industry. Although we are not there yet, we can clearly see the music and tech industries investing resources in pioneering towards these goals, and should keep a keen eye on the developments. However, the impact of blockchain on the future of the music industry will depend on the development of the technologies to overcome the issues mentioned above, such as the immutable ledger, as well as the challenges of scalability, reliability and market adoption.

Index